THE BROOKINGS INSTITUTION

The Brookings Institution—Devoted to Public Service through Research and Training in the Social Sciences—was incorporated on December 8, 1927. Broadly stated, the Institution has two primary purposes: the first is to aid constructively in the development of sound national policies; and the second is to offer training of a super-graduate character to students of the social sciences. The Institution will maintain a series of co-operating institutes, equipped to carry out comprehensive and inter-related research projects.

The responsibility for the final determination of the Institution's policies and its program of work and for the administration of its endowment is vested in a self-perpetuating board of trustees. It is the function of the trustees to make possible the conduct of scientific research under the most favorable conditions, and to safeguard the independence of the research staff in the pursuit of their studies and in the publication of the results of such studies. It is not a part of their function to determine, control, or influence the conduct of particular investigations or the conclusions reached; but only to approve the principal fields of investigation to which the available funds are to be allocated, and to satisfy themselves with reference to the intellectual competence and scientific integrity of the staff. Major responsibility for "formulating general policies and co-ordinating the activities of the various divisions of the Institution" is vested in the president. The by-laws provide also that "there shall be an advisory council selected by the president from among the scientific staff of the Institution and representing the different divisions of the Institution."

THE INSTITUTE FOR GOVERNMENT RESEARCH

OF

THE BROOKINGS INSTITUTION

STUDIES IN ADMINISTRATION No. 40

CONGRESSIONAL APPORTIONMENT

BY
LAURENCE F. SCHMECKEBIER

GREENWOOD PRESS, PUBLISHERS
WESTPORT, CONNECTICUT

Library of Congress Cataloging in Publication Data

Schmeckebier, Laurence Frederick, 1877-1959.
   Congressional apportionment.

   Reprint of the ed. published by Brookings
Institution, Washington, and issued as no. 40 of
Studies in administration.
   Includes bibliographical references.
   1. United States. Congress. House--Election
districts. 2. Apportionment (Election law)--U-
nited States. I. Title. II. Series: Brookings
Institution, Washington, D. C. Institute for
Government Research. Studies in administration ;
no. 40.
JK1341.S35   328.73'07'345   74-4731
ISBN 0-8371-7486-4

PREFACE

In January 1941 the President will submit to Congress a statement of the apportionment population in each state, and an apportionment of 435 members among the several states according to the methods of major fractions and equal proportions. Unless Congress takes other action within sixty calendar days, a new apportionment according to the method of major fractions will go into effect.

Apportionment of representatives is important both because of equitable representation in the House of Representatives and by reason of its effect on the election of the President, the electoral vote of each state being the number of representatives plus two.

In view of the importance of the subject this volume contains a description of the five modern workable methods of apportionment and a discussion of their relative advantages. It includes also a discussion of the question whether the aliens should be counted in making the apportionment, and whether the disfranchised voter should be taken into account. The last chapter is devoted to apportionment within the states, in many of which the inequities are more pronounced than in the case of the apportionment among the states.

There is no discussion of the size of the House of Representatives, as that presents a problem in legislative organization not concerned with apportionment. Each of the five modern methods of apportionment may be applied to any size of House, and will give results consistent with the principle on which the method is based.

The author desires to express his indebtedness to Dr. Edward V. Huntington, Dr. Calvert L. Dedrick, and Mr. Morris B. Ullman for assistance on mathematical problems. It should be added that these gentlemen are not responsible for any conclusions or opinions. The author is also indebted to Miss L. Esther Breck and Mrs. Medora M. Richardson, for the preparation of many of the tables and the checking of the results and to Mr. Sheldon B. Akers and Miss Louise Bebb for computations and mathematical assistance.

Laurence F. Schmeckebier

December 1940

CONTENTS

CHAPTER I

IMPORTANCE OF APPORTIONMENT

One of the most earnestly discussed questions considered by the Constitutional Convention was that pertaining to the composition of Congress. The conflicting interests of the large and small states led to the compromise that the states should have equality of representation in the Senate, but that they should elect members to the House of Representatives according to their population. Coupled with representation according to population was the requirement that direct taxes should also be apportioned in the same manner. Thus increased representation meant increased direct taxation.

The Sixteenth Amendment, effective in 1913, provides that taxes on income may be levied and collected "without apportionment among the several states, and without regard to any census of enumeration." Therefore at the present time the apportionment of representatives is the only constitutional requirement dependent upon the census of population.

In order to provide the population basis for the apportionment the Constitution provided that the first enumeration should be made within three years after the first meeting of Congress, and "within every subsequent term of ten years." The Constitution does not state that a new apportionment must be made after each census, but such a requirement may be inferred from the provisions quoted above.

Congress has made provision for a new apportionment after every census except that of 1920. Consequently the apportionment in effect after the census of 1910 continued in force until after the census of 1930, although there had been material shifts in population between 1910 and 1920.[1]

Section 22 of the census act of June 18, 1929 (46 Stat. L. 26)

[1] The 1910 apportionment which continued in effect and a new apportionment by the method of major fractions are given in App. C. The apportionments for 1920 by the five modern methods are given on p. 64.

I

provides for an automatic apportionment after each census.

If representation in the House of Representatives is to be based on population, it is essential that there be a periodic adjustment of the apportionment consonant with the changes in the number of inhabitants. Any neglect to make such adjustments gives undue weight to a portion of the population, and is subversive of the democratic process.

An inequitable apportionment extends its effect beyond the membership of the House of Representatives, and also has a direct bearing upon the election of a President, as the number of presidential electors from each state is the number of representatives plus two. In a close election the result might be decided by the electoral votes of a state or group of states which had representation in the House out of proportion to its population.[2]

The automatic system of apportionment provided by existing law is desirable in that it prescribes in advance the method of computation, and thus avoids the dangers of members being influenced by the fact that their state might lose or gain a representative as the result of the use of a particular method. It is, however, desirable to evaluate the several methods which have been recognized by law or which have been proposed.

The problem of equitable apportionment is not as easy as it seems. If the apportionment population of the United States were 130,500,000 and if the membership of the House of Representatives is fixed at 435, there would be exactly one member for each 300,000 persons. Then if the population of each state is an exact multiple of 300,000 there would be no question regarding the number of members to be assigned to each state—the apportionment of each state would be determined by dividing 300,000 into its population.

Difficulty arises from the circumstance that seldom if ever will any ratio of population to representatives divide exactly into the population of any state. In every case there is a remainder which may vary from a small to a large fraction of the

---

[2] It was suggested in 1928 that as a result of the failure to pass an apportionment act the electoral college to be chosen that year would be unconstitutionally composed. See William Starr Myers, "An Unconstitutional President," *North American Review*, Vol. 226, pp. 385–89.

ratio. At every apportionment since the adoption of the Constitution there has been a controversy over the selection of the states that will receive an additional member for its fractional population above the ratio. In modern methods of apportionment the ratio of a representative to population is not a part of the original computation; as will be shown later it is a secondary result reached after the apportionment has been made.

Modern methods of apportioning representatives are based on principles which are well known to students of mathematics, but which are not likely to be familiar to persons who have neglected their mathematics during their mature years. However, as will be shown on later pages, the application of any modern method to an apportionment involves merely a simple problem of multiplication.

CHAPTER II

FACTORS AND DEFINITIONS

In order to avoid repetition, certain factors which are common to two or more methods of apportionment are described below.

Ratio. The apportionment ratio is obtained by dividing the population of the entire country by the number of representatives. Thus the total population of the country in 1910 was 91,569,325; dividing this by 435 gives a ratio of 210,504. This is the natural ratio. Formerly in the computation of the apportionment by the method of major fractions (to be discussed later) a revised ratio was used as explained on page 16. No modern method of apportioning representatives uses any ratio in determining the results. A ratio is often referred to in connection with modern methods, but it is obtained after the apportionment is made from the priority list described on later pages. The ratio as thus determined varies with the different methods and may be any number between the priority list number that applies to the last number (the 435th under recent apportionments) and the next succeeding number. Commonly it is the number midway between these two.

After the census of 1930 the natural ratio was 278,376. The accompanying table shows for each method, based on the census of 1930, the last priority list number used, the succeeding priority list number, and the number midway between, commonly used as the ratio.

DERIVATION OF RATIO FROM PRIORITY LIST

Method	Last Priority List Number Used	Next Priority List Number	Number Midway between 2 and 3, Commonly Used as the Ratio[a]
1	2	3	4
Smallest divisors........	297,778	294,407	296,093
Harmonic mean..........	282,911	282,140	282,526
Equal proportions.......	280,747	280,669	280,708
Major fractions.........	280,212	279,212	279,712
Greatest divisors........	265,865	265,806	265,835

[a] Some of these numbers are not the same as those given on p. 19 of *Apportionment of Representatives in Congress*, Hearings before the House Committee on the Census, 70 Cong. 3 sess., 1940. The discrepancy is not material, as any number between those given in columns 2 and 3 may be used.

4

Quota. The quota is the number of representatives assigned to a state under any method of apportionment. It is, in fact, the apportionment. Under all modern methods it is always a whole number and is obtained by means of a priority list as explained on later pages. Under some proposed methods and some obsolete methods quotas were obtained by using a ratio arbitrarily selected or a ratio obtained by dividing the entire population by the number of representatives. Thus if the ratio is 250,000 and the population of a state is 852,500, the quota is 3.41. This may be called the exact quota and it is almost universally fractional. Consequently it cannot be used directly for apportionment. Under some methods which are unworkable the fraction may be dropped, the next higher number may be used, a fraction less than half may be dropped, the next higher number may be used if the fraction is one-half or more, or the exact quota may be used as an intermediate step. These various dispositions of the fractions are considered in the discussion of the several methods.

Major fractions and units and minor fractions. If the ratio as determined above is divided into the population of a state, the quotient will be a whole number and a fraction. If the fraction is one-half or more it is known as a major fraction; if it is less than one-half it is known as a minor fraction. The term "major unit" is here used to mean the sum of all whole numbers for a particular state plus an additional number for each major fraction. Thus if the quotient for one state is 8.75 and for another state 8.65, the number of major units would be 18. As far as is known the term "major unit" has not heretofore been used in the discussions of apportionment.

Paradoxes. A paradox is a phenomenon or action which has contradictory qualities or phases. Several methods of apportionment result in what have become known as the population paradox and the Alabama paradox.

The population paradox is so named because with a fixed ratio of representation an increase in the total population may result in a decrease in the size of the House.

An example of the population paradox is given in the table

below, which shows that a fixed ratio of 250,000 per district will result in a House of 435 members with a population of 102,750,113, but will give only 391 members if the population

APPORTIONMENTS RESULTING FROM USE OF FIXED QUOTA OF 250,000[a]

State	Apportionment Based on Total Population of 102,750,113		Apportionment Based on Total Population of 102,958,798	
	Hypothetical Population	Number of Representatives	Hypothetical Population	Number of Representatives
Alabama	2,375,002	10	2,368,416	9
Arizona	125,004	1	333,326	1
Arkansas	1,625,002	7	1,615,380	6
California	3,375,002	14	3,370,369	13
Colorado	875,001	4	857,140	3
Connecticut	1,375,002	6	1,363,633	5
Delaware	125,003	1	333,325	1
Florida	875,002	4	857,141	3
Georgia	2,875,001	12	2,869,563	11
Idaho	375,003	2	333,329	1
Illinois	6,625,001	27	6,622,640	26
Indiana	2,875,002	12	2,869,564	11
Iowa	2,375,004	10	2,368,418	9
Kansas	1,625,003	7	1,615,381	6
Kentucky	2,375,005	10	2,368,419	9
Louisiana	1,625,005	7	1,615,383	6
Maine	625,004	3	599,998	2
Maryland	1,375,003	6	1,363,634	5
Massachusetts	3,875,001	16	3,870,966	15
Michigan	3,625,001	15	3,620,688	14
Minnesota	2,375,003	10	2,368,417	9
Mississippi	1,625,004	7	1,615,382	6
Missouri	3,375,001	14	3,370,368	13
Montana	375,006	2	333,332	1
Nebraska	1,125,001	5	1,111,110	4
Nevada	125,001	1	333,323	1
New Hampshire	375,004	2	333,330	1
New Jersey	3,125,001	13	3,119,999	12
New Mexico	375,002	2	333,328	1
New York	10,375,001	42	10,373,492	41
North Carolina	2,375,006	10	2,368,420	9
North Dakota	625,003	3	599,997	2
Ohio	5,875,001	24	5,872,339	23
Oklahoma	1,875,001	8	1,866,665	7
Oregon	625,005	3	599,999	2
Pennsylvania	8,875,001	36	8,873,238	35
Rhode Island	625,001	3	599,995	2
South Carolina	1,625,001	7	1,615,379	6
South Dakota	625,002	3	599,996	2
Tennessee	2,375,001	10	2,368,415	9
Texas	4,625,001	19	4,621,620	18
Utah	375,005	2	333,331	1
Vermont	375,001	2	333,327	1
Virginia	2,125,001	9	2,117,646	8
Washington	1,375,001	6	1,363,632	5
West Virginia	1,375,004	6	1,363,635	5
Wisconsin	2,625,001	11	2,619,046	10
Wyoming	125,002	1	333,324	1
Total	102,750,113	435	102,958,798	391

[a] From E. V. Huntington, *Methods of Apportionment in Congress*, 76 Cong. 3 sess., S. Doc. 304, p. 19.

is increased to 102,958,798. The population figures in this table are hypothetical but are not beyond the range of possibility. The apportionment given results from the use of any one of the three following methods: fixed ratio with major fractions, fixed ratio with harmonic fractions, and fixed ratio with geometric fractions. Each of these three methods is discussed in Chapter V.

The so-called Alabama paradox may result in a state's losing a representative even if the size of the House is increased. It derives its name from the fact that it was first noted after the census in 1880, when a proposed apportionment would have resulted in the loss of a seat to Alabama, although the size of the House was increased from 299 to 300.

After the census of 1890 a proposed apportionment resulted in a gain of one member for Arkansas with a membership of 359, a loss at 360, and a gain at 361. Under the census of 1900 a proposed apportionment resulted in a gain of one for Colorado with a House at 350 to 356, a loss at 357, and a gain at 358. Under the same plan Maine lost at 382, gained from 383 to 385, lost at 386, gained at 377 and 388, lost at 389 and 390, gained at 391 and thereafter. Commenting on this, Representative Littlefield said:

... In Maine comes and out Maine goes. The House increases in size and still she is out. It increases a little more in size, and then, forsooth, in she comes. A further increase, and out she goes, and then a little further increase and in she comes. God help the State of Maine when mathematics reach for her and undertake to strike her down in this manner in connection with her representation on this floor—more cruel even than the chairman of this great committee.[1]

Average population per district. The average population per district in a state is obtained by dividing the population of a state by the number of representatives.[2] It is consequently the same as average population per representative. Thus in Rhode Island the population in 1930 was 687,497; as the state has two representatives the average population per district is 687,497 divided by 2, or 343,749. It should be remembered that

---

[1] *Cong. Record*, 56 Cong. 2 sess., Vol. 34, Pt. 1, p. 593.

[2] This is sometimes called average size of district. The term "size" is not used here because it may be confused with "area."

the average population per district is derived from the state population and representation and not from the population and representation of the entire country. The average population per district for each state is shown in Chapter IX.

Individual share in a representative. Each individual may be conceived to have a share in a representative. Such a share would be the number of representatives divided by the population of the state. As the number of representatives from Rhode Island is 2 and the population is 687,497, the share of each individual is 2 divided by 687,497 or .000,002,9. This may be expressed as 2.9 per million. Like the average population per district, the individual share in a representative is derived from the population and representation of the state.

Absolute and relative differences. The absolute difference between two numbers is obtained by subtracting the smaller from the larger. The relative difference is the percentage by which the larger exceeds the smaller and is obtained by dividing the smaller amount into the difference. Thus if a piece of property costing $500 is sold for $600 and another piece costing $1,000 is sold for $1,100, the absolute difference in the profit is the same in each case, namely $100. But the relative difference in one case is 500 divided into 100, or 20 per cent; in the other case it is 1,000 divided into 100, or 10 per cent.

Priority lists. The modern methods of computing apportionment—equal proportions, major fractions, harmonic mean, smallest divisors, and greatest divisors—assign the representatives to each state by means of priority lists, which indicate the apportionment to each state for any desired size of the House of Representatives. As the Constitution provides that one representative shall be assigned to each state, no question of priority would exist if the House consisted of 48 members. Each state would obtain one representative regardless of its population. Therefore the priority list begins with the forty-ninth member of the House (the second member for some state), and when complete it shows which states would receive additional members for any size of House larger than 48.

The priority list numbers are obtained by multiplying the

population of each state successively by the multipliers applicable to the second member, the third member, and so on. A different series of multipliers is used for each of the five methods discussed. Tables of multipliers to be used are given in Chapter III under the discussion of each method, where the mathematical derivation of the multipliers is also explained. It is obvious that the process need be applied only for a few representatives in excess of the number expected to be apportioned to each state.

In the preparation of a priority list the product resulting from each computation should be placed on a separate card, which should contain the name of the state and a figure showing the number of members from the state corresponding to the multiplier used.

There is given below a brief summary of the computation of a priority list using the method of equal proportions and based on the 1930 census. Under the method of equal proportions the multipliers to be used for the second and third members after one member has been assigned to each state are 0.707,106,78 and 0.408,248,29.

Thus in a priority list using the method of equal proportions and based on the census of 1930 the two priority list numbers for the second and third members from New York would be derived as follows:

12,587,967 (population) ×0.707,106,78 (multiplier for second member) = 8,901,037 (priority number)

12,587,967 (population) ×0.408,248,29 (multiplier for third member) = 5,139,016 (priority number)

The resulting cards for New York would then read:

8,901,037 New York 2

5,139,016 New York 3

The cards for the second and third members for Pennsylvania would read:

6,810,357 Pennsylvania 2

3,931,961 Pennsylvania 3

The cards for all members from all states should then be

arranged in descending order of the priority numbers, the cards being numbered consecutively beginning with 49. The first card is numbered 49 as one representative has already been assigned to each of the 48 states. The priority list would then read in part as follows:

PORTION OF PRIORITY LIST BY METHOD OF EQUAL PROPORTIONS, BASED ON CENSUS OF 1930

Total Number of Representatives from All States	Priority Number	State	Cumulative Total of Representatives from Each State
49...........	8,901,037	New York	2
50...........	6,810,357	Pennsylvania	2
51...........	5,395,499	Illinois	2
52...........	5,139,016	New York	3
***			
56...........	3,931,961	Pennsylvania	3
***			
100...........	1,329,006	Kansas	2
***			
200...........	633,732	Ohio	11
***			
384...........	318,338	Oklahoma	8
***			
432...........	282,893	New York	45
433...........	281,873	Indiana	12
434...........	280,837	Louisiana	8
435...........	280,747	Oklahoma	9
436...........	280,669	Rhode Island	3
437...........	280,001	New Mexico	2

A line is then drawn below the number (in the first column) representing the membership which has been determined upon. Then for each state the last entry above the line in the fourth column (cumulative total of representatives for each state) shows the number of representatives to which the state is entitled. Thus for a House of 435 members, reading up from 435, the members apportioned to the last four states above the line would be Oklahoma 9, Louisiana 8, Indiana 12, and New York 45. If the membership were increased to 436 Rhode Island would obtain an additional member, making 3; if increased to 437 New Mexico would obtain an additional member, making 2. If the membership were decreased to 434 Oklahoma would be reduced to 8, but Louisiana, Indiana, New York, and all other states would remain the same.

It should be noted that under any method the very large states will receive several members before a small state will receive a second member.

As different multipliers are used in the several methods, the products will not be the same and the order of priority may differ, but for each method the steps in preparing the list and its use will be as indicated above.

Priority lists, based on the censuses of 1930 and 1940, are given in Appendixes A and B.

By use of the table of multipliers the preparation of a priority list for any of the modern systems of apportionment is a simple job of multiplication. With the aid of a computing machine a list for any method may be prepared in a few hours.

Population. In the counting of the population for the apportionment of representatives, the Constitution specifically excludes Indians not taxed. Unless otherwise noted, all the population figures used in this volume are those for the apportionment population, that is, beginning with 1870, the total population minus the Indians not taxed. Prior to the Civil War the apportionment population comprised free persons and three-fifths of other persons in the states, and excluded the Indians not taxed.

The tables in Appendix C show for each state the total population and the apportionment population as reported for each census as well as the number of representatives assigned at the succeeding apportionment. For the census of 1870 and for each census from 1900 to 1930 inclusive, the number of Indians not taxed as reported by the census is the difference between the total population and the apportionment population. For 1880 and 1890 the Indians were apparently not included in the total population. For 1940 the apportionment population includes the Indians, as all Indians are now regarded as subject to taxation. For 1880, 1890, and 1940, therefore, the apportionment population is the same as the total population. In the official reports the apportionment population is variously referred to as the constitutional population, the federal population, and the representative population. The total apportionment population includes only the inhabitants of the states, and does not include the population of the District of Columbia, the territories, and the possessions.

CHAPTER III

MODERN METHODS OF APPORTIONMENT

There are five modern systems of apportionment which are mathematically correct, which are easily applied through the use of a priority list, and which avoid paradoxes. These methods are designated as follows:

Major fractions
Equal proportions
Harmonic mean
Smallest divisors
Greatest divisors

While these methods are all mathematically correct, each one starts with a different premise and the results may be different. For each one the discussion will show how the method is derived and applied, will give algebraic proof of its correctness, and will include empirical tests comparing the results of each method with the results of the other four methods.

In every case the empirical test compares the apportionment to two states by two methods. If the size of the House is fixed, an incorrect apportionment can be remedied only by a transfer of a representative from one state to another state. The empirical test shows the results of such a transfer. Obviously a single test between two states does not prove that the same result will be reached by comparing all the other pairs of states. However, a comparison of any two states by the methods indicated will yield the same conclusion. The universal applicability of each of the modern methods is shown in the algebraic proof. On the other hand a single example that does not meet the test disproves the applicability of the method.

Two of the modern methods—major fractions and equal proportions—are recognized by statute. The other three methods—harmonic mean, smallest divisors, and greatest divisors—have been discussed in committees and in the literature, but have never received statutory recognition.

METHODS RECOGNIZED BY STATUTE

The permanent apportionment section of the Census Act of June 18, 1929 (46 Stat. L. 26) provides that the President shall report to Congress apportionments of representatives by three methods: (1) by the method used at the last preceding census, (2) by the method of major fractions, and (3) by the method of equal proportions.[1] In practice the reports are reduced to two, as the apportionment after the last preceding census was made by the method of major fractions. The act further provides that if Congress fails to pass an apportionment act the apportionment should be made by the method used at the last preceding one. The method last used before 1930 was that of major fractions. After the census of 1930 the methods of major fractions and equal proportions gave the same result.

Method of Major Fractions

By the method of major fractions the difference between the representation of any two states is the smallest possible when measured by the absolute difference in the individual share in a representative.

The method of major fractions was devised by Professor Walter F. Willcox of Cornell University in 1910.[2] It was used after the censuses of 1910 and 1930. After the census of 1930 it gave the same results as the method of equal proportions. Section 22 of the act of June 18, 1929 (46 Stat. L. 26) and the amendatory act of April 25, 1940 (54 Stat. L. 162) provide that the President shall report to Congress the results of apportionment by the methods of major fractions and equal proportions.

Application of Method of Major Fractions

The computation of the relative claims of each state is made

[1] The act of 1929 was amended by the act of Apr. 25, 1940 (54 Stat. L. 162), but the act of 1940 made no change in the methods to be reported; it merely changed the date on which the report should be made.

[2] Walter F. Willcox, "The Apportionment of Representatives," *American Economic Review, Supplement,* Vol. 6, pp. 1–16.

by means of a priority list, as described on page 8, which is computed by dividing the population of the state successively by the arithmetic mean between succeeding representatives. The divisors begin with $1\frac{1}{2}$ for the second representative and increase in arithmetical progression for each additional representative, the divisors being $1\frac{1}{2}$, $2\frac{1}{2}$, $3\frac{1}{2}$, etc. This may be expressed in the form of an equation as follows:

$$P_{\text{(Priority list figure)}} = \frac{\text{Population of any state } (A)}{(\text{Its next higher assignment } (k) \text{ minus one}) + (\text{one-half})}$$

$$= \frac{A}{(k-1) + \frac{1}{2}}.$$

As one representative has already been assigned to each state the priority numbers for the second and third representatives will be as follows:

$$P_2 = \frac{A}{(2-1) + \frac{1}{2}} \qquad P_3 = \frac{A}{(3-1) + \frac{1}{2}}$$

$$= \frac{A}{1\frac{1}{2}} \qquad\qquad = \frac{A}{2\frac{1}{2}}$$

$$= A \times \text{reciprocal of } 1.5 \qquad = A \times \text{reciprocal of } 2.5$$

$$= A \times 0.666,666,67 \qquad = A \times 0.4$$

The last figures in the equations above are the first two multipliers in the table on page 15, which gives all the multipliers to be used successively for the population of each state in order to obtain the figures for the priority list. Thus the priority numbers based on the census of 1930 for the second and third representatives from New York are as follows:

Priority number for second representative from New York = Population $\times$ 0.666,666,67 = 12,587,967 $\times$ 0.666,666,67 = 8,391,978.

Priority number of third representative from New York = Population $\times$ 0.4 = 12,587,967 $\times$ 0.4 = 5,035,187.

The name of the method of major fractions will be misleading to many persons. It implies for the first step a division of the

Multipliers for Priority List for Method of Major Fractions[a]
(k = successive numbers of representatives)

k	Multiplier	k	Multiplier	k	Multiplier	k	Multiplier
		14	0.0740 7407	27	0.0377 3585−	40	0.0253 1646
2	0.6666 6667	15	.0689 6552	28	.0363 6364	41	.0246 9136
3	.4000 0000	16	.0645 1613	29	.0350 8772	42	.0240 9639
4	.2857 1429	17	.0606 0606	30	.0338 9831	43	.0235 2941
5	.2222 2222	18	.0571 4286	31	.0327 8689	44	.0229 8851
6	.1818 1818	19	.0540 5405+	32	.0317 4603	45	.0224 7191
7	.1538 4615+	20	.0512 8205+	33	.0307 6923	46	.0219 7802
8	.1333 3333	21	.0487 8049	34	.0298 5075−	47	.0215 0538
9	.1176 4706	22	.0465 1163	35	.0289 8551	48	.0210 5263
10	.1052 6316	23	.0444 4444	36	.0281 6901	49	.0206 1856
11	.0952 3810	24	.0425 5319	37	.0273 9726	50	.0202 0202
12	.0869 5652	25	.0408 1633	38	.0266 6667	51	.0198 0198
13	.0800 0000	26	.0392 1569	39	.0259 7403	52	.0194 1748

[a] E. V. Huntington, *Methods of Apportionment*, p. 10.

total population of the country by the number of representatives. This will give the average number of persons in each district, which number may be called the natural ratio. If this number is divided into the population of each state the result would be a whole number and a fraction. Thus if a true method of major fractions is used each state will receive a representative for each whole number and one for each fraction of one-half or more.

Seldom if ever can the method described in the preceding paragraph be applied to a House of fixed size. The division by the natural ratio will give too many or too few major fractions. Thus with an initial divisor of 435 representatives and the use of the natural ratio, the apportionment by states gave 439 major units after the census of 1910 and 433 major units after the census of 1930.[3] These apportionments will be considered in more detail in a later paragraph.

Originally the apportionment by this method was obtained by using an arbitrary ratio that would yield the required number of major fractions. As stated by Professor Willcox: "It is not obtained by any mathematical formula. It is a process of cutting and trying."[4] Later it was found that a priority list de-

[3] The term "major units" is here used to mean the sum of all whole numbers plus an additional number for each major fraction. Thus 8.75 and 8.65 would make 18 major units. The number of major units is equal to the number of representatives.

[4] *Apportionment of Representatives*, Hearing before the House Committee on the Census, 70 Cong. 1 sess., on H.R. 130, February ... 1928, p. 89.

rived by a division of the state population by 1½, 2½, etc., as described on preceding pages, will yield the same result.

If we revert to the apportionment made after the census of 1910, we find that the population base for the entire country was 91,569,325; dividing this by 435 gives a natural ratio per district of 210,504. If this ratio is divided into the population of the several states and seats assigned according to a true method of major fractions the total number of seats would be 439.

To meet this situation the apportionment was adjusted by using an assumed ratio of 211,877, which "is merely the halfway or midpoint between Iowa's quotient [in the priority list], 211,883, and Ohio's quotient [in the priority list] 211,872, which would have received the 436th member. By using this divisor, 211,877, each state secured in 1910 one representative for each full quota (211,877), and one for each major fraction."[5] The same result would be reached by taking as the revised ratio any number between 211,883 and 211,872.

The adjustments in 1910 are shown in the following table.

ADJUSTMENT OF MAJOR FRACTIONS IN APPORTIONMENT
BASED ON CENSUS OF 1910[a]

State	Population	True Method of Major Fractions		Adjusted Method of Major Fractions	
		Exact Quota Based on Natural Ratio of 210,504 Persons per District	Number of Representatives	Exact Quota Based on Revised Ratio of 211,877 Persons per District	Number of Representatives
Mississippi..........	1,797,114	8.54	9	8.48	8
New Mexico........	316,983	1.50	2	1.49	1
Ohio..............	4,767,121	22.65	23	22.49	22
Texas.............	3,896,542	18.51	19	18.39	18
Total...........	—	—	53	—	49
Other states.......	b	—	386	—	386
All states........	—	—	439	—	435

[a] *Apportionment of Representatives in Congress amongst the Several States,* Hearing before the House Committee on the Census, 69 Cong. 2 sess., on H.R. 13471, p. 17.
[b] No change was made in the assignment to these states, as the division of the population of the state by the natural ratio and by the revised ratio did not change any fraction from a major fraction to a minor fraction or vice versa.

After the census of 1930 the apportionment was made by means of the priority list, which does not require any assumed ratio. At that time the natural ratio of 280,675 (122,093,455 divided by 435) yielded only 433 major units. However, if any

[5] *Apportionment of Representatives,* 70 Cong. 1 sess., H. Rept. 1137, p. 10.

figure between the priority number for the 435th member (280,212) and the priority number for the 436th member (279,212) is used for the ratio, the result will be 435 major units. In other words it is not necessary to assume any ratio. However, 435 major units cannot be obtained by dividing by the natural ratio, but can be derived only by using an assumed or derived ratio. Priority lists for the method of major fractions, based on the censuses of 1930 and 1940, are given in Appendixes A and B.

The method of major fractions gives the smallest possible difference in the individual share in a representative, if the inequality is measured on the basis of absolute differences, but it is not a method of major fractions if the natural ratio is taken as the divisor.

Empirical Tests of Method of Major Fractions[6]

The correctness of the method of major fractions, on the basis of the absolute difference in the share in a representative, may

[6] The algebraic proof of the correctness of the method of major fractions in equalizing the representation when measured by the absolute difference in the share in a representative is as follows:

Designate the population of two states as A and B; designate the number of representatives assigned to State A as a, and the number assigned to State B as b. The share in a representative will then be the number of representatives divided by the population, or $\dfrac{a}{A}$ and $\dfrac{b}{B}$. Under what conditions would it be fairer to assign an additional representative to State A in preference to State B? If an additional representative is assigned to State A, the absolute difference in the share in a representative would be expressed by the following fraction:

$$\frac{a+1}{A} - \frac{b}{B}.$$

If an additional representative is assigned to State B the absolute difference would be expressed by the fraction

$$\frac{b+1}{B} - \frac{a}{A}.$$

If the assignment of the additional representative to A is correct, the absolute difference will be smaller than if the additional representative had been assigned to B. This may be expressed as follows:

$$\frac{a+1}{A} - \frac{b}{B} < \frac{b+1}{B} - \frac{a}{A}.$$

If the terms are transposed the relationship is not changed and we get

be tested by a comparison of any two states. On the following pages comparisons are made between two states under an apportionment by the method of major fractions and by each of the other four methods. If every pair of states were compared, the method of major fractions would show the smaller absolute difference in the individual share in a representative.

The minimum relative difference per share in a representative and in the average population per district is effected by the method of equal proportions; the minimum absolute difference in the average population per district is achieved by the method of harmonic mean; the minimum absolute representation surplus is effected by the method of smallest divisors; the minimum absolute representative deficiency is effected by the method of greatest divisors. Tests based on these criteria are given in the discussion of those methods.

The methods of major fractions and equal proportions gave the same apportionment for a House of 435 members after the census of 1930; therefore, tests of the method of major fractions based on the census of 1930 would give the same results as the tests of method of equal proportions given on pages 28–32. Accordingly, all the tests for the method of major fractions will be based on the census of 1920.

$$\frac{a+1}{A} + \frac{a}{A} < \frac{b+1}{B} + \frac{b}{B}$$

$$\frac{a+(a+1)}{A} < \frac{b+(b+1)}{B}.$$

By taking the reciprocals we get

$$\frac{A}{a+(a+1)} > \frac{B}{b+(b+1)}$$

$$\frac{A}{2a+1} > \frac{B}{2b+1}$$

$$\frac{A}{a+\frac{1}{2}} > \frac{B}{b+\frac{1}{2}}.$$

Therefore it follows that State A deserves the additional assignment when its population divided by its present assignment plus $\frac{1}{2}$ is greater than the population of State B divided by its present assignment plus $\frac{1}{2}$.

Taking up a comparison of the method of major fractions with the method of equal proportions we find that the differences in the apportionment were as follows:

APPORTIONMENT BY METHODS OF MAJOR FRACTIONS AND EQUAL
PROPORTIONS, CENSUS OF 1920

State	Population	Major Fractions	Equal Proportions
New Mexico........	353,428	1	2
New York..........	10,380,589	43	42
North Carolina......	2,559,123	11	10
Rhode Island.......	604,397	2	3
Vermont...........	352,428	1	2
Virginia...........	2,309,187	10	9

A comparison of the absolute difference in the individual share in a representative for the states of North Carolina and Vermont, according to these two methods, is shown in the succeeding table:

INDIVIDUAL SHARE IN A REPRESENTATIVE, BASED ON CENSUS OF 1920,
METHODS OF MAJOR FRACTIONS AND EQUAL PROPORTIONS

State	Population	Major Fractions		Equal Proportions	
		Number of Representatives	Individual Share	Number of Representatives	Individual Share
North Carolina.....	2,559,123	11	.000,004,30	10	.000,003,91
Vermont...........	352,428	1	.000,002,84	2	.000,005,68
Absolute difference..	—	—	.000,001,46	—	.000,001,77

If the smaller absolute difference in the individual share is taken as the criterion, North Carolina will receive 11 representatives and Vermont 1, as indicated by the method of major fractions.

The differences in apportionment between the methods of major fractions and of harmonic mean, after the census of 1920, were as follows:

APPORTIONMENT BY METHODS OF MAJOR FRACTIONS AND HARMONIC
MEAN, CENSUS OF 1920

State	Population	Major Fractions	Harmonic Mean
New Mexico........	353,428	1	2
New York..........	10,380,589	43	42
North Carolina.....	2,559,123	11	10
Rhode Island.......	604,397	2	3
Vermont...........	352,428	1	2
Virginia...........	2,309,187	10	9

A comparison of the absolute difference in the individual share for Virginia and New Mexico yields the following result:

INDIVIDUAL SHARE IN A REPRESENTATIVE, BASED ON CENSUS OF 1920, METHODS OF MAJOR FRACTIONS AND HARMONIC MEAN

State	Population	Major Fractions		Harmonic Mean	
		Number of Representatives	Individual Share	Number of Representatives	Individual Share
New Mexico........	353,428	1	.000,002,83	2	.000,005,66
Virginia...........	2,309,187	10	.000,004,33	9	.000,003,90
Absolute difference..	—	—	.000,001,50	—	.000,001,76

If the absolute difference in the individual share is taken as the criterion, Virginia will receive 10 representatives and New Mexico 1, as the difference is smaller by the method of major fractions.

Turning to the method of smallest divisors we find the following differences in apportionment based on the census of 1920:

APPORTIONMENT BY METHODS OF MAJOR FRACTIONS AND SMALLEST DIVISORS, CENSUS OF 1920

State	Population	Major Fractions	Smallest Divisors	State	Population	Major Fractions	Smallest Divisors
Arizona.......	309,495	1	2	Ohio..........	5,759,394	24	23
Illinois........	6,485,280	27	26	Oregon........	783,389	3	4
Louisiana.....	1,798,509	7	8	Pennsylvania..	8,720,017	36	34
Montana......	541,511	2	3				
				Rhode Island..	604,397	2	3
Nebraska.....	1,296,372	5	6	Vermont......	352,428	1	2
New Mexico...	353,428	1	2	Virginia.......	2,309,187	10	9
New York.....	10,380,589	43	41				
North Carolina.	2,559,123	11	10				

A comparison of the individual share for Louisiana and Virginia yields the following result:

INDIVIDUAL SHARE IN A REPRESENTATIVE, BASED ON CENSUS OF 1920, METHODS OF MAJOR FRACTIONS AND SMALLEST DIVISORS

State	Population	Major Fractions		Smallest Divisors	
		Number of Representatives	Individual Share	Number of Representatives	Individual Share
Louisiana..........	1,798,509	7	.000,003,89	8	.000,004,45
Virginia...........	2,309,187	10	.000,004,33	9	.000,003,90
Absolute difference..	—	—	.000,000,44	—	.000,000,55

As the absolute difference in the individual share is less by the method of major fractions than by the method of smallest divisors, the apportionment of 7 members to Louisiana and 10 members to Virginia, as made by the method of major fractions, is correct if the smaller absolute difference in individual share is the criterion.

After the census of 1920 there were the following differences in apportionment by the methods of major fractions and greatest divisors:

APPORTIONMENT BY METHODS OF MAJOR FRACTIONS AND GREATEST
DIVISORS, CENSUS OF 1920

State	Population	Major Fractions	Greatest Divisors
Idaho.............	430,442	2	1
Illinois.............	6,485,280	27	28
New Hampshire.....	443,083	2	1
New York..........	10,380,589	43	45
North Dakota......	643,953	3	2
Ohio..............	5,759,394	24	25
Pennsylvania.......	8,720,017	36	37
South Dakota.......	631,239	3	2
Texas.............	4,663,228	19	20
Utah..............	448,388	2	1
Washington........	1,354,596	6	5

A comparison of the individual share for Washington and Texas yields the following result:

INDIVIDUAL SHARE IN A REPRESENTATIVE, BASED ON CENSUS OF 1920,
METHODS OF MAJOR FRACTIONS AND GREATEST DIVISORS

State	Population	Major Fractions		Greatest Divisors	
		Number of Representatives	Individual Share	Number of Representatives	Individual Share
Texas.............	4,663,228	19	.000,004,07	20	.000,004,28
Washington........	1,354,596	6	.000,004,43	5	.000,003,69
Absolute difference..	—	—	.000,000,36	—	.000,000,59

As the absolute difference in the individual share is less by the method of major fractions than by the method of greatest divisors, the apportionment of 6 members to Washington and 19 members to Texas, as made by the method of major fractions, is correct if the smaller absolute difference in individual share is the criterion.

Method of Equal Proportions

By the method of equal proportions the difference between the representation of any two states is the smallest possible when measured both by the relative difference in the average population per district and also by the relative difference in the individual share in a representative.

This method was developed by Professor Edward V. Huntington of Harvard University in 1920.[7] It has never been used in any congressional apportionment, although after the census of 1930 it gave the same results as the method of major fractions, which was prescribed by statute. Section 22 of the act of June 18, 1929 (46 Stat. L. 26) and the amendatory act of April 25, 1940 (54 Stat. L. 162) provide that the President shall report to Congress the results of apportionments by the methods of equal proportions and major fractions.

Application of the Method of Equal Proportions

This method uses the following process of computation: State A deserves an additional representative when its population, divided by the geometric mean of its present assignment of representatives and of its next higher assignment, is greater than the population of any other state divided by the geometric mean of the assignment to such other state and its next higher assignment.

In order to compute the relative claims of each state a priority list is prepared as described on page 8. The figures for the priority list are obtained by dividing the population of the state by the geometric means of successive numbers of representatives. As the geometric mean of two numbers is the square root of their product,[8] this process may be expressed in the form of an

---

[7] See Edward V. Huntington, "A New Method of Apportionment of Representatives," *Quarterly Publication of the American Statistical Association*, Vol. 17, pp. 859–70; "The Apportionment of Representatives in Congress," *Transactions of the American Mathematical Society*, Vol. 30, pp. 85–110. *Methods of Apportionment*, 76 Cong. 3 sess., S. Doc. 304.

[8] The geometric mean is a method of averaging ratios. The geometric mean (m) of two numbers (a) and (b) may be expressed as follows:

$$\frac{m}{a} = \frac{b}{m}, \quad \text{or} \quad m^2 = ab, \quad \text{or} \quad m = \sqrt{ab}.$$

Thus the geometric mean of 4 and 16 is $\sqrt{4 \times 16}$ or $\sqrt{64}$ or 8.

equation as follows:

$$P \text{ (Priority list figure)} = \frac{\text{Population of any state } (A)}{\text{Geometric mean of its next higher assignment } (k) \text{ and its present assignment } (k-1)}$$

$$= \frac{A}{\sqrt{k(k-1)}}.$$

As one representative has already been assigned the priority numbers for the second and third will be as follows:

$$P_2 = \frac{A}{\sqrt{2(2-1)}} \qquad\qquad P_3 = \frac{A}{\sqrt{3(3-1)}}$$

$$= \frac{A}{\sqrt{2(1)}} \qquad\qquad = \frac{A}{\sqrt{3(2)}}$$

$$= \frac{A}{\sqrt{2}} \qquad\qquad = \frac{A}{\sqrt{6}}$$

$$= \frac{A}{1.414,213,6} \qquad\qquad = \frac{A}{2.449,489,7}$$

$$= A \times \text{reciprocal of } 1.414,213,6 \qquad = A \times \text{reciprocal of } 2.449,489,7$$

$$= A \times 0.707,106,78 \qquad\qquad = A \times 0.408,248,29$$

The last figures in the equations above are the first two multipliers in the table on page 24, which gives all the multipliers to be used successively for the population of each state in order to obtain the figures for the priority list. Thus the priority numbers based on the census of 1930 for the second and third representatives from New York are derived as follows:

Priority number for second representative from New York = Population $\times$ 0.707,106,78 = 12,587,967 $\times$ 0.707,106,78 = 8,901,037.

Priority number for third representative from New York = Population $\times$ 0.408,248,29 = 12,587,967 $\times$ 0.408,248,29 = 5,139,016.

Priority lists for the method of equal proportions, based on the censuses of 1930 and 1940 are given in Appendixes A and B.

k	Multiplier	k	Multiplier	k	Multiplier	k	Multiplier
		14	0.0741 2493	27	0.0377 4257	40	0.0253 1848
2	0.7071 0678	15	.0690 0656	28	.0363 6965−	41	.0246 9324
3	.4082 4829	16	.0645 4972	29	.0350 9312	42	.0240 9813
4	.2886 7513	17	.0606 3391	30	.0339 0318	43	.0235 3104
5	.2236 0680	18	.0571 6620	31	.0327 9129	44	.0229 9002
6	.1825 7419	19	.0540 7381	32	.0317 5003	45	.0224 7333
7	.1543 0335−	20	.0512 9892	33	.0307 7287	46	.0219 7935−
8	.1336 3062	21	.0487 9500	34	.0298 5407	47	.0215 0662
9	.1178 5113	22	.0465 2421	35	.0289 8855+	48	.0210 5380
10	.1054 0926	23	.0444 5542	36	.0281 7181	49	.0206 1965+
11	.0953 4626	24	.0425 6283	37	.0273 9983	50	.0202 0305+
12	.0870 3883	25	.0408 2483	38	.0266 6904	51	.0198 0295+
13	.0800 6408	26	.0392 2323	39	.0259 7622	52	.0194 1839

[a] Huntington, *Methods of Apportionment*, p. 6.

Empirical Tests of Method of Equal Proportions[9]

The correctness of the apportionment may be tested by a comparison of any two states. On the following pages comparisons are made between two states under an apportionment by

[9] The algebraic proof that the method of equal proportions provides less inequality between states both in respect to the relative difference in average population per district and in respect to the share of the individual in a representative is given below.

The first problem is to find a method of assignment of representatives among the states so that the relative difference in average population of districts between any two states is as small as possible.

Designate the population of two states as A and B; designate the number of representatives assigned to State A as a, and the number of representatives assigned to State B as b. The average population of the districts in any state is the total population divided by the number of representatives, or $\dfrac{A}{a}$ and $\dfrac{B}{b}$.

Under what conditions would it be fairer to assign an additional representative to State A in preference to State B? If an additional representative is assigned to A the relative difference in average population per district would be expressed by the following fraction:

$$\frac{\left(\dfrac{B}{b}\right) - \left(\dfrac{A}{a+1}\right)}{\left(\dfrac{A}{a+1}\right)}.$$

If an additional representative is assigned to B the relative difference in average population per district would be expressed by the following fraction:

$$\frac{\left(\dfrac{A}{a}\right) - \left(\dfrac{B}{b+1}\right)}{\left(\dfrac{B}{b+1}\right)}.$$

If the assignment of the additional representative to A is correct, the relative differ-

the method of equal proportions and by each of the other four methods. If every pair of states were compared the method of

ence will be smaller than if the additional representative had been assigned to B. This may be expressed as follows:

$$\frac{\left(\frac{B}{b}\right) - \left(\frac{A}{a+1}\right)}{\left(\frac{A}{a+1}\right)} < \frac{\left(\frac{A}{a}\right) - \left(\frac{B}{b+1}\right)}{\left(\frac{B}{b+1}\right)}.$$

By separating the fractions we get

$$\frac{\left(\frac{B}{b}\right)}{\left(\frac{A}{a+1}\right)} - \frac{\left(\frac{A}{a+1}\right)}{\left(\frac{A}{a+1}\right)} < \frac{\left(\frac{A}{a}\right)}{\left(\frac{B}{b+1}\right)} - \frac{\left(\frac{B}{b+1}\right)}{\left(\frac{B}{b+1}\right)}.$$

As any number divided by itself is 1 we can dispense with the fractions

$$\frac{\left(\frac{A}{a+1}\right)}{\left(\frac{A}{a+1}\right)} \quad \text{and} \quad \frac{\left(\frac{B}{b+1}\right)}{\left(\frac{B}{b+1}\right)}$$

and write

$$\frac{\left(\frac{B}{b}\right)}{\left(\frac{A}{a+1}\right)} - 1 < \frac{\left(\frac{A}{a}\right)}{\left(\frac{B}{b+1}\right)} - 1$$

We can add 1 to each side without changing the relationship and the result will be

$$\frac{\left(\frac{B}{b}\right)}{\left(\frac{A}{a+1}\right)} < \frac{\left(\frac{A}{a}\right)}{\left(\frac{B}{b+1}\right)}$$

If we multiply each side by both denominators the relationship will not be changed and we obtain the following:

$$\frac{\left(\frac{B}{b}\right)}{\left(\frac{A}{a+1}\right)} \times \left(\frac{A}{a+1}\right) \times \left(\frac{B}{b+1}\right) < \frac{\left(\frac{A}{a}\right)}{\left(\frac{B}{b+1}\right)} \times \left(\frac{A}{a+1}\right) \times \left(\frac{B}{b+1}\right)$$

$$\left(\frac{B}{b}\right) \times \left(\frac{B}{b+1}\right) < \left(\frac{A}{a}\right) \times \left(\frac{A}{a+1}\right)$$

$$\frac{B^2}{b(b+1)} < \frac{A^2}{a(a+1)}.$$

We can take the square root of both sides without changing the relationship, and we

equal proportions would show the smaller relative difference in average population per district and in individual share in a representative.

The minimum absolute difference in the average population per district is effected by the method of harmonic mean; the

get

$$\frac{B}{\sqrt{b(b+1)}} < \frac{A}{\sqrt{a(a+1)}}.$$

For convenience we can turn this around to read

$$\frac{A}{\sqrt{a(a+1)}} > \frac{B}{\sqrt{b(b+1)}}.$$

As the square root of the product of two numbers is the geometric mean of these two numbers it follows that State A deserves the additional representative when its population divided by the geometric mean of its present assignment and of its next higher assignment is greater than the population of State B divided by the geometric mean of B's present assignment and of its next higher assignment.

The second problem is to find a method of assignment of representatives among the states so that the relative difference in the share in a representative between any two states is as small as possible.

If the population of two states is designated by A and B and the number of representatives by a and b as before, the share in a representative is the number of representatives divided by the population, or $\frac{a}{A}$ and $\frac{b}{B}$. If an additional representative is assigned to A the relative difference per share of a representative would be

$$\frac{\left(\frac{a+1}{A}\right) - \left(\frac{b}{B}\right)}{\left(\frac{b}{B}\right)}.$$

If an additional representative is assigned to B the relative difference in the share of a representative would be expressed by the following fraction:

$$\frac{\left(\frac{b+1}{B}\right) - \left(\frac{a}{A}\right)}{\left(\frac{a}{A}\right)}.$$

If the assignment of an additional representative to A is correct the relative difference will be smaller than if the additional representative had been assigned to B. This may be expressed as follows:

$$\frac{\left(\frac{a+1}{A}\right) - \left(\frac{b}{B}\right)}{\left(\frac{b}{B}\right)} < \frac{\left(\frac{b+1}{B}\right) - \left(\frac{a}{A}\right)}{\left(\frac{a}{A}\right)}.$$

75136

minimum absolute difference in the share in a representative is effected by the method of major fractions; the minimum ab-

By separating the fractions we get:

$$\frac{\left(\frac{a+1}{A}\right)}{\left(\frac{b}{B}\right)} - \frac{\left(\frac{b}{B}\right)}{\left(\frac{b}{B}\right)} < \frac{\left(\frac{b+1}{B}\right)}{\left(\frac{a}{A}\right)} - \frac{\left(\frac{a}{A}\right)}{\left(\frac{a}{A}\right)}.$$

As any number divided by itself is 1 we can dispense with the fractions and write

$$\frac{\left(\frac{a+1}{A}\right)}{\left(\frac{b}{B}\right)} - 1 < \frac{\left(\frac{b+1}{B}\right)}{\left(\frac{a}{A}\right)} - 1.$$

We can add 1 to each side without changing the relationship, and the result will be:

$$\frac{\left(\frac{a+1}{A}\right)}{\left(\frac{b}{B}\right)} < \frac{\left(\frac{b+1}{B}\right)}{\left(\frac{a}{A}\right)}.$$

If we multiply each side by both denominators the relationship will not be changed, and we obtain the following

$$\frac{\left(\frac{a+1}{A}\right)}{\left(\frac{b}{B}\right)} \times \frac{b}{B} \times \frac{a}{A} < \frac{\left(\frac{b+1}{B}\right)}{\left(\frac{a}{A}\right)} \times \frac{b}{B} \times \frac{a}{A}$$

or

$$\frac{a+1}{A} \times \frac{a}{A} < \frac{b+1}{B} \times \frac{b}{B}$$

or

$$\frac{a(a+1)}{A^2} < \frac{b(b+1)}{B^2}.$$

We can take the square root of both sides without changing the relationship and we get

$$\frac{\sqrt{a(a+1)}}{A} < \frac{\sqrt{b(b+1)}}{B}.$$

By taking the reciprocals we get

$$\frac{A}{\sqrt{a(a+1)}} > \frac{B}{\sqrt{b(b+1)}}.$$

As the square root of the product of two numbers is the geometric mean of these two numbers, it follows that State A deserves the additional representative when its population divided by the geometric mean of its present assignment and its next higher assignment is greater than the population of State B divided by the geometric mean of B's present assignment and its next higher assignment.

solute representation surplus is effected by the method of smallest divisors; the minimum absolute representation deficiency is effected by the method of greatest divisors. Tests based on these criteria are given in the discussions of those methods.

The first comparison, based on the census of 1930, will be between the methods of equal proportions and harmonic mean. These methods show the following differences:

APPORTIONMENT BY METHODS OF EQUAL PROPORTIONS
AND HARMONIC MEAN, CENSUS OF 1930

State	Population	Equal Proportions	Harmonic Mean
Arizona	389,375	1	2
Indiana	3,238,480	12	11
Louisiana	2,101,593	8	7
New Mexico	395,982	1	2
Oklahoma	2,382,222	9	8
Rhode Island	687,497	2	3

We shall examine in detail the differences between Louisiana and Rhode Island, and shall first compare the average population per district, which is as follows:

AVERAGE POPULATION PER DISTRICT, BASED ON CENSUS OF 1930,
METHODS OF EQUAL PROPORTIONS AND HARMONIC MEAN

State	Population	Equal Proportions		Harmonic Mean	
		Number of Representatives	Average Population per District	Number of Representatives	Average Population per District
Louisiana	2,101,593	8	262,699	7	300,228
Rhode Island	687,497	2	343,748	3	229,166
Absolute difference	—	—	81,049	—	71,062
Relative difference	—	—	30.9%	—	31.0%

The absolute difference between Louisiana and Rhode Island in average population per district is less by the method of harmonic mean, and if the absolute difference is the criterion the method of harmonic mean should be used and 7 representatives should be apportioned to Louisiana and 3 to Rhode Island.[10] However the relative difference between the two states is less by the method of equal proportions, and if the relative difference is the criterion the method of equal proportions should be

[10] An apportionment by the method of harmonic mean will always show the smallest absolute difference in the average population of congressional districts if two states are compared.

used and 8 representatives assigned to Louisiana and 2 to Rhode Island.

We shall next compare the two states on the basis of the individual share in a representative, which results as follows:

INDIVIDUAL SHARE IN A REPRESENTATIVE, BASED ON CENSUS OF 1930,
METHODS OF EQUAL PROPORTIONS AND HARMONIC MEAN

State	Population	Equal Proportions		Harmonic Mean	
		Number of Representatives	Individual Share	Number of Representatives	Individual Share
Louisiana.........	2,101,593	8	.000,003,81	7	.000,003,33
Rhode Island......	687,497	2	.000,002,91	3	.000,004,36
Absolute difference..	—	—	.000,000,90	—	.000,001,03
Relative difference...	—	—	30.9%	—	31.0%

In this case the difference is less, both absolutely and relatively, in the apportionment made by the method of equal proportions, but the relative difference is the one to be taken into consideration. Combining these two tests we find the method of equal proportions is the one which gives the smaller difference in relative population per district, and also gives the smaller difference in the individual share in a representative.

It will be noted that the percentage difference is small in each case. As has been stated, the computation is based on a membership of 435; if the membership were increased to 436 the additional member allotted under the method of equal proportions would go to Rhode Island. Under the method of harmonic mean the apportionment to Rhode Island would be reduced to 2 if the membership were fixed at 429.

As the methods of equal proportions and major fractions give the same results with a House of 435 members apportioned according to the census of 1930 it is necessary to use the census of 1920 to compare the two methods, which show the following differences:

APPORTIONMENT BY METHODS OF EQUAL PROPORTIONS AND MAJOR
FRACTIONS, CENSUS OF 1920

State	Population	Equal Proportions	Major Fractions
New Mexico........	353,428	2	1
New York..........	10,380,589	42	43
North Carolina.....	2,559,123	10	11
Rhode Island.......	604,397	3	2
Vermont...........	352,428	2	1
Virginia...........	2,309,187	9	10

We shall examine in detail the differences between New York and Rhode Island, and shall first compare the average population per district, which is as follows:

AVERAGE POPULATION PER DISTRICT, BASED ON CENSUS OF 1920,
METHODS OF EQUAL PROPORTIONS AND MAJOR FRACTIONS

State	Population	Equal Proportions		Major Fractions	
		Number of Representatives	Average Population per District	Number of Representatives	Average Population per District
New York.........	10,380,589	42	247,157	43	241,409
Rhode Island.......	604,397	3	201,466	2	302,198
Absolute difference..	—	—	45,691	—	60,789
Relative difference...	—	—	22%	—	25%

The relative difference in the average population per district is smaller in an apportionment by the method of equal proportions, and therefore that method should be used if the relative difference in average population per district is the criterion.

Turning to the share of the individual in a representative we find that the apportionment by these two methods yields the following result:

INDIVIDUAL SHARE IN A REPRESENTATIVE, BASED ON CENSUS OF 1920,
METHODS OF EQUAL PROPORTIONS AND MAJOR FRACTIONS

State	Population	Equal Proportions		Major Fractions	
		Number of Representatives	Individual Share	Number of Representatives	Individual Share
New York.........	10,380,589	42	.000,004,05	43	.000,004,14
Rhode Island.......	604,397	3	.000,004,96	2	.000,003,31
Absolute difference..	—	—	.000,000,91	—	.000,000,83
Relative difference...	—	—	22%	—	25%

If the absolute difference of the individual share is taken as the criterion, the apportionment should be made by the method of major fractions, as that method will always give a smaller figure for that difference. If the relative difference is taken as the criterion, the method of equal proportions should be used, as an apportionment by that method will always result in the smallest possible variation in the individual share.

The next comparison will be between the methods of equal proportions and of greatest divisors. The census of 1930 gave the following differences in representation by the two methods:

APPORTIONMENT BY METHODS OF EQUAL PROPORTIONS AND
GREATEST DIVISORS, CENSUS OF 1930

State	Population	Equal Proportions	Greatest Divisors	State	Population	Equal Proportions	Greatest Divisors
Arkansas	1,854,444	7	6	New Hampshire	465,292	2	1
California	5,668,241	20	21	New Jersey	4,041,319	14	15
Colorado	1,034,849	4	3	New York	12,587,967	45	47
Idaho	441,536	2	1	Ohio	6,646,633	24	25
Illinois	7,630,388	27	28	Oklahoma	2,382,222	9	8
Louisiana	2,101,593	8	7	Pennsylvania	9,631,299	34	36
Maine	797,418	3	2	Utah	505,741	2	1
Michigan	4,842,052	17	18	Washington	1,552,423	6	5
Montana	524,729	2	1	Wisconsin	2,931,721	10	11

Examination will be made in detail of the differences between Ohio and Louisiana. Comparisons on the basis of average population per district and of individual share in a representative give the following results:

AVERAGE POPULATION PER DISTRICT, BASED ON CENSUS OF 1930,
METHODS OF EQUAL PROPORTIONS AND GREATEST DIVISORS

State	Population	Equal Proportions		Greatest Divisors	
		Number of Representatives	Average Population per District	Number of Representatives	Average Population per District
Louisiana	2,101,593	8	262,699	7	300,228
Ohio	6,646,633	24	276,943	25	265,865
Absolute difference	—	—	14,244	—	34,363
Relative difference	—	—	5%	—	13%

INDIVIDUAL SHARE IN A REPRESENTATIVE, BASED ON CENSUS OF 1930,
METHODS OF EQUAL PROPORTIONS AND GREATEST DIVISORS

State	Population	Equal Proportions		Greatest Divisors	
		Number of Representatives	Individual Share	Number of Representatives	Individual Share
Louisiana	2,101,593	8	.000,003,81	7	.000,003,33
Ohio	6,646,633	24	.000,003,61	25	.000,003,76
Absolute difference	—	—	.000,000,20	—	.000,000,43
Relative difference	—	—	5%	—	13%

These examples show that in the case of average population per district and individual share in a representative the use of the method of equal proportions gives a smaller relative difference in the representation of the two states.

One more method remains to be considered—that of the smallest divisors. The census of 1930 gave the following differences in representation by the methods of equal proportions and smallest divisors:

APPORTIONMENT BY METHODS OF EQUAL PROPORTIONS AND
SMALLEST DIVISORS, CENSUS OF 1930

State	Population	Equal Proportions	Smallest Divisors	State	Population	Equal Proportions	Smallest Divisors
Arizona	389,375	1	2	Oregon	950,379	3	4
Illinois	7,630,388	27	26	Pennsylvania	9,631,299	34	33
Indiana	3,238,480	12	11	Rhode Island	687,497	2	3
New Mexico	395,982	1	2	South Dakota	673,005	2	3
New York	12,587,967	45	43	Texas	5,824,601	21	20
North Dakota	673,340	2	3	Vermont	359,611	1	2
Ohio	6,646,633	24	23				

A comparison between the apportionment for Ohio and Rhode Island by these methods results as follows:

AVERAGE POPULATION PER DISTRICT, BASED ON CENSUS OF 1930,
METHODS OF EQUAL PROPORTIONS AND SMALLEST DIVISORS

State	Population	Equal Proportions		Smallest Divisors	
		Number of Representatives	Average Population per District	Number of Representatives	Average Population per District
Ohio	6,646,633	24	276,943	23	288,984
Rhode Island	687,497	2	343,748	3	229,166
Absolute difference	—	—	66,805	—	59,818
Relative difference	—	—	24%	—	26%

INDIVIDUAL SHARE IN A REPRESENTATIVE, BASED ON CENSUS OF 1930,
METHODS OF EQUAL PROPORTIONS AND SMALLEST DIVISORS

State	Population	Equal Proportions		Smallest Divisors	
		Number of Representatives	Individual Share	Number of Representatives	Individual Share
Ohio	6,646,633	24	.000,003,61	23	.000,003,46
Rhode Island	687,497	2	.000,002,91	3	.000,004,36
Absolute difference	—	—	.000,000,70	—	.000,000,90
Relative difference	—	—	24%	—	26%

These examples give the same result as those for the method of greatest divisors: the relative difference in the average population per district and in the individual share in a representative is less in the case of the method of equal proportions.

METHODS NOT RECOGNIZED BY STATUTE

Three methods which are mathematically correct have been developed during recent years, but none of them has been recognized by law. These are the method of harmonic mean, the method of smallest divisors, and the method of greatest divisors. The basis and the limitations of each are described in the following pages.

Method of Harmonic Mean

By the method of harmonic mean the difference between the representation of any two states is the smallest possible when measured by the absolute difference of the average population per district. The method of harmonic mean was first developed by E. V. Huntington in 1921 but was later abandoned by him in favor of the method of equal proportions. It has never been used in an apportionment.

Application of Method of Harmonic Mean

This method uses the following process of computation. State *A* deserves an additional representative when its population divided by the harmonic mean of its present assignment of representatives and of its next higher assignment of representatives is greater than the population of any other state divided by the harmonic mean of the present assignment to such other state and its next higher assignment.

In order to compute the relative claims of each state a priority list is prepared as described on page 8. The figures for the priority list are obtained by multiplying the population of the state by the harmonic means of successive numbers of representatives.[11]

As the harmonic mean of two numbers is twice their product divided by their sum this process may be expressed in the form

[11] The harmonic mean is a method of averaging absolute differences. The harmonic mean (H) of two numbers (a) and (b) may be expressed as

$$H = \frac{2(a \times b)}{a + b}.$$

Thus the harmonic mean of 2 and 3 is

$$\frac{2(2 \times 3)}{2 + 3} = \frac{12}{5} = 2\frac{2}{5}.$$

of an equation as follows:

$$P \text{ (Priority list figure)} = \frac{\text{Population of any state } (A)}{\text{Harmonic mean of its next higher assignment } (k) \text{ and of its present assignment } (k-1)}$$

$$= \frac{A}{\left(\dfrac{2(k-1)k}{(k-1)+k}\right)}.$$

As one representative has already been assigned the priority numbers for the second and third would be as follows:

$$P_2 = \frac{A}{\left(\dfrac{2(2-1)2}{(2-1)+2}\right)} \qquad P_3 = \frac{A}{\left(\dfrac{2(3-1)3}{(3-1)+3}\right)}$$

$$= \frac{A}{\left(\dfrac{2(2)}{1+2}\right)} \qquad\qquad = \frac{A}{\left(\dfrac{2(2)3}{2+3}\right)}$$

$$= \frac{A}{\frac{4}{3}} \qquad\qquad\qquad = \frac{A}{\frac{12}{5}}$$

$$= A \times \tfrac{3}{4} \qquad\qquad\quad = A \times 5/12$$

$$= A \times 0.75 \qquad\qquad = A \times 0.416,666,67$$

The last figures in the equations above are the first two multipliers in the table on page 35, which gives all the multipliers to be used successively for the population of the state in order to obtain the figures for the priority list. Thus the priority numbers based on the census of 1930 for the second and third representatives from New York are derived as follows:

Priority number for second representative from New York = Population ×0.75 = 12,587,967 ×0.75 = 9,440,975.

Priority number for third representative from New York = Population × 0.416,666,67 = 12,587,967 × 0.416,666,67 = 5,244,985.

The priority list for the method of harmonic mean, based on the census of 1930, is given in Appendix A.

MULTIPLIERS FOR PRIORITY LIST FOR METHOD OF HARMONIC MEAN[a]
(*k* = successive numbers of representatives)

k	Multiplier	k	Multiplier	k	Multiplier	k	Multiplier
		14	0.0741 7582	27	0.0377 4929	40	0.0253 2051
2	0.7500 0000	15	.0690 4762	28	.0363 7566	41	.0246 9512
3	.4166 6667	16	.0645 8333	29	.0350 9852	42	.0240 9988
4	.2916 6667	17	.0606 6176	30	.0339 0805 −	43	.0235 3267
5	.2250 0000	18	.0571 8954	31	.0327 9570	44	.0229 9154
6	.1833 3333	19	.0540 9357	32	.0317 5403	45	.0224 7475 −
7	.1547 6190	20	.0513 1579	33	.0307 7652	46	.0219 8068
8	.1339 2857	21	.0488 0952	34	.0298 5740	47	.0215 0786
9	.1180 5556	22	.0465 3680	35	.0289 9160	48	.0210 5496
10	.1055 5556	23	.0444 6640	36	.0281 7460	49	.0206 2075 −
11	.0954 5455 −	24	.0425 7246	37	.0274 0240	50	.0202 0408
12	.0871 2121	25	.0408 3333	38	.0266 7141	51	.0198 0392
13	.0801 2821	26	.0392 3077	39	.0259 7841	52	.0194 1931

[a] Huntington, *Methods of Apportionment*, p. 9.

The method of harmonic mean has been confused with the so-called method of minimum range, which is a selective test of apportionments and not a method.[12] The method of harmonic mean has also been confused with the method of smallest divisors, in the statement that "by it [method of harmonic mean] every decimal fraction [in a quota] entitles the state to a representative."[13] The method described in the preceding quotation is that of smallest divisors or included fractions. As has been shown the methods of smallest divisors and harmonic mean are computed from different bases and do not give the same results.

Empirical Tests of Method of Harmonic Mean[14]

The correctness of the method of harmonic mean, on the basis of the absolute difference in the average population per

[12] *Science, New Series*, Vol. 69, 1929, p. 164.

[13] The same.

[14] The algebraic proof of the method of harmonic mean is given below. The problem is to find a method of assigning representatives among the states so that the difference between the representation of two states is the smallest possible when measured by the absolute difference in the average population per district.

Designate the population of two states as A and B; designate the number of representatives assigned to State A as a and the number assigned to State B as b. The average population of the districts in any state is the population divided by the number of representatives or

$$\frac{A}{a} \quad \text{and} \quad \frac{B}{b}.$$

Under what conditions would it be fairer to assign an additional representative to State B?

If an additional representative is assigned to A, the absolute difference in average pop-

district, may be tested by a comparison of any two states. On the following pages comparisons are made between two states under an apportionment by the method of harmonic mean and by each of the other four methods. If every pair of states were compared, the method of harmonic mean would show the smaller absolute difference in average population per district.

---

ulation per district may be expressed as

$$\frac{B}{b} - \frac{A}{a+1}.$$

If an additional representative is assigned to State B, the absolute difference in average population per district would be

$$\frac{A}{a} - \frac{B}{b+1}.$$

If the assignment of an additional representative to A is correct the absolute difference will be smaller than if the additional representative had been assigned to B. This may be expressed as follows:

$$\frac{B}{b} - \frac{A}{a+1} < \frac{A}{a} - \frac{B}{b+1}.$$

By transposing we get

$$\frac{B}{b} + \frac{B}{b+1} < \frac{A}{a} + \frac{A}{a+1}$$

$$\frac{A}{a} + \frac{A}{a+1} > \frac{B}{b} + \frac{B}{b+1}$$

$$A\left(\frac{1}{a} + \frac{1}{a+1}\right) > B\left(\frac{1}{b} + \frac{1}{b+1}\right).$$

Since the harmonic mean (H) of two numbers is equal to twice their product divided by their sum

$$H \text{ of } a \text{ and } a+1 = \frac{2a(a+1)}{a+(a+1)} \text{ and}$$

$$\frac{1}{H \text{ of } a \text{ and } a+1} = \frac{1}{\left(\frac{2a(a+1)}{a+(a+1)}\right)} \text{ or } \frac{a+(a+1)}{2a(a+1)}$$

Multiplying both sides of the equation by 2, we have

$$\frac{2}{H \text{ of } a \text{ and } a+1} = \frac{a+(a+1)}{a(a+1)} \equiv \frac{a}{a(a+1)} + \frac{(a+1)}{a(a+1)} = \frac{1}{a+1} + \frac{1}{a}$$

Likewise

$$\frac{2}{H \text{ of } b \text{ and } b+1} = \frac{1}{b+1} + \frac{1}{b}$$

The minimum relative difference in the average population per district and in the minimum relative difference in the share in a representative are effected by the method of equal proportions; the minimum absolute difference in the share of a representative is effected by the method of major fractions; the minimum absolute representation surplus is effected by the method of smallest divisors; the minimum absolute representation deficiency is effected by the method of greatest divisors. Tests based on these criteria are given in the discussion of those methods.

The first comparison, based on the census of 1930, will be with the method of equal proportions.

APPORTIONMENT BY METHODS OF HARMONIC MEAN AND EQUAL
PROPORTIONS, CENSUS OF 1930

State	Population	Harmonic Mean	Equal Proportions
Arizona............	389,375	2	1
Indiana............	3,238,480	11	12
Louisiana..........	2,101,593	7	8
New Mexico........	395,982	2	1
Oklahoma..........	2,382,222	8	9
Rhode Island.......	637,497	3	2

We shall examine in detail the differences between Louisiana and Rhode Island, giving attention only to the absolute differences in average population per district. As the absolute difference is less if 7 representatives are assigned to Louisiana and 3 to Rhode Island, as shown in the table on page 38, the apportionment by the method of harmonic mean should be followed if the absolute difference is the criterion.

Therefore the inequality above may be written

$$\frac{2A}{H \text{ of } a \text{ and } a+1} > \frac{2B}{H \text{ of } b \text{ and } b+1}$$

$$\frac{A}{H \text{ of } a \text{ and } a+1} > \frac{B}{H \text{ of } b \text{ and } b+1}$$

It therefore follows that measured by absolute differences in average population per district, State A is entitled to an additional representative when its population divided by the harmonic mean of its present assignment and of its next higher assignment is greater than the population of State B divided by the harmonic mean of its present assignment and of its next higher assignment.

AVERAGE POPULATION PER DISTRICT, BASED ON CENSUS OF 1930,
METHODS OF HARMONIC MEAN AND EQUAL PROPORTIONS

State	Population	Harmonic Mean		Equal Proportions	
		Number of Representatives	Average Population per District	Number of Representatives	Average Population per District
Louisiana..........	2,101,593	7	300,228	8	262,699
Rhode Island.......	687,497	3	229,166	2	343,748
Absolute difference..	—	—	71,062	—	81,049
Relative difference...	—	—	31.0%	—	30.9%

The next comparison will be with the method of major fractions. After the census of 1930 the results of apportionments by the methods of equal proportions and major fractions were the same for a House of 435 members, and consequently any differences between the method of harmonic mean and the method of major fractions are the same as those given above for the method of harmonic mean and equal proportions. Turning to the census of 1920 we find the following differences between the methods of harmonic mean and major fractions.

APPORTIONMENT BY METHODS OF HARMONIC MEAN AND MAJOR
FRACTIONS, CENSUS OF 1920

State	Population	Harmonic Mean	Major Fractions
New Mexico........	353,428	2	1
New York..........	10,380,589	42	43
North Carolina.....	2,559,123	10	11
Rhode Island.......	604,397	3	2
Vermont...........	352,428	2	1
Virginia...........	2,309,187	9	10

A comparison of the absolute difference in average population per district in Virginia and Rhode Island yields the following result:

AVERAGE POPULATION PER DISTRICT BASED ON CENSUS OF 1920,
METHODS OF HARMONIC MEAN AND MAJOR FRACTIONS

State	Population	Harmonic Mean		Major Fractions	
		Number of Representatives	Average Population per District	Number of Representatives	Average Population per District
Virginia............	2,309,187	9	256,576	10	230,919
Rhode Island.......	604,397	3	201,466	2	302,199
Absolute difference..	—	—	55,110	—	71,280

As the absolute difference is smaller by the method of harmonic mean the proper apportionment is 9 to Virginia and 3 to Rhode Island if the absolute difference is the criterion.

Use of the methods of harmonic mean and of greatest divisors resulted in the following differences in apportionment after the census of 1930.

APPORTIONMENT BY METHODS OF HARMONIC MEAN AND
GREATEST DIVISORS, CENSUS OF 1930

State	Population	Harmonic Mean	Greatest Divisors	State	Population	Harmonic Mean	Greatest Divisors
Arizona.......	389,375	2	1	New Hampshire	465,292	2	1
Arkansas......	1,854,444	7	6	New Jersey....	4,041,319	14	15
California.....	5,668,241	20	21	New Mexico...	395,982	2	1
Colorado......	1,034,849	4	3	New York.....	12,587,967	45	47
Idaho.........	441,536	2	1	Ohio..........	6,646,633	24	25
Illinois........	7,630,388	27	28	Pennsylvania..	9,631,299	34	36
Indiana.......	3,238,480	11	12	Rhode Island..	687,497	3	2
Maine........	797,418	3	2	Utah	505,741	2	1
Michigan......	4,842,052	17	18	Washington ..	1,552,423	6	5
Montana......	524,729	2	1	Wisconsin.....	2,931,721	10	11

By comparing the absolute difference in average population per district in California and Washington we obtain the following:

AVERAGE POPULATION PER DISTRICT, BASED ON CENSUS OF 1930,
METHODS OF HARMONIC MEAN AND GREATEST DIVISORS

State	Population	Harmonic Mean		Greatest Divisors	
		Number of Representatives	Average Population per District	Number of Representatives	Average Population per District
California..........	5,668,241	20	283,412	21	269,916
Washington........	1,552,423	6	258,737	5	310,485
Absolute difference..	—	—	24,675	—	40,569

As the absolute difference is smaller by the method of harmonic mean the proper apportionment is 20 to California and 6 to Washington if the absolute difference is the criterion.

The following differences in apportionment resulted from the methods of harmonic mean and smallest divisors after the census of 1930.

APPORTIONMENT BY METHODS OF HARMONIC MEAN AND
SMALLEST DIVISORS, CENSUS OF 1930

State	Population	Harmonic Mean	Smallest Divisors	State	Population	Harmonic Mean	Smallest Divisors
Illinois.......	7,630,388	27	26	Oregon.......	950,379	3	4
Louisiana.....	2,101,593	7	8	Pennsylvania..	9,631,299	34	33
New York.....	12,587,967	45	43	South Dakota.	673,005	2	3
North Dakota.	673,340	2	3	Texas........	5,824,601	21	20
Ohio.........	6,646,633	24	23	Vermont......	359,611	1	2
Oklahoma.....	2,382,222	8	9				

Comparison of the absolute difference in the average population per district in Ohio and Oregon results as follows:

AVERAGE POPULATION PER DISTRICT, BASED ON CENSUS OF 1930,
METHODS OF HARMONIC MEAN AND SMALLEST DIVISORS

State	Population	Harmonic Mean		Smallest Divisors	
		Number of Representatives	Average Population per District	Number of Representatives	Average Population per District
Ohio..............	6,646,633	24	276,943	23	288,984
Oregon...........	950,379	3	316,793	4	237,594
Absolute difference..	—	—	39,850	—	51,390

As the absolute difference in average population per district is smaller by the method of harmonic mean the proper apportionment is 24 to Ohio and 3 to Oregon if the absolute difference is the criterion.

Method of Smallest Divisors

Under the method of smallest divisors the difference between any two states is the smallest possible when measured by what is termed the absolute representation surplus, which is the absolute difference between the number of representatives of an over-represented state and the number of representatives of an under-represented state multiplied by the population of the over-represented state divided by the population of the under-represented state.[15]

[15] A state is over-represented with respect to another state if it has a smaller average population per district; it is under-represented if it has a larger average population per district. Thus an example of over-representation is Louisiana with an average per district of 262,699 as compared with Ohio with an average of 276,943, as 262,699 is less than 276,943. Conversely Ohio is under-represented with respect to Louisiana.

The absolute representation surplus may be expressed as the absolute difference between a and b (A/B) in which the letters represent the following:

A = population of over-represented state

B = population of under-represented state

a = number of representatives assigned to State A

b = number of representatives assigned to State B

The method of smallest divisors was first discussed by E. V. Huntington in 1922. It is the same as the method of included fractions. It has never been used in an apportionment.

Application of Method of Smallest Divisors

In order to compute the relative claims of each state a priority list is prepared as described on page 8. The figures in the priority list are obtained by dividing the population by successive numbers of representatives beginning with 1. This may be expressed in the form of an equation as follows:

$$P \text{ (Priority list number)} = \frac{\text{Population of any state } (A)}{\text{Next higher assignment } (k) \text{ minus 1}}$$

$$= \frac{A}{k - 1} \cdot$$

As one representative has already been assigned to each state the priority numbers for the second and third representatives will be as follows:

$$P2 = \frac{A}{2 - 1} \qquad\qquad P3 = \frac{A}{3 - 1}$$

$$= \frac{A}{1} \qquad\qquad\qquad = \frac{A}{2}$$

$$= A \times \text{reciprocal of 1} \qquad = A \times \text{reciprocal of 2}$$

$$= A \times 1 \qquad\qquad\qquad = A \times 0.5$$

The last figures in the equations above are the first two multipliers in the table on page 42, which gives all the multipliers to be used successively for the population of each state in order to obtain the figures for the priority list. Thus the priority numbers for the second and third representatives from New York are derived as follows:

Priority number for second representative from New York = Population × 1 = 12,587,967 × 1 = 12,587,967.

Priority number for third representative from New York = Population × 0.5 = 12,587,967 × 0.5 = 6,293,984.

MULTIPLIERS FOR PRIORITY LIST FOR METHOD OF SMALLEST DIVISORS[a]
(k = successive numbers of representatives)

k	Multiplier	k	Multiplier	k	Multiplier	k	Multiplier
		14	0.0769 2308	27	0.0384 6154	40	0.0256 4103
2	1.0000 0000	15	.0714 2857	28	.0370 3704	41	.0250 0000
3	0.5000 0000	16	.0666 6667	29	.0357 1429	42	.0243 9024
4	.3333 3333	17	.0625 0000	30	.0344 8276	43	.0238 0952
5	.2500 0000	18	.0588 2353	31	.0333 3333	44	.0232 5581
6	.2000 0000	19	.0555 5556	32	.0322 5806	45	.0227 2727
7	.1666 6667	20	.0526 3158	33	.0312 5000	46	.0222 2222
8	.1428 5714	21	.0500 0000	34	.0303 0303	47	.0217 3913
9	.1250 0000	22	.0476 1905 −	35	.0294 1176	48	.0212 7660
10	.1111 1111	23	.0454 5455 −	36	.0285 7143	49	.0208 3333
11	.1000 0000	24	.0434 7826	37	.0277 7778	50	.0204 0816
12	.0909 0909	25	.0416 6667	38	.0270 2703	51	.0200 0000
13	.0833 3333	26	.0400 0000	39	.0263 1579	52	.0196 0784

[a] Huntington, *Methods of Apportionment*, p. 14.

The priority list for the method of greatest divisors based on the census of 1930 is given in Appendix A.

The computation method described above is different from that given in the 1940 hearings where the procedure for applying the method of smallest divisors is described as follows:

It must be understood at the start that all modern methods assign representatives to state after state after the first 48, in an order of priority which varies with the method adopted. The question then arises: How is that order of priority determined under the method of smallest divisors? I answered that it is determined by the rule or principle that each representative after the first 48 is assigned to the state which at that point has the largest population per representative or, what amounts to the same thing, the largest average size of district. Thus on the rack or frame before you the forty-ninth representative goes to New York because that state had the largest population. The average population of a New York district when the state has two representatives, is 6,293,983, a number smaller than the total population of Pennsylvania, Illinois, or Ohio, but greater than the total population of Texas; consequently the fiftieth representative goes to

Pennsylvania, the fifty-first to Illinois, the fifty-second to Ohio, and the fifty-third to New York because Texas has less than one-half the population of New York. By continuing this process the difference between the largest and the smallest average size of a district is reduced progressively until the results illustrated . . . are reached.[16]

The apportionment resulting from the use of the multipliers given on page 42 and from the process quoted from the hearings will be the same, but the use of the multipliers is much simpler and less confusing. For a given size of House the method of smallest divisors gives the same result as the method of included fractions if the ratio used is any number between the priority list number for the last number in the size of House selected and the priority list number for a House with one more member. Thus on the basis of the 1930 census the priority list number for the method of smallest divisors for the 435th member is 297,778; the priority list number for the 436th member is 294,407. If we divide the population of each state by any number between 297,778 and 294,407, and assign a seat for each whole number and for each fraction, which is the method of included fractions, the apportionment will be the same as that reached by the method of smallest divisors.

It should be borne in mind, however, that the use of the method of included fractions with a fixed ratio applied to different population bases may lead to a population paradox.

Empirical Tests of Method of Smallest Divisors[17]

The correctness of the method of smallest divisors, on the basis of smallest absolute representation surplus, may be tested by a comparison of any two states. On the following pages com-

---

[16] *Apportionment of Representatives in Congress*, Hearings before the House Committee on the Census, 76 Cong. 3 sess., 1940, Statement of Walter F. Willcox, p. 16.

[17] The algebraic proof of the correctness of the method of smallest divisors in equalizing representation when measured by the absolute representation surplus is as follows: Designate the population of two states by A and B; designate the number of representatives assigned to State A as a, and the number assigned to State B as b.

The representation surplus of State A with reference to State B, provided State A is the over-represented state of the pair, is the number of representatives of State A less the number of representatives of State B multiplied by the population of State A divided by the population of State B, or $a - b(A/B)$. The representation surplus of

parisons are made between two states under an apportionment by the method of smallest divisors and by each of the other four methods. If every pair of states were compared, the method of smallest divisors would show the smaller absolute representation surplus.

The minimum relative difference in the average population per district and the minimum relative difference in the share in a representative are effected by the method of equal proportions; the minimum absolute difference in the share in a representative is effected by the method of major fractions; the minimum absolute difference in the average population per district is effected by the method of harmonic mean; the minimum absolute representation deficiency is effected by the method of greatest divisors.

While the test here given is complicated it is the only one that can be applied; it is "more artificial and less important" than the tests for the methods of major fractions, equal proportions, and harmonic mean.[18]

State B with reference to State A will be similarly $b - a(B/A)$.

For the next higher representation the expressions will be $(a+1) - b(A/B)$ and $(b+1) - a(B/A)$. Therefore if the assignment of the next representative to State A is correct, the relationship may be expressed as follows:

$$(a + 1) - b\left(\frac{A}{B}\right) < (b + 1) - a\left(\frac{B}{A}\right).$$

This may be reduced as follows:

$$(a + 1) + a\left(\frac{B}{A}\right) < (b + 1) + b\left(\frac{A}{B}\right)$$

$$1 + \frac{a(A + B)}{A} < 1 + \frac{b(A + B)}{B}$$

$$\frac{a}{A} < \frac{b}{B}$$

$$\frac{A}{a} > \frac{B}{b}.$$

Therefore the next representative should be assigned to A when the population of A divided by the number of representatives of A is greater than the population of B divided by the number of representatives of B.

[18] Zechariah Chafee, Jr., "Congressional Reapportionment," *Harvard Law Review*, Vol. 42, 1929, p. 1028.

In the case of any pair of states the absolute representation surplus is the absolute difference between (1) the representation of the over-represented state and (2) the representation of the under-represented state multiplied by the population of the over-represented state divided by the population of the under-represented state. It may be expressed as follows:

$S = a - b(A/B)$ in which

S is the absolute representation surplus

A is the population of the over-represented state

B is the population of the under-represented state

a is the number of representatives of the over-represented state

b is the number of representatives of the under-represented state

Any state is over-represented with respect to another state if it has a smaller average population per representative.

Any state is under-represented with respect to another state if it has a larger average population per representative.

In applying this test it should be remembered that the over-represented state by the test for one apportionment is the under-represented state by the test for another apportionment.

The first comparisons based on the census of 1930 will be with the method of equal proportions. The differences in apportionment under these two methods are as follows:

APPORTIONMENT BY METHODS OF SMALLEST DIVISORS AND EQUAL PROPORTIONS, CENSUS OF 1930

State	Population	Smallest Divisors	Equal Proportions	State	Population	Smallest Divisors	Equal Proportions
Arizona.......	389,375	2	1	Oregon.......	950,379	4	3
Illinois.......	7,630,388	26	27	Pennsylvania..	9,631,299	33	34
Indiana.......	3,238,480	11	12	Rhode Island..	687,497	3	2
New Mexico...	395,982	2	1	South Dakota.	673,005	3	2
New York....	12,587,967	43	45	Texas........	5,824,601	20	21
North Dakota.	673,340	3	2	Vermont......	359,611	2	1
Ohio.........	6,646,633	23	24				

We shall examine in detail the difference between Ohio and Rhode Island, giving attention only to the absolute representation surplus. The last column in the following table gives the results of the test described above.

ABSOLUTE REPRESENTATION SURPLUS, CENSUS OF 1930, METHODS
OF SMALLEST DIVISORS AND EQUAL PROPORTIONS
(Population: Ohio 6,646,633; Rhode Island 687,497)

State	Number of Representatives	Average Population per Representative	Absolute Representation Surplus
METHOD OF SMALLEST DIVISORS: Ohio......................	23	288,984	$23\left(\dfrac{687,497}{6,646,633}\right)=2.38$
Rhode Island[a]...............	3	229,166	$3 \qquad\qquad =3.00$
Difference................	—	—	0.62
METHOD OF EQUAL PROPORTIONS: Ohio[a]......................	24	276,943	$24 \qquad\qquad =24.00$
Rhode Island...............	2	343,748	$2\left(\dfrac{6,646,633}{687,497}\right)=19.34$
Difference................	—	—	4.66

[a] Over-represented state by reason of having the smaller average population per representative.

As the difference in representation surplus by the method of smallest divisors is absolutely less than by the method of equal proportions the apportionment of 23 members to Ohio and 3 to Rhode Island as made by the method of smallest divisors is correct if the smaller absolute representation surplus is the criterion.

Differences in apportionment after the census of 1930 by the methods of smallest divisors and harmonic mean are as follows:

APPORTIONMENT BY METHODS OF SMALLEST DIVISORS AND
HARMONIC MEAN, CENSUS OF 1930

State	Population	Smallest Divisors	Harmonic Mean	State	Population	Smallest Divisors	Harmonic Mean
Illinois........	7,630,388	26	27	Oregon........	950,379	4	3
Louisiana.....	2,101,593	8	7	Pennsylvania..	9,631,299	33	34
New York.....	12,587,967	43	45	South Dakota.	673,005	3	2
North Dakota.	673,340	3	2	Texas.........	5,824,601	20	21
Ohio..........	6,646,633	23	24	Vermont......	359,611	2	1
Oklahoma.....	2,382,222	9	8				

The difference between Oregon and Texas will be examined in detail, attention being paid only to the absolute representation surplus. The last column in the table on page 47 gives the results of the test described on page 45.

As the difference in representation surplus by the method of smallest divisors is absolutely less than by the method of harmonic mean, the apportionment of 20 members to Texas and 4 members to Oregon as made by the method of smallest divisors

ABSOLUTE REPRESENTATION SURPLUS, CENSUS OF 1930, METHODS
OF SMALLEST DIVISORS AND HARMONIC MEAN
(Population: Texas 5,824,601; Oregon 950,379)

State	Number of Representatives	Average Population per Representative	Absolute Representation Surplus
METHOD OF SMALLEST DIVISORS: Texas....................	20	291,230	$20\left(\dfrac{950,379}{5,824,601}\right)=3.2$
Oregon[a]....................	4	237,595	$=4.0$
Difference................	—	—	0.8
METHOD OF HARMONIC MEAN: Texas[a]....................	21	277,362	$21 = 21.0$
Oregon....................	3	316,793	$3\left(\dfrac{5,824,601}{950,379}\right)=18.3$
Difference................	—	—	2.7

[a] Over-represented state by reason of having the smaller average population per representative.

is correct if the smaller absolute representation surplus is the criterion.

The next test will be a comparison of the methods of smallest divisors and major fractions. After the census of 1930 an apportionment by the method of major fractions gave the same result as one by the method of equal proportions with a House of 435 members. Consequently any differences between the method of smallest divisors and the method of major fractions based on the census of 1930 will be the same as those given above for the methods of smallest divisors and equal proportions. Therefore the results of the census of 1920 will be used for the comparison, the differences being as follows:

APPORTIONMENT BY METHODS OF SMALLEST DIVISORS AND
MAJOR FRACTIONS, CENSUS OF 1920

State	Population	Smallest Divisors	Major Fractions	State	Population	Smallest Divisors	Major Fractions
Arizona.......	309,495	2	1	North Carolina	2,559,123	10	11
Illinois.......	6,485,280	26	27	Ohio.........	5,759,394	23	24
Louisiana.....	1,798,509	8	7	Oregon.......	783,389	4	3
Montana.....	541,511	3	2	Pennsylvania..	8,720,017	34	36
Nebraska.....	1,296,372	6	5	Rhode Island..	604,397	3	2
New Mexico...	353,428	2	1	Vermont......	352,428	2	1
New York.....	10,380,589	41	43	Virginia......	2,309,187	9	10

The difference between Montana and Virginia will be examined in detail, attention being paid only to the absolute representation surplus. The last column in the following table gives the results of the test described on page 45.

ABSOLUTE REPRESENTATION SURPLUS, CENSUS OF 1920, METHODS
OF SMALLEST DIVISORS AND MAJOR FRACTIONS
(Population: Virginia, 2,309,187; Montana, 541,511)

State	Number of Representatives	Average Population per Representative	Absolute Representation Surplus
METHOD OF SMALLEST DIVISORS:			
Virginia....................	9	256,576	$9\left(\dfrac{541,511}{2,309,187}\right)=2.07$
Montana[a]..................	3	180,504	$3 = 3.00$
Difference................	—	—	0.93
METHOD OF MAJOR FRACTIONS:			
Virginia[a]...................	10	230,919	$10 = 10.00$
Montana...................	2	270,756	$2\left(\dfrac{2,309,187}{541,511}\right)= 8.53$
Difference................	—	—	1.47

[a] Over-represented state by reason of having the smaller average population per representative.

As the difference in representation surplus by the method of smallest divisors is less absolutely than by the method of major fractions, the apportionment of 9 members to Virginia and 3 to Montana as made by the method of smallest divisors is correct if the smaller absolute representation surplus is the criterion.

Differences in apportionment after the census of 1930 by the methods of smallest divisors and greatest divisors are as follows:

APPORTIONMENT BY METHODS OF SMALLEST DIVISORS AND
GREATEST DIVISORS, CENSUS OF 1930

State	Population	Smallest Divisors	Greatest Divisors	State	Population	Smallest Divisors	Greatest Divisors
Arizona.......	389,375	2	1	New York.....	12,587,967	43	47
Arkansas......	1,854,444	7	6	North Dakota.	673,340	3	2
California.....	5,668,241	20	21	Ohio..........	6,646,633	23	25
Colorado......	1,034,849	4	3	Oklahoma.....	2,382,222	9	8
Idaho.........	441,536	2	1	Oregon........	950,379	4	3
Illinois........	7,630,388	26	28	Pennsylvania..	9,631,299	33	36
Indiana.......	3,238,480	11	12	Rhode Island..	687,497	3	2
Louisiana.....	2,101,593	8	7				
				South Dakota..	673,005	3	2
Maine........	797,418	3	2	Texas.........	5,824,601	20	21
Michigan......	4,842,052	17	18	Utah.........	505,741	2	1
Montana......	524,729	2	1				
				Vermont......	359,611	2	1
New Hampshire	465,292	2	1	Washington...	1,552,423	6	5
New Jersey....	4,041,319	14	15	Wisconsin.....	2,931,721	10	11
New Mexico...	395,982	2	1				

The difference between California and Colorado will be examined in detail, attention being paid only to the absolute representation surplus. The last column in the following table gives the results of the test described on page 45.

ABSOLUTE REPRESENTATION SURPLUS, CENSUS OF 1930, METHODS
OF SMALLEST DIVISORS AND GREATEST DIVISORS
(Population: California, 5,668,241; Colorado, 1,034,849)

State	Number of Representatives	Average Population per Representative	Absolute Representation Surplus
METHOD OF SMALLEST DIVISORS:			
California.................	20	283,412	$20\left(\dfrac{1,034,849}{5,668,241}\right)=2.0$
Colorado[a].................	4	258,712	$4 \qquad\qquad =4.0$
Difference................	—	—	2.0
METHOD OF GREATEST DIVISORS:			
California[a].................	21	269,916	$21 \qquad\qquad =21.00$
Colorado...................	3	344,950	$3\left(\dfrac{5,668,241}{1,034,849}\right)=15.15$
Difference................	—	—	5.85

[a] Over-represented state by reason of having the smaller average population per representative.

As the difference in representation surplus by the method of smallest divisors is less absolutely than by the method of greatest divisors, the apportionment of 20 members to California and 4 members to Colorado, as made by the method of smallest divisors, is correct if the smaller absolute representation surplus is the criterion.

Method of Greatest Divisors

By the method of greatest divisors the difference between any two states is the smallest possible when measured by what is termed the absolute representation deficiency, which is the difference between the number of representatives of an under-represented state and the number of representatives of the over-represented state multiplied by the population of the under-represented state divided by the population of the over-represented state.[19]

The absolute representation deficiency may be expressed as the absolute difference between b and $a(B/A)$, in which the letters represent the following:

A = population of over-represented state

[19] For the purpose of this method a state is over-represented with respect to another state if it has a smaller average population per district; it is under-represented with respect to another state if it has a larger average population per district. Thus under this method an example of over-representation would be Louisiana with an average per district of 262,699 compared with Ohio with an average per district of 276,943, as 262,699 is less than 276,943. Conversely Ohio is under-represented with respect to Louisiana.

B = population of under-represented state
a = number of representatives assigned to State A
b = number of representatives assigned to State B

The present process of computation of the method of greatest divisors was developed by Professor Victor d'Hondt of the University of Ghent in 1855. The method is the same as the method of rejected fractions, which was used from 1790 to 1830, except that the early use of the method employed a fixed ratio of representation. Its present form, which is described below, does not use a fixed ratio, and has not been used in an apportionment.

Application of the Method of Greatest Divisors

The process for determining priority by the method of greatest divisors is as follows: State A deserves an additional representative when its population divided by its present assignment plus 1 is greater than the population of State B divided by its present assignment plus 1.

In order to compute the relative claims of each state a priority list is prepared as described on page 8. The figures in the priority list are obtained by dividing the population of the state by successive numbers of representatives beginning with 2. This may be expressed in the form of an equation as follows:

$$P \text{ (Priority list figure)} = \frac{\text{Population of any state } (A)}{\text{Its present assignment plus 1 } (k+1)}$$

$$= \frac{A}{k+1}.$$

As one representative has already been assigned to each state the priority numbers for the second and third representatives will be as follows:

$$P2 = \frac{A}{1+1} \qquad\qquad P3 = \frac{A}{2+1}$$

$$= \frac{A}{2} \qquad\qquad\qquad = \frac{A}{3}$$

$$= A \times \text{reciprocal of 2} \qquad = A \times \text{reciprocal of 3}$$
$$= A \times 0.5 \qquad\qquad = A \times 0.333,333,33$$

The last figures in the equations above are the first two multipliers in the following table, which gives all the multipliers to be used successively for the population of each state in order to obtain the figures for the priority list. Thus the priority numbers, based on the census of 1930, for the second and third representatives from New York are derived as follows:

Priority number for second representative from New York = Population $\times 0.5 = 12{,}587{,}967 \times 0.5 = 6{,}293{,}984$.

Priority number for third representative from New York = Population $\times$ 0.333,333,33 = 12,587,967 $\times$ 0.333,333,33 = 4,195,989.

MULTIPLIERS FOR PRIORITY LIST FOR METHOD OF GREATEST DIVISORS[a]
(*k* = successive numbers of representatives)

k	Multiplier	k	Multiplier	k	Multiplier	k	Multiplier
		14	0.0714 2857	27	0.0370 3704	40	0.0250 0000
2	0.5000 0000	15	.0666 6667	28	.0357 1429	41	.0243 9024
3	.3333 3333	16	.0625 0000	29	.0344 8276	42	.0238 0952
4	.2500 0000	17	.0588 2353	30	.0333 3333	43	.0232 5581
5	.2000 0000	18	.0555 5556	31	.0322 5806	44	.0227 2727
6	.1666 6667	19	.0526 3158	32	.0312 5000	45	.0222 2222
7	.1428 5714	20	.0500 0000	33	.0303 0303	46	.0217 3913
8	.1250 0000	21	.0476 1905 −	34	.0294 1176	47	.0212 7660
9	.1111 1111	22	.0454 5455 −	35	.0285 7143	48	.0208 3333
10	.1000 0000	23	.0434 7826	36	.0277 7778	49	.0204 0816
11	.0909 0909	24	.0416 6667	37	.0270 2703	50	.0200 0000
12	.0833 3333	25	.0400 0000	38	.0263 1579	51	.0196 0784
13	.0769 2308	26	.0384 6154	39	.0256 4103	52	.0192 3077

[a] Huntington, *Methods of Apportionment*, p. 15.

The priority list for the method of smallest divisors based on the census of 1930 is given in Appendix A.

For a given size of House the method of greatest divisors gives the same result as the method of rejected fractions if the ratio used is any number between the priority list number for the last member in the size of House selected and the priority list number for a House with one more member. Thus on the basis of the 1930 census the priority list number for the method of greatest divisors for the 435th member is 265,865; the priority list number for the 436th member is 265,806. If we divide the population of each state by any number between 265,865 and

265,806, and assign a seat for each whole number and disregard the fractions, which is the method of rejected fractions, the apportionment will be the same as that reached by the method of greatest divisors.

It should be borne in mind, however, that the use of the method of rejected fractions with a fixed ratio applied to different population bases may lead to the population paradox.

Empirical Tests of Method of Greatest Divisors[20]

The correctness of the method of greatest divisors, on the basis of the smallest absolute representation deficiency, may be tested by a comparison of any two states. On the following pages

[20] The algebraic proof of the correctness of the method of greatest divisors in equalizing representation when measured by the absolute representation deficiency is as follows: Designate the population of two states as A and B; designate the number of representatives assigned to State A as a, and the number assigned to State B as b. The representation deficiency relative to State B will then be shown if the population of State B is divided by the population of State A, the quotient multiplied by the number of representatives from State A, and from the product the number of representatives from State B subtracted, or $a(B/A) - b$. The representation deficiency of State B with reference to State A will be similarly $b(A/B) - a$.

If the assignment of an additional representative to A is correct, the absolute representation deficiency will be smaller than if the additional representative had been assigned to B. This may be expressed as follows:

$$(a + 1)\frac{B}{A} - b < (b + 1)\frac{A}{B} - a$$

$$(a + 1)\frac{B}{A} - (b + 1) < (b + 1)\frac{A}{B} - (a + 1)$$

$$(a + 1)\frac{B}{A} + (a + 1) < (b + 1)\frac{A}{B} + (b + 1)$$

$$a + 1)\left(\frac{B}{A} + 1\right) < (b + 1)\left(\frac{A}{B} + 1\right)$$

$$(a + 1)\left(\frac{A + B}{A}\right) < (b + 1)\left(\frac{A + B}{B}\right)$$

$$\frac{a + 1}{A} < \frac{b + 1}{B}$$

$$\frac{A}{a + 1} > \frac{B}{b + 1} .$$

Therefore the additional representative should be assigned to A when its population divided by its present representation plus 1 is greater than the population of B divided by its present representation plus 1.

comparisons are made between two states under an apportionment by the method of greatest divisors and by each of the other four methods. If every pair of states were compared, the method of greatest divisors would show the smaller absolute difference in the representation deficiency.

The minimum relative difference in the average population per district and in the minimum relative difference in the share in a representative are effected by the method of equal proportions; the minimum absolute difference in the share in a representative is effected by the method of major fractions; the minimum absolute difference in the average population per district is effected by the method of harmonic mean; the minimum absolute representation surplus is effected by the method of smallest divisors.

While the test here given is complicated it is the only one that can be applied; it is "more artificial and less important" than the tests for the methods of major fractions, equal proportions, and harmonic mean.[21]

In the case of any pair of states the absolute deficiency representation is the absolute difference between (1) the representation of the under-represented state and (2) the representation of the over-represented state multiplied by the population of the under-represented state divided by the population of the over-represented state. It may be expressed as follows:

$D = b - (aB/A)$ in which

D is the absolute representation deficiency

A is the population of the over-represented state

B is the population of the under-represented state

a is the number of representatives of the over-represented state

b is the number of representatives of the under-represented state

Any state is over-represented with respect to another state if it has a smaller average population per representative.

[21] Chafee, "Congressional Reapportionment," *Harvard Law Review*, Vol. 42, 1929, p. 1028.

Any state is under-represented with respect to another state if it has a larger average population per representative.

In applying this test it should be remembered that the over-represented state for the test by one apportionment is the under-represented state for the test by another apportionment.

The first comparison based on the census of 1930 will be with the method of equal proportions. The differences in apportionment under the two methods are as follows:

APPORTIONMENT BY METHODS OF GREATEST DIVISORS AND
EQUAL PROPORTIONS, CENSUS OF 1930

State	Population	Greatest Divisors	Equal Proportions	State	Population	Greatest Divisors	Equal Proportions
Arkansas	1,854,444	6	7	New Hampshire	465,292	1	2
California	5,668,241	21	20	New Jersey	4,041,319	15	14
Colorado	1,034,849	3	4	New York	12,587,967	47	45
Idaho	441,536	1	2	Ohio	6,646,633	25	24
Illinois	7,630,388	28	27	Oklahoma	2,382,222	8	9
Louisiana	2,101,593	7	8	Pennsylvania	9,631,299	36	34
Maine	797,418	2	3	Utah	505,741	1	2
Michigan	4,842,052	18	17	Washington	1,552,423	5	6
Montana	524,729	1	2	Wisconsin	2,931,721	11	10

We shall examine in detail the difference between Ohio and Louisiana, giving attention only to the absolute representation deficiency. The last column in the accompanying table gives the results of the test described on page 53.

ABSOLUTE REPRESENTATION DEFICIENCY, CENSUS OF 1930, METHODS
OF GREATEST DIVISORS AND EQUAL PROPORTIONS
(Population: Ohio, 6,646,633; Louisiana, 2,101,593)

State	Number of Representatives	Average Population per Representative	Absolute Representation Deficiency
METHOD OF GREATEST DIVISORS:			
Ohio[a]	25	265,865	$25\left(\dfrac{2,101,593}{6,646,633}\right)=7.90$
Louisiana	7	300,228	$7 \qquad\qquad =7.00$
Difference	—	—	0.90
METHOD OF EQUAL PROPORTIONS:			
Ohio	24	276,943	$24 \qquad\qquad =24.00$
Louisiana[a]	8	262,699	$8\left(\dfrac{6,646,633}{2,101,593}\right)=25.30$
Difference	—	—	1.30

[a] Over-represented state by reason of having the smaller average population per representative.

As the difference in representation deficiency by the method of greatest divisors is absolutely less by the method of greatest divisors, the apportionment of 25 members to Ohio and 7 to

Louisiana, as made by the method of greatest divisors, is correct if the smaller absolute representation deficiency is the criterion.

The next test will be a comparison between the methods of greatest divisors and major fractions. After the census of 1930 an apportionment by the method of major fractions gave the same result as the one by the method of equal proportions with a House of 435 members. Consequently any differences between the method of greatest divisors and the method of major fractions based on the census of 1930 will be the same as those given above for the methods of greatest divisors and equal proportions. Therefore the results of the census of 1920 will be used for the comparison, the differences being indicated in the accompanying table.

APPORTIONMENT BY METHODS OF GREATEST DIVISORS AND
MAJOR FRACTIONS, CENSUS OF 1920

State	Population	Greatest Divisors	Major Fractions	State	Population	Greatest Divisors	Major Fractions
Idaho.........	430,442	1	2	Pennsylvania..	8,720,017	37	36
Illinois........	6,485,280	28	27	South Dakota..	631,239	2	3
New Hampshire	443,083	1	2	Texas.........	4,663,228	20	19
New York.....	10,380,589	45	43	Utah.........	448,388	1	2
North Dakota..	643,953	2	3	Washington...	1,354,596	5	6
Ohio.........	5,759,394	25	24				

The differences between Washington and Texas will be examined in detail, attention being paid only to the absolute representation deficiency. The last column in the following table gives the results of the test described on page 53.

ABSOLUTE REPRESENTATION DEFICIENCY, CENSUS OF 1920, METHODS
OF GREATEST DIVISORS AND MAJOR FRACTIONS
(Population: Texas, 4,663,228; Washington, 1,354,596)

State	Number of Representatives	Average Population per Representative	Absolute Representation Deficiency
METHOD OF GREATEST DIVISORS:			
Texas[a].....................	20	233,161	$20\left(\dfrac{1,354,596}{4,663,228}\right)=5.80$
Washington................	5	270,919	$5\phantom{\left(\dfrac{1,354,596}{4,663,228}\right)}=5.00$
Difference................	—	—	0.80
METHOD OF MAJOR FRACTIONS:			
Texas.....................	19	245,433	$19\phantom{\left(\dfrac{4,663,228}{1,354,596}\right)}=19.00$
Washington[a]................	6	225,766	$6\left(\dfrac{4,663,228}{1,354,596}\right)=20.64$
Difference................	—	—	1.64

[a] Over-represented state by reason of having the smaller average population per representative.

As the difference in representation deficiency by the method of greatest divisors is less absolutely than by the method of major fractions, the apportionment of 20 members to Texas and 5 to Washington, as made by the method of greatest divisors, is correct if the smaller absolute representation deficiency is the criterion.

Differences in apportionment after the census of 1930 by the methods of greatest divisors and harmonic mean are as follows:

APPORTIONMENT BY METHODS OF GREATEST DIVISORS AND
HARMONIC MEAN, CENSUS OF 1930

State	Population	Greatest Divisors	Harmonic Mean	State	Population	Greatest Divisors	Harmonic Mean
Arizona.......	389,375	1	2	New Hampshire	465,292	1	2
Arkansas......	1,854,444	6	7	New Jersey....	4,041,319	15	14
California.....	5,668,241	21	20	New Mexico...	395,982	1	2
Colorado......	1,034,849	3	4	New York.....	12,587,967	47	45
Idaho.........	441,536	1	2	Ohio..........	6,646,633	25	24
Illinois........	7,630,388	28	27	Pennsylvania..	9,631,299	36	34
Indiana.......	3,238,480	12	11	Rhode Island..	687,497	2	3
Maine........	797,418	2	3	Utah.........	505,741	1	2
Michigan......	4,842,052	18	17	Washington...	1,552,423	5	6
Montana......	524,729	1	2	Wisconsin.....	2,931,721	11	10

The difference between California and Colorado will be examined in detail, attention being paid only to the absolute representation deficiency. The last column in the following table gives the results of the test described on page 53.

ABSOLUTE REPRESENTATION DEFICIENCY, CENSUS OF 1930, METHODS
OF GREATEST DIVISORS AND HARMONIC MEAN
(Population: California, 5,668,241; Colorado, 1,034,849)

State	Number of Representatives	Average Population per Representative	Absolute Representation Deficiency
METHOD OF GREATEST DIVISORS: California[a].................	21	269,916	$21\left(\dfrac{1,034,849}{5,668,241}\right)=3.78$
Colorado...................	3	344,950	$3\phantom{\left(\dfrac{1,034,849}{5,668,241}\right)}=3.00$
Difference................	—	—	0.78
METHOD OF HARMONIC MEAN: California..................	20	283,412	$20\phantom{\left(\dfrac{5,668,241}{1,034,849}\right)}=20.00$
Colorado[a]..................	4	258,712	$4\left(\dfrac{5,668,241}{1,034,849}\right)=21.88$
Difference................	—	—	1.88

[a] Over-represented state by reason of having the smaller average population per representative.

As the difference in representation deficiency by the method of greatest divisors is less absolutely than by the method of harmonic mean, the apportionment of 21 members to California and 3 members to Colorado, as made by the method of greatest divisors, is correct if the smaller absolute representation deficiency is the criterion.

Differences in apportionment after the census of 1930 between methods of greatest divisors and smallest divisors are as follows:

APPORTIONMENT BY METHODS OF GREATEST DIVISORS AND
SMALLEST DIVISORS, CENSUS OF 1930

State	Population	Greatest Divisors	Smallest Divisors	State	Population	Greatest Divisors	Smallest Divisors
Arizona.......	389,375	1	2	New York.....	12,587,967	47	43
Arkansas......	1,854,444	6	7	North Dakota.	673,340	2	3
California.....	5,668,241	21	20	Ohio..........	6,646,633	25	23
Colorado......	1,034,849	3	4	Oklahoma.....	2,382,222	8	9
Idaho.........	441,536	1	2	Oregon........	950,379	3	4
Illinois........	7,630,388	28	26	Pennsylvania..	9,631,299	36	33
Indiana.......	3,238,480	12	11	Rhode Island..	687,497	2	3
Louisiana.....	2,101,593	7	8	South Dakota..	673,005	2	3
Maine........	797,418	2	3	Texas.........	5,824,601	21	20
Michigan......	4,842,052	18	17	Utah.........	505,741	1	2
Montana......	524,729	1	2	Vermont......	359,611	1	2
New Hampshire	465,292	1	2	Washington...	1,552,423	5	6
New Jersey....	4,041,319	15	14	Wisconsin.....	2,931,721	11	10
New Mexico...	395,982	1	2				

The difference between Wisconsin and Arkansas will be examined in detail, attention being paid only to the absolute representation deficiency. The last column in the following table gives the results of the test described on page 53.

ABSOLUTE REPRESENTATION DEFICIENCY, CENSUS OF 1930, METHODS
OF GREATEST DIVISORS AND SMALLEST DIVISORS
(Population: Wisconsin, 2,931,721; Arkansas, 1,854,444)

State	Number of Representatives	Average Population per Representative	Absolute Representation Deficiency
METHOD OF GREATEST DIVISORS: Wisconsin[a]...............	11	266,520	$11\left(\dfrac{1,854,444}{2,931,721}\right) = 6.6$
Arkansas...................	6	309,074	$6 = 6.0$
Difference................	—	—	0.6
METHOD OF SMALLEST DIVISORS: Wisconsin.................	10	293,172	$10 = 10.0$
Arkansas[a]..................	7	264,921	$7\left(\dfrac{2,931,721}{1,854,444}\right) = 11.1$
Difference................	—	—	1.1

[a] Over-represented state by reason of having the smaller average population per representative.

As the difference in representation deficiency by the method of greatest divisors is less absolutely than by the method of smallest divisors, the apportionment of 11 members to Wisconsin and 6 members to Arkansas, as made by the method of greatest divisors, is correct if the smaller absolute representation deficiency is the criterion.

The method of greatest divisors has been at times confused with the method of minimum range. They are not the same, as is shown by the following comparison of apportionments made by the two methods.

APPORTIONMENT BY METHODS OF GREATEST DIVISORS AND MINIMUM RANGE[a]

State	Population	Greatest Divisors	Minimum Range
A...............	726,000	8	7
B...............	539,000	6	6
C...............	335,000	3	4
Total..........	1,600,000	17	17

[a] Adapted from E. V. Huntington, *Methods of Apportionment*, p. 31.

The method of minimum range is discussed on page 81.

CHAPTER IV

RELATIVE MERITS OF THE SEVERAL MODERN METHODS

All the methods described in the preceding chapter have several common features. Each one is based on a definite mathematical formula, which is proved to be correct, both algebraically and empirically, if we adopt the premise on which it is based. Each one uses a priority list which is easily computed and which may be verified by any one who can multiply correctly. None of them leads to inconsistencies or paradoxes. Each one can be used for any size of House. In none of them is a population ratio part of the computation, although a ratio which is without significance may be derived from the final apportionment.

No one of the methods is more complicated than any other in its application and computation, although the statements of the purposes of the method of greatest divisors and smallest divisors require some concentration and the empirical tests of these methods are somewhat involved.

Notwithstanding the fact that the five modern methods have many features in common, all are founded on different premises and generally give different results. The relative desirability of the five methods is described in this chapter.

OBJECTIVES OF THE SEVERAL METHODS

The results achieved by the five modern methods are as follows:

The method of equal proportions most nearly equalizes the average population per district and the individual share in a representative if the inequality is measured by the relative difference.

The method of major fractions most nearly equalizes the individual share in a representative if the inequality is measured by the absolute difference.

The method of harmonic mean most nearly equalizes the average population per district if the inequality is measured by the absolute difference.

The method of greatest divisors most nearly equalizes the representation deficiency of each state.

The method of smallest divisors most nearly equalizes the representation surplus of each state.

In choosing a method it is therefore necessary to determine its objective. If the absolute difference in the share of a representative is the criterion, the method of major fractions should be used; if the absolute difference in the average population per district is the test, the method of harmonic mean is indicated. If the relative difference both in average population per district and in individual share in a representative is the criterion, the method of equal proportions should be used.

Mathematicians generally agree that the significant feature of a difference is its relation to the smaller number and not its absolute quantity. Thus the increase of 50 horsepower in the output of two engines would not be of any significance if one engine already yielded 10,000 horsepower, but it would double the efficiency of a plant of only 50 horsepower. It has been shown above that the relative difference between two apportionments is always least if the method of equal proportions is used. Moreover, the method of equal proportions is the only one that uses relative differences, the methods of harmonic mean and major fraction being based on absolute differences. In addition, the method of equal proportions gives the smallest relative difference for both average population per district and individual share in a representative. No other method takes account of both these factors. Therefore the method of equal proportions gives the most equitable distribution of representatives among the states.

As the method of smallest divisors was energetically advocated in 1940 at the hearings before the House Committee on the Census it seems desirable to devote special attention to the claims regarding it.

In the hearings on apportionment in 1940 it was stated "that if the main purpose of apportionment is to make the average population of congressional districts as nearly equal as possible, that purpose is best secured by the method of smallest divisors."[1]

Supporting this statement, the witness made the following statement:

The differences between the largest and smallest average size of districts by each of the three methods are shown below:

Method	Average Population per Representative		
	Largest	Smallest	Difference
Major fractions.......	395,982	86,390	309,592
Greatest divisors......	524,729	86,390	438,339
Smallest divisors......	294,900	86,390	208,510

If the difference between the largest and smallest average population per district under the method of major fractions is taken as 100, the difference under the method of greatest divisors is 141 and that under the method of smallest divisors 67.

The statement in the preceding quotation is not a test of the method of smallest divisors, but applies to the so-called method of minimum range, which is shown on page 81 to be not a method, but a selective test between other methods, and to be unworkable because it is subject to the Alabama paradox. Apportionments by the method of smallest divisors and by the test of minimum range may not be the same, as is shown in the following example.

APPORTIONMENT BY METHODS OF SMALLEST DIVISORS AND MINIMUM RANGE[a]

State	Population	Smallest Divisors	Minimum Range
A..............	726,000	7	8
B..............	539,000	5	5
C..............	335,000	4	3
Total..........	1,600,000	16	16

[a] Adapted from E. V. Huntington, *Methods of Apportionment*, p. 30.

The statement quoted is also erroneous because the state with the smallest average population per representative is Nevada,

[1] *Apportionment of Representatives in Congress*, Hearings before the House Committee on the Census, 76 Cong. 3 sess., 1940, testimony of Walter F. Willcox, p. 16.

which had a population of only 86,390, and which, under the constitutional provision, would receive a representative no matter how small its population.

Moreover, a single positive example does not establish the validity of a method, but a single negative example, either actual or hypothetical, will suffice to demonstrate its failure. The accompanying table gives the population of nine states in 1920. If the entire population of the country had been included in these states, the apportionments by the methods of smallest divisors and equal proportions for a House of 147 members would have been as indicated in the table.

APPORTIONMENT OF 147 MEMBERS BY METHODS OF SMALLEST
DIVISORS AND EQUAL PROPORTIONS[a]

State	Population	Smallest Divisors		Equal Proportions	
		Number of Repre- sentatives	Average Population per District	Number of Repre- sentatives	Average Population per District
New York.........	10,380,589	41	253,185	42	247,157
Pennsylvania......	8,720,017	34	256,471	36	242,223
Illinois............	6,485,280	26	249,434	27	240,196
Ohio.............	5,759,394	23	250,408	24	239,975
Louisiana.........	1,798,509	8	224,814	7	256,930
Nebraska.........	1,296,372	6	216,062	5	259,274
Oregon...........	783,389	4	195,847	3	261,130
Montana..........	541,511	3	180,504	2	270,756
Arizona..........	309,495	2	154,748	1	309,495
Total..........	36,074,556	147	—	147	—
Range..........	—	—	101,723	—	69,520

[a] Huntington, *Methods of Apportionment*, p. 26.

Under the method of smallest divisors Pennsylvania has the largest average population per district, 256,471, and Arizona has the smallest, 154,748, a difference of 101,723. Under the method of equal proportions Arizona has the largest average, 309,495, and Ohio has the smallest, 239,975, a difference of 69,520. As the difference is less by the method of equal proportions, it is evident that the method of smallest divisors will not always give the smallest difference.

At the hearings in 1928 the claim just discussed regarding the equalization of average population of congressional districts was made for the method of major fractions, which, it was stated, makes "the average population of congressional districts in small, medium and large states nearly as equal as Congress can make it the same."[2] Neither the method of smallest divisors nor the method of major fractions equalizes as nearly as possible the population of the districts in the small, medium, and large states.

In the discussion of the methods of equal proportions and harmonic mean it was shown both algebraically and empirically that the smallest relative difference in average population per district was obtained by the method of equal proportions and that the smallest absolute difference in average population per district was reached by the method of harmonic mean. The method of smallest divisors merely tends to most nearly equalize the absolute representation surplus as defined in the discussion of that method. The method of major fractions most nearly equalizes the individual share in a representative if the absolute difference is the criterion.

APPORTIONMENTS BY THE SEVERAL METHODS

Owing to the vagaries of figures, all the methods for a given size of House may give the same result for a given state, or two methods may give the same result for all states. Thus for a House of 435 members the same apportionment for all states was reached under the census of 1920 by the methods of major fractions and harmonic mean, and under the census of 1930 by the methods of equal proportions and major fractions. Notwithstanding these coincidences, the distribution of representatives among the states generally varies considerably according to the method used.

The tables on pages 64 and 65 show apportionments under the censuses of 1920 and 1930 by the five methods that have been considered.[3] In these tables the states are divided into five groups according to population, as follows: very small states, which would receive one representative regardless of their population; small states with populations between 300,000 and

---

[2] *Apportionment of Representatives*, Hearing before the House Committee on the Census, 70 Cong. 1 sess., on H.R. 130, 1928, testimony of Walter F. Willcox, p. 88.

[3] Apportionments by the methods of major fractions and equal proportions under the census of 1940 are given in App. C.

APPORTIONMENT UNDER CENSUS OF 1920 BY FIVE METHODS

States	Population	Equal Proportions	Major Fractions	Harmonic Mean	Smallest Divisors	Greatest Divisors
Very small states						
Nevada..........	75,820	1	1	1	1	1
Wyoming.........	193,487	1	1	1	1	1
Delaware........	223,003	1	1	1	1	1
Total..........	492,310	3	3	3	3	3
Small states						
Arizona..........	309,495	1	1	1	2	1
Vermont.........	352,428	2	1	2	2	1
New Mexico......	353,428	2	1	2	2	1
Idaho...........	430,442	2	2	2	2	1
New Hampshire....	443,083	2	2	2	2	1
Utah............	448,388	2	2	2	2	1
Montana.........	541,511	2	2	2	3	2
Rhode Island.....	604,397	3	2	3	3	2
South Dakota.....	631,239	3	3	3	3	2
North Dakota.....	643,953	3	3	3	3	2
Maine...........	768,014	3	3	3	3	3
Oregon..........	783,389	3	3	3	4	3
Colorado.........	939,161	4	4	4	4	4
Florida..........	968,470	4	4	4	4	4
Total..........	8,217,398	36	33	36	39	28
Medium-sized states						
Nebraska........	1,296,372	5	5	5	6	5
Washington......	1,354,596	6	6	6	6	5
Connecticut......	1,380,631	6	6	6	6	6
Maryland........	1,449,661	6	6	6	6	6
West Virginia.....	1,463,701	6	6	6	6	6
South Carolina.....	1,683,724	7	7	7	7	7
Arkansas.........	1,752,204	7	7	7	7	7
Kansas..........	1,769,257	7	7	7	7	7
Mississippi.......	1,790,618	7	7	7	7	7
Louisiana........	1,798,509	7	7	7	8	7
Oklahoma........	2,028,283	8	8	8	8	8
Virginia..........	2,309,187	9	10	9	9	10
Tennessee........	2,337,885	10	10	10	10	10
Alabama.........	2,348,174	10	10	10	10	10
Minnesota........	2,385,656	10	10	10	10	10
Iowa............	2,404,021	10	10	10	10	10
Kentucky........	2,416,630	10	10	10	10	10
North Carolina....	2,559,123	10	11	10	10	11
Wisconsin........	2,631,305	11	11	11	11	11
Georgia..........	2,895,832	12	12	12	12	12
Indiana..........	2,930,390	12	12	12	12	12
New Jersey........	3,155,900	13	13	13	13	13
Missouri.........	3,404,055	14	14	14	14	14
California........	3,426,031	14	14	14	14	14
Michigan.........	3,668,412	15	15	15	15	15
Massachusetts.....	3,852,356	16	16	16	16	16
Total..........	60,492,513	248	250	248	250	249
Large states						
Texas...........	4,663,228	19	19	19	19	20
Ohio............	5,759,394	24	24	24	23	25
Illinois...........	6,485,280	27	27	27	26	28
Pennsylvania......	8,720,017	36	36	36	34	37
New York........	10,380,589	42	43	42	41	45
Total..........	36,008,508	148	149	148	143	155
Grand total.....	105,210,729	435	435	435	435	435

APPORTIONMENT UNDER CENSUS OF 1930, BY FIVE METHODS

States	Population	Equal Proportions	Major Fractions	Harmonic Mean	Smallest Divisors	Greatest Divisors
Very small states						
Nevada...........	86,390	1	1	1	1	1
Wyoming.........	223,630	1	1	1	1	1
Delaware.........	238,380	1	1	1	1	1
Total...........	548,400	3	3	3	3	3
Small states						
Vermont.........	359,611	1	1	1	2	1
Arizona...........	389,375	1	1	2	2	1
New Mexico.......	395,982	1	1	2	2	1
Idaho............	441,536	2	2	2	2	1
New Hampshire....	465,292	2	2	2	2	1
Utah.............	505,741	2	2	2	2	1
Montana.........	524,729	2	2	2	2	1
South Dakota.....	673,005	2	2	2	3	2
North Dakota.....	673,340	2	2	2	3	2
Rhode Island......	687,497	2	2	3	3	2
Maine............	797,418	3	3	3	3	2
Oregon...........	950,379	3	3	3	4	3
Total...........	6,863,905	23	23	26	30	18
Medium-sized states						
Colorado.........	1,034,849	4	4	4	4	3
Nebraska.........	1,375,123	5	5	5	5	5
Florida...........	1,468,191	5	5	5	5	5
Washington.......	1,552,423	6	6	6	6	5
Connecticut.......	1,606,897	6	6	6	6	6
Maryland.........	1,631,522	6	6	6	6	6
West Virginia......	1,729,199	6	6	6	6	6
South Carolina.....	1,738,760	6	6	6	6	6
Arkansas.........	1,854,444	7	7	7	7	6
Kansas...........	1,879,498	7	7	7	7	7
Mississippi........	2,008,154	7	7	7	7	7
Louisiana.........	2,101,593	8	8	7	8	7
Oklahoma.........	2,382,222	9	9	8	9	8
Virginia...........	2,421,829	9	9	9	9	9
Iowa.............	2,470,420	9	9	9	9	9
Minnesota........	2,551,583	9	9	9	9	9
Kentucky.........	2,614,575	9	9	9	9	9
Tennessee........	2,616,497	9	9	9	9	9
Alabama.........	2,646,242	9	9	9	9	9
Georgia..........	2,908,446	10	10	10	10	10
Wisconsin........	2,931,721	10	10	10	10	11
North Carolina.....	3,167,274	11	11	11	11	11
Indiana..........	3,238,480	12	12	11	11	12
Missouri.........	3,629,110	13	13	13	13	13
Total...........	53,559,052	192	192	189	191	188
Large states						
New Jersey.......	4,041,319	14	14	14	14	15
Massachusetts.....	4,249,598	15	15	15	15	15
Michigan.........	4,842,052	17	17	17	17	18
California.........	5,668,241	20	20	20	20	21
Texas............	5,824,601	21	21	21	20	21
Ohio.............	6,646,633	24	24	24	23	25
Illinois...........	7,630,388	27	27	27	26	28
Pennsylvania......	9,631,299	34	34	34	33	36
New York.........	12,587,967	45	45	45	43	47
Total...........	61,122,098	217	217	217	211	226
Grand total.....	122,093,455	435	435	435	435	435

1,000,000; medium-sized states with populations between 1,000,-
000 and 4,000,000; and large states with populations of over
4,000,000. Owing to increases in population the states in each
group are not the same for the two censuses.

Recapitulation of the distribution of representatives among
the several groups of states, based on the censuses of 1920 and
1930, gives the following results.

DISTRIBUTION OF REPRESENTATIVES AMONG SEVERAL GROUPS OF STATES,
BASED ON CENSUSES OF 1920 AND OF 1930

Group of States	Equal Proportions	Major Fractions	Harmonic Mean	Smallest Divisors	Greatest Divisors
Census of 1920:					
Very small states........	3	3	3	3	3
Small states............	36	33	36	39	28
Medium-sized states.....	248	250	248	250	249
Large states...........	148	149	148	143	155
Total..............	435	435	435	435	435
Census of 1930:					
Very small states........	3	3	3	3	3
Small states............	23	23	26	30	18
Medium-sized states.....	192	192	189	191	188
Large states...........	217	217	217	211	226
Total..............	435	435	435	435	435

Under the censuses of 1920 and 1930 the small states as a
group receive larger representation by the method of smallest
divisors than by any other method, and the large states receive
a larger representation by the method of greatest divisors than
by any other method; and this result will always follow the use
of these methods. It has sometimes been supposed (1) that in
an apportionment by the method of smallest divisors the large
states would have larger average populations per district than
the small states, and (2) that in an apportionment by the
method of greatest divisors the small states would have larger
average populations per district than the large states.

While apportionments based on the censuses of 1920 and 1930
apparently support these two statements, the result is what
might be termed a mathematical accident. That the statements
are not universally true is shown by the two following examples.
In both examples the states have the same total population, the
size of House is the same, and each state has the same number
of representatives, but the populations of the individual states
are different. The first example will show an apportionment by

the methods of major fractions and smallest divisors, both of which give the same result for the assumed populations.

APPORTIONMENT BY METHODS OF MAJOR FRACTIONS AND
SMALLEST DIVISORS[a]

State	Population	Number of Representatives	Average Population per District
A.............	2,000,016	9	222,224
B.............	1,750,008	8	218,751
C.............	1,379,994	6	229,999
D.............	1,149,990	5	229,998
E.............	749,994	3	249,998
F.............	499,998	2	249,999
Total.........	7,530,000	33	228,182

[a] Huntington, *Methods of Apportionment*, p. 39.

In this example each of the four large states has a smaller average population per district than either of the two small states, and for each of the two largest states the average is smaller than for the country as a whole. This disproves the statement that by the method of smallest divisors the average population per district is smallest in the small states.

The next example will show an apportionment by the methods of major fractions and greatest divisors, both of which give the same results for the assumed facts.

APPORTIONMENT BY METHODS OF MAJOR FRACTIONS AND
GREATEST DIVISORS[a]

State	Population	Number of Representatives	Average Population per District
A.............	2,106,279	9	234,031
B.............	1,895,664	8	236,958
C.............	1,349,958	6	224,993
D.............	1,124,940	5	224,988
E.............	631,893	3	210,631
F.............	421,266	2	210,633
Total..........	7,530,000	33	228,182

[a] Huntington, *Methods of Apportionment*, p. 39.

In this example each of the four large states has a greater average population per district than either of the two small states, and for each of the two largest states the average is greater than for the country as a whole. This disproves the statement that by the method of greatest divisors the average population per district is smallest in the large states.

The two foregoing examples also disprove the statement that the method of major fractions avoids discrimination between the large and small states. In the first example each of the large states has a smaller average population per district than either of the small states. In the second example these conditions are reversed, and each of the large states has a larger average population per district than either of the small states.

At the hearings in 1928 it was stated: "Inevitably, inherently, in the method of equal proportions, the average population of a congressional district in a group of small states is less than the average population of a congressional district in the very large state."[4]

The statement quoted above might be true under certain conditions, but it has no mathematical basis, and is not "inevitably" and "inherently" characteristic of the method of equal proportions. In fact an apportionment by the method of equal proportions after the census of 1930 gave results directly contrary to this statement. The average population per district by that method for all the very large states was 277,060, while the average for the small states was 281,668. Turning to the individual states we find that only five of the small states had smaller averages than the average for all the very large states, while seven had larger averages. The same five are the only small states with averages lower than the lowest average for the very large states. The figures for the several states are given in the table on page 69.

The method of equal proportions has been called a "novel method"[5] but this description is not accurate either as regards time or characteristics. As a period of almost 20 years has elapsed since it was devised it has sufficient age not to be classed as novel. It is based on sound mathematical principles which have been recognized for many years, although one of them (the geometric mean) was not applied to the problem of apportion-

[4] *Apportionment of Representatives*, Hearing before the House Committee on the Census, 70 Cong. 1 sess., on H.R. 130, 1928, Testimony of Walter F. Willcox, p. 63.

[5] *Apportionment of Representatives in Congress*, Hearings before the House Committee on the Census, 76 Cong. 3 sess., 1940, testimony of Walter F. Willcox, p. 16.

AVERAGE POPULATION PER DISTRICT IN SMALL AND VERY LARGE STATES BY METHOD
OF EQUAL PROPORTIONS, BASED ON CENSUS OF 1930
(Figures in italics are for small states for which the average population per district
is less than average population per district in all very large states.)

States	Population	Number of Representatives	Average Population per District
Small states			
Vermont............	359,611	1	359,611
Arizona.............	389,375	1	389,375
New Mexico.........	395,982	1	395,982
Idaho..............	441,536	2	*220,768*
New Hampshire......	465,292	2	*232,646*
Utah...............	505,741	2	*252,870*
Montana...........	524,729	2	*262,364*
South Dakota ...	673,005	2	336,502
North Dakota.......	673,340	2	336,670
Rhode Island........	687,497	2	343,748
Maine..............	797,418	3	*265,806*
Oregon.............	950,379	3	316,793
Total............	6,863,905	23	298,431
Very large states			
New Jersey..........	4,041,319	14	288,666
Massachusetts.......	4,249,598	15	283,307
Michigan...........	4,842,052	17	284,827
California..........	5,668,241	20	283,412
Texas..............	5,824,601	21	277,362
Ohio..............	6,646,633	24	276,943[a]
Illinois.............	7,630,388	27	282,607
Pennsylvania........	9,631,299	34	283,274
New York..........	12,587,967	45	279,733
Total............	61,122,098	217	281,668

Smallest average population per district among very large states.

ment until the development of the method of alternate ratios,
which preceded the method of equal proportions. It is true that
it has never been used in an actual apportionment, but that is
likewise true of all the other modern methods with the exception of the method of major fractions.

Considering the methods separately we thus find that as compared with the method of equal proportions the method of
smallest divisors gives larger representation to the small states;
that the method of greatest divisors gives larger representation
to the large states; that the method of harmonic mean tends to
give a larger representation to the small states, but not as great
as the method of smallest divisors; and that the method of major fractions tends to favor the large states, but not to the same
degree as the method of greatest divisors. The method of equal
proportions tends to give the most equitable distribution among
the states regardless of size.

CONCLUSIONS

The relative merits of the several methods were summed up as follows in 1929 in the report of the Committee of the National Academy of Sciences:[6]

There are five methods of apportionment now known which are unambiguous (that is, lead to a workable solution), and should be considered at this time.

These five methods are—
Method of smallest divisors
Method of harmonic mean
Method of equal proportions
Method of major fractions
Method of greatest divisors

. . . .

After full consideration of these various methods your committee is of the opinion that on mathematical grounds, the method of equal proportions is the method to be preferred. Each of the other four methods listed is, however, consistent with itself and unambiguous.

The essential mathematical characteristics of the five methods are as follows:

Let the population of a State A and the number of Representatives assigned to it according to a selected method of apportionment be a, and let B and b represent the corresponding numbers for a second State. Under an ideal apportionment the population A/a, B/b of the congressional districts in the two States should be equal, as well as the numbers a/A, b/B of Representatives per person in each State. In practice it is impossible to bring this desirable result about for all pairs of States.

In the opinion of this committee the best test of a desirable apportionment so far proposed is the following:

"An apportionment of Representatives to the various States, when the total number of Representatives is fixed, is mathematically satisfactory if for every pair of States the discrepancy between the numbers A/a and B/b cannot be decreased by assigning one more Representative to the State A and one fewer to the State B or vice versa, or if the two numbers a/A and b/B have the same property.

"For the purposes of discussion let A/a be larger than B/b so that the State A is underrepresented as compared with B. If the 'discrepancy' between A/a and B/b is defined to be the percentage discrepancy, that is, the difference $A/a - B/b$ divided by the smaller B/b of the two numbers A/a, B/b and if the discrepancy between

[6] The committee consisted of Raymond Pearl, chairman, G. A. Bliss, E. W. Brown, and L. P. Eisenhart.

b/B and a/A is measured in the same way, the test above leads to an apportionment which satisfies the test when applied to either the pair A/a, B/b, or the pair a/A, b/B. The method so determined has been called the method of equal proportions."

If the test is applied only to the pair a/A, b/B, and if the discrepancy between these numbers is interpreted to be the absolute difference $b/B - a/A$, another method of apportionment called the "method of major fractions" is uniquely determined. If, on the other hand, the test is applied only to the absolute difference of the pair A/a, B/b, a third method, called the "method of harmonic mean," is similarly defined.

It has been shown that there are two further methods of apportionment determined by the test set down above when applied to the differences $b - aB/A$, $bA/B - a$. These are called, respectively, the "method of smallest divisors," and the "method of greatest divisors."

The methods thus briefly characterized mathematically are the five methods in the list above. Each method in the list favors the larger States as compared with the methods which precede it. . . .

The method of the harmonic mean and the method of major fractions are symmetrically situated on the list. Mathematically there is no reason for choosing between them. . . .

The method of equal proportions is preferred by the committee because it satisfies the test proposed above when applied either to sizes of congressional districts or to numbers of representatives per person, and because it occupies mathematically a neutral position with respect to emphasis on larger and smaller States.[7]

The following is a summary of the report on methods of apportionment made in 1921 by the Census Advisory Committee of the Department of Commerce:[8]

1. It is clear that the Constitution requires that the allocation of representatives among the several states shall be proportionate to the distribution of population. It is not equally clear that there is anything in the constitutional requirement which suggests that one of the forms in which such apportionment ratios or proportion may be expressed should be preferred to another.

2. The "method of major fractions" utilizes only one of several ways of expressing apportionment ratios. The "method of equal proportions" utilizes all of these ways without inconsistency. The latter method, therefore, has a broader basis.

3. There is no mathematical or logical ground for preferring the one form of expression of the apportionment ratio used in the method of

[7] *Apportionment of Representatives in Congress*, Hearings before the House Committee on the Census, 76 Cong. 3 sess., 1940, pp. 70–71.

[8] The committee consisted of W. S. Rossiter, chairman, C. W. Doten, E. F. Gay, W. C. Mitchell, E. R. A. Seligman, and A. A. Young.

major fractions to other forms of expression. These other forms lead, when similar processes of computation are employed, to different and therefore inconsistent results.

4. The method of major fractions logically implies preference for a special meaning which may be attached to one of the forms in which apportionment ratios may be expressed. To attach to ratios meanings which vary with the forms in which the ratios are expressed is to interpret them as something else than ratios.

5. In the "method of major fractions" the "nearness" of the ratios of representatives and population for the several states is measured by absolute differences. The "method of equal proportions" utilizes relative differences. The relative scale is to be preferred.[9]

It has been claimed that the large states or the small states are favored in varying degrees by the several methods, and at various times in the hearings and the debates the argument has been advanced that as the Federal Convention gave the small states larger proportionate representation in the Senate by making the representation from each state equal, it was the intention to give the large states any advantage that might result from apportionment in the House. There is nothing in the debates or in the Constitution that supports such a contention.

The constitutional provision is clear and unambiguous: "Representatives and direct taxes shall be apportioned among the several states which may be included within this Union, according to their respective numbers."

There is nothing in the clause that connotes any conflict between large and small states, either singly or as groups. The apportionment is to be according to the respective numbers. The Constitution contemplates equality, but as it is impossible to attain absolute mathematical equality, the apportionment must be such as to reduce inequality to a minimum. As explained on preceding pages varying differences are used in the several methods to measure the degree or amount of inequality, but both the weight of authority and the equity of the apportionment indicate that the method of equal proportions is more desirable than any other method that has been devised.

[9] *Apportionment of Representatives in Congress amongst the Several States,* Hearing before House Committee on the Census, 69 Cong. 2 sess., on H.R. 13471, Jan. 19, 1927, Pt. 2, p. 58.

CHAPTER V

DISCARDED METHODS OF APPORTIONMENT

Methods of apportionment which may lead to paradoxes or which are otherwise unsatisfactory are discussed in this chapter. Some of these have been used, but others have never progressed beyond the proposal stage. The methods are as follows:

Fixed ratio with rejected fractions (Jefferson method) used from 1790 to 1830

Fixed ratio with major fractions, used in 1840

Vinton method, used from 1850 to 1900

Modified Vinton method

Alternate ratios

Webster method

Fixed ratio with geometric fractions

Fixed ratio with included fractions

Fixed ratio with harmonic fractions

Minimum range

Inverse minimum range

Each of these will be described in turn.

The examples given in this chapter to show the defects of the several methods are hypothetical. This fact, however, does not detract from their value, as a proper method of apportionment must meet every conceivable variation in population no matter how fantastic. This being the case, a single example that shows an inconsistency or a paradox is sufficient to condemn the method.

Most of the discarded methods make use of a fixed ratio. No method has been devised which uses a fixed ratio and avoids the paradoxes.

FIXED RATIO WITH REJECTED FRACTIONS

The method of fixed ratio with rejected fractions, the one devised by Jefferson, was used after each census from 1790 to 1830, inclusive. Under this method a representative is assigned for every whole number in the quota, and the fractions are disregarded. Thus a state with an exact quota of 3.9 gets 3 representatives. This method is subject to the population paradox,[1] namely, that an increase in population may be accompanied by a decrease in the size of the House.

FIXED RATIO WITH MAJOR FRACTIONS

Under the method of fixed ratio with major fractions, used in the apportionment made in 1840, after dividing the population of each state by the ratio selected a representative is assigned for every whole number in the quotient, and one for every fraction which is over one-half. Under this method a state with a quota of 3.51 gets 4 representatives and a state with a quota of 3.49 gets 3. An apportionment by this method equalizes as nearly as possible the individual share in a representative, if the inequalities are measured by absolute differences. The method is subject to the population paradox, as an increase in population may result in a decrease in the size of the House. This is shown by the example on page 6.

VINTON METHOD

The Vinton method, which was used from 1850 to 1900, is based on a fixed ratio and a fixed size of House. In this method the population of the country is divided by the number of members of the House to give the ratio or number of persons for each district. This ratio is then divided into the population of each state to give the exact quota for each state. After assigning one representative to each state whose quota is less than one, in order to meet the constitutional requirement that each state is entitled to one representative, each of the other states receives a representative for each whole number in its exact quota. The remaining representatives are then assigned in order to the states having the highest fractions. It might be called the method of highest fractions, although this term has not been used so far as is known to the writer.

The highest fractions used to complete the membership of the

[1] E. V. Huntington, *Methods of Apportionment*, p. 18.

House may not include all the major fractions; likewise they may include some minor fractions.[2]

The Vinton method is subject to the Alabama paradox, as a state may lose a member if the size of the House is increased. This is shown in the following examples:

EXAMPLES OF VINTON METHOD[a]

I. HOUSE OF 100 MEMBERS; TOTAL POPULATION 1,000,000; RATIO 10,000

State	Population	Exact Quota	Tentative Quota	Assigned Quota after Using Highest Fractions
A.......	453,320	45.332	45	45
B.......	443,310	44.331	44	44
C.......	103,370	10.337	10	11[b]
Total.......	1,000,000	100.000	99	100

II. HOUSE OF 101 MEMBERS; TOTAL POPULATION 1,000,000; RATIO 9,901

State	Population	Exact Quota	Tentative Quota	Assigned Quota after Using Highest Fractions
A.......	452,170	45.669	45	46[c]
B.......	442,260	44.668	44	45[c]
C.......	105,570	10.663	10	10
Total.......	1,000,000	101.000	99	101

[a] Adapted from Huntington, *Methods of Apportionment*, pp. 28, 29.
[b] Additional representative, necessary to give 100 members, assigned to this state because it has the highest fraction in the exact quota.
[c] Additional representatives, necessary to give 101 members, assigned to these two states because they have the highest fractions in the exact quota.

In the examples given the total population is unchanged, but the size of the House is increased from 100 to 101, thus changing the ratio from 10,000 to 9,901. In the second example the population of States *A* and *B* has decreased both relatively and absolutely; the population of State *C* has increased both relatively and absolutely. Nevertheless States *A* and *B* each receive an additional representative and State *C*, with an increase in population, loses a representative.

MODIFIED VINTON METHOD

The modified Vinton method, which has never been used in an apportionment, is based on a fixed ratio and a fixed size of House. In this method the population of the country is divided by the number of members of the House to give the ratio or number of persons for each district. This ratio is then divided

[2] In the examples given it will be noted that in the first all the exact quotas are minor fractions and that in the second all the exact quotas are major fractions.

into the population of each to give the exàct quota for each state. After assigning one representative to each state whose quota is less than one, in order to meet the constitutional requirement, each of the other states receives a representative for each whole number in its exact quota. Up to this point the procedure is the same as in the original Vinton method.

The fraction for each state is then divided by the population of the state to obtain a ratio of the fraction to the population. Additional seats are then assigned in the order of the states having the highest ratios. The method is illustrated by the following example.

STEPS IN APPORTIONMENT BY MODIFIED VINTON METHOD, FOR
HOUSE OF 100 MEMBERS[a]
(Total population 25,000,000; ratio 250,000)

State	Population	Exact Quota	First Assignment	Fraction	Ratio of Fraction to Population[b]	Assigned Quota
1	2	3	4	5	6	7
A.....	12,972,500	51.89	51	.89	.007	51
B.....	11,000,000	44.00	44	.00	.000	44
C.....	345,000	1.38	1	.38	.110	2[c]
D....	342,500	1.37	1	.37	.108	2[c]
E.....	340,000	1.36	1	.36	.106	1
Total....	25,000,000	100.00	98	—	—	100

[a] Adapted from Huntington, *Methods of Apportionment*, p. 38.
[b] Column 5 divided by column 2; five decimals omitted.
[c] Additional representative assigned because of largest ratios of fraction to population.

The modified Vinton method is subject to the Alabama paradox, as a state may lose a member if the size of the House is increased, with no change in population of the several states. This is shown by the example in the accompanying table:

APPORTIONMENT BY MODIFIED VINTON METHOD, FOR HOUSE
OF 100 AND 101 MEMBERS[a]

State	Population	House of 100 Members (Ratio 5,000)	House of 101 Members (Ratio 4,905)
A..............	154,550	30	31
B..............	154,500	30	31
C..............	154,450	30	31
D.............	7,400	2	2
E..............	7,350	2	2
F..............	7,300	2	2
G..............	7,250	2	1
H.............	7,200	2	1
Total..........	500,000	100	101

[a] Huntington, *Methods of Apportionment*, pp. 29, 38.

By increasing the House from 100 to 101 members, States *G* and *H* each lose a member, although there is no change in the population of any of the states.

ALTERNATE RATIOS

The method of alternate ratios, which was proposed by Dr. Joseph A. Hill in 1911 but which has never been used in an apportionment, is based on a fixed ratio and a fixed size of House. It was the first one to use the geometric mean and was a forerunner of the method of equal proportions; it was discarded by Dr. Hill for the method of equal proportions when that method was developed.[3]

This method is described by Dr. Hill as follows:

1. Compute the exact quotas to which the states are severally entitled on the basis of population and the total number of representatives to be apportioned. [Up to this point the procedure is the same as in the Vinton method.]

2. Determine the number of representatives to be assigned for fractions, by adding the whole numbers in the exact quotas and subtracting the total from total number of representatives to be apportioned.

3. Compute for each state the two ratios that will result if the fraction is (first) disregarded or is (second) counted as a unit.

4. Obtain [a priority list by taking] the product of these ratios.

5. Rank the states in the order of the size of these products [or this priority list].

6. Assign the representatives to be assigned for fractions in the order of this ranking [until sufficient additional members are assigned to make a House of the size desired].[4]

The working of this method is illustrated by the example given in the table on page 78.

[3] *Apportionment of Representatives in Congress amongst the Several States*, Hearing before the House Committee on the Census, 69 Cong. 2 sess., on H.R. 13471, 1927, p. 16.

[4] *Apportionment of Representatives*, 62 Cong., 1 sess., H. Rept. 12, p. 51. The working of the method is fully explained in this report.

STEPS IN METHOD OF ALTERNATE RATIOS FOR HOUSE OF 75 MEMBERS[a]
(Total population 7,500,000; ratio 100,000)

State	Population	Exact Quota	First Assign-ment	Ratio		Index of Priority[d]	Assigned Quota
				Not Counting Fractions[b]	Counting Each Fraction as a Whole Number[c]		
1	2	3	4	5	6	7	8
A.....	3,688,000	36.88	36	102,444	99,676	10,211	36
B	3,156,000	31.56	31	101,806	98,625	10,041	31
C.....	154,000	1.54	1	154,000	77,000	11,858	2[e]
D....	355,000	3.55	3	118,333	88,750	10,502	4[e]
E.....	147,000	1.47	1	147,000	73,500	10,805	2[e]
Total....	7,500,000	75.00	72[f]	—	—	—	75[f]

[a] Adapted from Joseph A. Hill in *Apportionment of Representatives*, 62 Cong. 1 sess., H. Rept. 12, p. 52.
[b] Obtained by dividing population (column 2) by whole numbers of quota, disregarding fractions, in column 3.
[c] Obtained by dividing population (column 2) by next higher whole number of quota (column 3).
[d] Product of two preceding columns; carried out to five significant figures only.
[e] Additional representative assigned by reason of higher value of index of priority in preceding column.
[f] Difference between these figures shows members to be assigned for fractions in exact quota.

The method of alternate ratios is subject to the Alabama paradox, as a state may lose a member if the size of the House is increased. This is shown in the following example:

APPORTIONMENT BY METHOD OF ALTERNATE RATIOS FOR HOUSE
OF 100 AND OF 101 MEMBERS[a]

State	Population	House of 100 Members (Ratio 5,000)	House of 101 Members (Ratio 4,905)
A.............	154,550	30	31
B.............	154,500	30	31
C.............	154,450	30	31
D.............	7,400	2	2
E.............	7,350	2	2
F.............	7,300	2	2
G.............	7,250	2	1
H.............	7,200	2	1
Total..........	500,000	100	101

[a] Huntington, *Methods of Apportionment*, p. 29.

Thus if the House is increased from 100 to 101 members a representative is lost by States *G* and *H* although the population of all the states remains the same.

WEBSTER METHOD

The Webster method, proposed in 1832, provided for a fixed size of House, a ratio determined by dividing the total number of members into the total population, and the assignment of members according to the nearest whole number in the exact quota. The last step is equivalent to a member for each whole number and an additional member for each major fraction. Thus with five states having a population of 20,000,000 and a House of 10 members, the ratio will be 2,000,000. A state with a population of 3,500,000 will have an exact quota of 1.75 and will receive 2 members, while a state with a population of 2,-500,000 will have an exact quota of 1.25 and will receive one member.

The following examples show that for every size of House ranging from 8 to 11 it is impossible to obtain a House of the desired size by this method.

EXAMPLES OF FAILURE OF WEBSTER METHOD[a]

State	Population	House of 8 Members (Ratio 2,500,000)		House of 9 Members (Ratio 2,222,222)		House of 10 Members (Ratio 2,000,000)		House of 11 Members (Ratio 1,818,182)	
		Exact Quota	Assigned Quota	Exact Quota	Assigned Quota	Exact Quota	Assigned Quota	Exact Quota	Assigned Quota
A.......	8,000,000	3.200	3	3.600	4	4.000	4	4.400	4
B.......	3,006,000	1.202	1	1.353	1	1.503	2	1.653	2
C.......	3,004,000	1.202	1	1.352	1	1.502	2	1.652	2
D.......	3,002,000	1.201	1	1.351	1	1.501	2	1.651	2
E.......	2,988,000	1.195	1	1.344	1	1.494	1	1.644	2
Total..	20,000,000	8	7	9	8	10	11	11	12

[a] Adapted from Huntington, *Methods of Apportionment*, p. 35.

With a House of 12 members the number of assigned seats would be 13. The Webster method has never been used in an apportionment.

FIXED RATIO WITH GEOMETRIC FRACTIONS

Under the method of fixed ratio with geometric fractions the population of each state is divided by the fixed ratio to give the exact quota or number of representatives from each state. Each state receives a representative for each whole number in its exact quota and an additional seat if the exact quota is greater than the geometric mean of the whole number already assigned and next higher number.[5]

With a ratio of 250,000 the computation of the quota would

---

[5] The geometric mean of two numbers is the square root of their product. Thus if a is the whole number already assigned, the next higher number will be $a + 1$ and the geometric mean will be $\sqrt{a(a+1)}$.

be as follows:

	State *A*	State *B*
Population.................................	862,500	867,500
Exact quota (population divided by ratio)..	3.45	3.47
Geometric mean..........................	$\sqrt{3 \times 4} = 3.464$	$\sqrt{3 \times 4} = 3.464$
Apportionment...........................	3	4

State *A* would receive three representatives as its exact quota is less than the geometric mean between 3 and 4; State *B* would receive four representatives as its exact quota is more than the geometric mean between 3 and 4. In an apportionment by this method the population of each district and the individual share in a representative are as near as possible to the ratio adopted, if the relative difference is the criterion.

With this method the size of the House cannot be fixed. Moreover it is subject to the population paradox, in that an increase in population may result in a smaller House even though the ratio remains the same. The hypothetical example given on page 6 shows that with an increase of population from 102,-750,113 to 102,958,798, the size of the House may decrease from 435 to 391. This method has never been used in an apportionment.

FIXED RATIO WITH INCLUDED FRACTIONS

Under the method of fixed ratio with included fractions, a representative is assigned for every whole number in the exact quota and one for every fraction, regardless of its size. Thus a state with an exact quota of 3.2 would obtain four representatives. This method has never been used; it is subject to the population paradox, as an increase in population may result in a decrease in the size of House.[6]

FIXED RATIO WITH HARMONIC FRACTIONS

Under the method of fixed ratios with harmonic fractions the population of each state is divided by the fixed ratio to give the exact quota or the number of representatives from each state. Each state receives a representative for each whole number in its exact quota, and an additional seat if the exact quota is greater than the harmonic mean between the whole number al-

[6] Huntington, *Methods of Apportionment*, p. 17.

ready assigned and the next higher number.[7] The method was proposed by James Dean in 1832.[8] With a ratio of 250,000 the computation of the quota would be as follows:

	State A	State B
Population..........................	852,500	857,500
Exact quota (population divided by ratio)..	3.41	3.43
Harmonic mean......................	$\dfrac{2(3\times4)}{7}=3.428$	$\dfrac{2(3\times4)}{7}=3.428$
Apportionment	3	4

State A would receive three representatives as its exact quota is less than the harmonic mean between 3 and 4; State B would receive four representatives as its exact quota is greater than the harmonic mean between 3 and 4.

In an apportionment by this method the population of each district is as near as possible to the ratio adopted, if the inequality is measured by the absolute difference.

With this method the size of the House cannot be fixed. Moreover it is subject to the population paradox, in that an increase in population may result in a smaller House even though the ratio remains the same. The hypothetical example given on page 6 shows that with an increase of population from 102,-750,113 to 102,958,798 the size of the House may decrease from 435 to 391. This method was never used in an apportionment.

MINIMUM RANGE

There has been considerable confusion in the use of the term minimum range. At times it has been used for a method of computation of an apportionment, which it is not, and at times it has been employed to describe a test for making a selection between other methods of apportionment. As it can be applied as a test or criterion for selection between methods, it will be referred to as the test of minimum range and not as a method.

The concept that underlies the test of minimum range is that

---

[7] The harmonic mean of two numbers is twice their product divided by their sum. Thus if a is the whole number already assigned, the next higher number will be $a+1$ and the harmonic mean will be $\dfrac{2a(a+1)}{a+(a+1)}$.

[8] 22 Cong. 1 sess., S. Doc. 119, pp. 19–21.

the best apportionment is one that reduces to a minimum the absolute difference between the highest and lowest average population per district. The application of the test to modern methods is illustrated by the following examples:

SELECTION OF METHOD OF APPORTIONMENT BY TEST OF MINIMUM
RANGE FOR HOUSE OF 16 MEMBERS[a]

State	Population	Apportionment by Method of Smallest Divisors		Apportionment by Methods of Harmonic Mean, Equal Proportions, and Major Fractions		Apportionment by Method of Greatest Divisors	
		Number of Repre-sentatives	Average Population per District	Number of Repre-sentatives	Average Population per District	Number of Repre-sentatives	Average Population per District
A.......	726,000	7	103,714	7	103,714	8	90,750
B.......	539,000	5	107,800	6	89,833	5	107,800
C.......	335,000	4	83,750	3	111,667	3	111,667
Total....	1,600,000	16	—	16	—	16	—
Range...	—	—	24,050	—	21,834	—	20,917 (minimum)

[a] Adapted from Huntington, *Methods of Apportionment*, p. 30.

As the absolute difference between the highest and lowest average population per district under the conditions given above is lowest with an apportionment made by the method of greatest divisors, that method meets the test of minimum range and is the best if that difference is the criterion. However, under other conditions another method might be indicated. If the size of the House is increased to 17 members, the population remaining the same, the test of minimum range would indicate either the method of harmonic mean or smallest divisors as is shown in the table below.

SELECTION OF METHOD OF APPORTIONMENT BY TEST OF MINIMUM
RANGE FOR HOUSE OF 17 MEMBERS[a]

State	Population	Apportionment by Methods of Smallest Divisors and Harmonic Mean		Apportionment by Methods of Equal Proportions, Major Fractions, and Greatest Divisors	
		Number of Representatives	Average Popula-tion per District	Number of Representatives	Average Popula-tion per District
A...........	726,000	7	103,714	8	90,750
B...........	539,000	6	89,833	6	89,833
C...........	335,000	4	83,750	3	111,667
Total........	1,600,000	17	—	17	—
Range.......	—	—	19,964 (minimum)	—	21,834

[a] Huntington, *Methods of Apportionment*, p. 30.

Every other method of apportionment that has been proposed is based on a mathematical formula resulting in a priority list, on a standard ratio for population of congressional districts, on the inclusion or rejection of fractions in the exact quota, or on a combination of these features. The test of minimum range uses none of these. It starts from an apportionment made by modern methods, and determines which one should be used.

It has been stated that the test for minimum range is the same as the method of harmonic mean.[9] This is erroneous. The method of harmonic mean affords a definite method of computation, but minimum range offers merely a selection. The examples on page 82 show that the method of harmonic mean meets the test of minimum range with a House of 17 members, but does not meet it with a House of 16 members.

A controlling defect in the test by minimum range is that it is subject to the Alabama paradox in that a state may lose a representative if the size of the House is increased, with no changes in the population of the several states. In the preceding examples, with a House of 16 members the test of minimum range indicates an apportionment by the method of greatest divisors, and State *A* receives 8 representatives. With a House of 17 members, the test of minimum range indicates an apportionment by the methods of smallest divisors or harmonic mean (both of which give identical results under the circumstances), and State *A* receives only 7 members, although the population of all three states remains the same. Therefore under the apportionments above made by the test of minimum range State *A* loses a representative if the House is increased from 16 to 17 members, although the population of all the states is the same.

[9] *Science, New Series,* Vol. 69, 1939, p. 165. There is a threefold confusion in this article. Not only is the test of minimum range stated to be the same as the method of harmonic mean, but the method of harmonic mean is identified with the method of smallest divisors or included fractions, by the statement that "by it [method of harmonic mean] every decimal fraction [in a quota] no matter how small entitles the state to a representative."

INVERSE MINIMUM RANGE

The process of inverse minimum range is also a selective test rather than a method. It is based on the concept that the best apportionment is one that reduces to a minimum the absolute difference between the highest and lowest individual share in a representative. Like the test of minimum range it is not based on a mathematical formula, on a priority list, on a standard ratio, on the inclusion or rejection of fractions in the exact quota, or on any combination of these features. It starts from an apportionment made by modern methods and determines which one should be used.

The application of the test to modern methods is illustrated by the example in the accompanying table:

APPORTIONMENT BY TEST OF INVERSE MINIMUM RANGE FOR HOUSE OF 16 MEMBERS[a]

State	Population	Apportionment by Methods of Smallest Divisors and Harmonic Mean		Apportionment by Method of Equal Proportions		Apportionment by Methods of Greatest Divisors and Major Fractions	
		Number of Representatives	Individual Share	Number of Representatives	Individual Share	Number of Representatives	Individual Share
A	729,000	7	.000,009,60	7	.000,009,60	8	.000,010,97
B	534,000	5	.000,009,36	6	.000,011,24	5	.000,009,36
C	337,000	4	.000,011,87	3	.000,008,90	3	.000,008,90
Total . . .	1,600,000	16		16		16	
Range . .	—	—	.000,002,51		.000,002,34		.000,002,07 (minimum)

[a] Adapted from Huntington, *Methods of Apportionment*, p. 31.

As the absolute difference is smallest by the methods of greatest divisors and major fractions, which give the same result under the conditions indicated, the test by the method of minimum range indicates the apportionment in the last column.

As in the case of the test of minimum range the test of inverse minimum range may indicate a different method under different conditions. In the example given above for a House of 16 members the test indicates the methods of greatest divisors and major fractions; as is shown below for a House of 17 members the test indicates the methods of harmonic mean and smallest divisors.

Even if the test of inverse minimum range were a method of computation, it is defective because it is subject to the Alabama

APPORTIONMENT BY TEST OF INVERSE MINIMUM RANGE FOR HOUSE OF 17 MEMBERS[a]

State	Population	Apprtionment by Methods of Equal Proportions, Major Fractions, and Greatest Divisors		Apportionment by Methods of Harmonic Mean and Smallest Divisors	
		Number of Representatives	Individual Share	Number of Representatives	Individual Share
A............	729,000	8	.000,010,97	7	.000,009,60
B............	534,000	6	.000,011,24	6	.000,011,24
C............	337,000	3	.000,008,90	4	.000,011,87
Total........	1,600,000	17	—	17	—
Range.......	—	—	.000,002,34	—	.000,002,27 (minimum)

[a] Huntington, *Methods of Apportionment*, p. 31.

paradox, as with an increase in the size of the House a state may lose a representative although the population of all the states is unchanged. In the apportionment by the tests given above State *A* receives 8 representatives in a House of 16 members; but for a House of 17 members receives only 7 representatives, although there has been no change in the population of the three states.

The test of inverse minimum range has never been used in an apportionment.

CHAPTER VI
THE COUNTING OF ALIENS

During recent years there have been several proposals that aliens be excluded from the apportionment population, but none of these has been adopted. The consideration of this matter naturally divides itself into two parts: (1) the constitutional aspects, and (2) the policy of excluding the aliens from the count.

CONSTITUTIONAL ASPECTS OF THE COUNTING OF ALIENS

The portions of the Constitution dealing with the subject are the third clause of section 2 of Article 1 and the Fourteenth Amendment. The third clause of section 2 of Article 1 reads as follows:

Representatives and direct taxes shall be apportioned among the several states which may be included in this Union according to their respective numbers, which shall be determined by adding to the whole number of free persons, including those bound to service for a term of years, and excluding Indians not taxed, three-fifths of other persons . . .

The pertinent part of section 2 of the Fourteenth Amendment, adopted to adjust the constitutional requirements to the abolition of slavery, reads as follows:

Representatives shall be apportioned among the several states according to their respective numbers, counting the whole number of persons in each state, excluding Indians not taxed.

It seems fairly conclusive that the aliens must be included in the apportionment population. Indians not taxed are specifically excluded and if one group of persons or inhabitants is excluded from the count, the general rules of construction require all other groups to be included.

It has been argued that there were no aliens in the country at the time the Constitution was adopted, and that consequently there was no occasion for the Constitutional Convention to insert any rule regarding their counting. But the framers of the Constitution were well aware that there would be aliens, as is shown by clause 4 of section 8 of Article 1, which gives Congress power "to establish an uniform rule of naturalization."

Notwithstanding the increasing immigration during the first half of the nineteenth century, no one seems to have raised the question of the relationship of aliens to apportionment. The census schedules of 1820 and 1830 provided for the enumeration of foreigners not naturalized, but the results do not seem to have been published. The census of 1850 was the first one which attempted to enumerate the foreign born, but not until 1890 was any attempt made to ascertain the number of aliens, and in 1890, 1900, and 1910 the returns regarding citizenship were tabulated only for males 21 years of age and over. The census of 1920 was the first one for which complete returns on citizenship of the foreign born were published.

By 1850 the foreign born numbered 11.5 per cent of the white population, and by 1890 the percentage had risen to 16.6. The fact that for over a hundred years there was no publication of the total number of aliens seems to indicate that public men were not interested in the subject. The apportionment debates contain no reference to the counting of aliens, and it seems likely that census figures would have been demanded if anyone had seriously believed that aliens should not be counted.

POLICY AS REGARDS COUNTING OF ALIENS

Regardless of the constitutional question involved, there arises the question of policy in regard to the counting of aliens for apportionment purposes. If the Constitution does not require the counting of aliens, the determination of whether they shall be counted becomes a matter of policy. If the Constitution requires the counting, there arises the question as to whether it is desirable to amend the Constitution so that aliens will be eliminated from the apportionment population. This again is a matter of policy.

The arguments for and against the inclusion of aliens are naturally not as conclusive from the standpoint of policy as they are from the constitutional side. The constitutional question involves merely the interpretation of the language of the Constitution, while the determination of policy rests entirely on political philosophy.

It might be said the representation should be based on all inhabitants, regardless of their civil and legal status, as aliens are generally allowed to own property, and have a stake in the country regardless of their right to vote. This argument had more force when both apportionment and direct taxes were based on the population, as originally provided by clause 3 of section 2 of Article 1 of the Constitution. Under this clause direct taxation and representation progressed in the same proportion. But the Sixteenth Amendment removed the relation between direct taxation and representation as it provides that "Congress shall have power to lay and collect taxes on incomes, from whatever source derived, without apportionment among the several states, and without regard to any census or enumeration."

The stronger argument seems to be that the apportionment population should be limited to citizens and that the aliens should be excluded from the count. At present aliens cannot vote in any state, and it seems logical that persons who cannot share in the election of a representative should not be counted in the apportionment. It is true that minors cannot vote and that there are other disqualifications for the suffrage in the various states, but most of these disqualifications cut across all groups of the population, and are not confined to a single one.[1]

Aliens have a different legal status from any other group of the population. Under the act of June 28, 1940 (54 Stat. L. 670) aliens must be registered and must give notice of any change of address. Until the foreign born become citizens it seems proper that they should not be counted in the apportionment population. As it is believed that the Constitution requires the inclusion of aliens, a constitutional amendment will be necessary to exclude them from the apportionment population. However, if a constitutional amendment is adopted basing apportionment

---

[1] The bearing of voting on apportionment will be discussed in the next chapter.

on voting, as is suggested in the next chapter, no amendment regarding aliens will be necessary.

Ten states, some of which have the largest percentage of aliens, exclude all or some aliens from the population base used for apportionment to one or both houses of the state legislature. In the apportionment for the state legislature the aliens are directly excluded by Maine, Nebraska, New York, and North Carolina. Apportionment is based on voters, who must be citizens, by Arizona, Kansas, Massachusetts, Rhode Island, and Tennessee. In California persons not eligible to become citizens are excluded; this eliminates the Japanese and Chinese. If the states exclude aliens from their own apportionment they cannot in good grace object to excluding them from the federal apportionment.[2]

The number of aliens in each state at the census of 1930 is shown in the table on page 90; figures for 1940 are not available. The table follows the census classification of "those having first papers," and "those not having first papers" (called aliens in the census reports). The foreign born having first papers are aliens, but they have made the first step toward citizenship, and it is deemed desirable to retain the census classification.

[2] The citations to the state constitutions are as follows: Arizona, Art. IV, [Pt] 2, sec. 1; Art. VII, sec. 2; California, Art. IV, sec. 6; Kansas, Art. II, sec. 2; Art. V, sec. 1; Maine, Art. IV, Pt. 1, sec. 2; Massachusetts, Amendment III, LXXI; Nebraska, Art. III, sec. 5; New York, Art. III, secs. 4–5; North Carolina, Art. II, secs. 4, 6; Rhode Island, Art. II, sec. 1; Art. V, sec. 1, Art. VI, sec. 1; Tennessee, Art. II, secs. 5–6; Art. IV, sec. 1. See New York State Constitutional Convention Committee, *Constitutions of the States and United States*, 1938.

ALIENS, CENSUS OF 1930

State	Total Population[a]	Having First Papers		Not Having First Papers	
		Number	Percentage of Total Population of State	Number	Percentage of Total Population of State
Alabama.................	2,646,248	1,145	b	2,901	0.1
Arizona.................	435,573	2,003	0.5	48,322	11.1
Arkansas................	1,854,482	500	b	1,591	0.1
California..............	5,677,251	84,891	1.5	506,876	8.9
Colorado...............	1,035,791	6,024	0.6	30,342	2.9
Connecticut.............	1,606,903	31,628	2.0	165,958	10.3
Delaware...............	238,380	1,438	0.6	5,041	2.1
Florida.................	1,468,211	4,201	0.3	28,802	2.0
Georgia.................	2,908,506	867	b	2,813	0.1
Idaho..................	445,032	2,112	0.5	7,101	1.6
Illinois.................	7,630,654	128,234	1.7	278,353	3.6
Indiana......	3,238,503	16,399	0.5	39,559	1.2
Iowa...................	2,470,939	7,763	0.3	22,826	0.9
Kansas.................	1,880,999	4,211	0.2	18,975	1.0
Kentucky...............	2,614,589	1,259	b	3,403	0.1
Louisiana...............	2,101,593	2,125	0.1	12,882	0.6
Maine..................	797,423	6,318	0.8	45,000	5.6
Maryland...............	1,631,526	8,193	0.5	25,971	1.6
Massachusetts...........	4,249,614	88,438	2.1	423,128	10.0
Michigan...............	4,842,325	142,524	2.9	251,269	5.2
Minnesota..............	2,563,953	23,438	0.9	47,909	1.9
Mississippi.............	2,009,821	392	b	2,462	0.1
Missouri...............	3,629,367	12,801	0.4	31,845	0.9
Montana...............	537,606	4,388	0.8	13,823	2.6
Nebraska...............	1,377,963	6,970	0.5	17,402	1.3
Nevada.................	91,058	1,128	1.2	6,587	7.2
New Hampshire..........	465,293	5,749	1.2	32,942	7.1
New Jersey.............	4,041,334	74,876	1.9	262,434	6.5
New Mexico.............	423,317	913	0.2	15,741	3.7
New York...............	12,588,066	313,037	2.5	1,065,974	8.5
North Carolina...........	3,170,276	618	b	1,868	0.1
North Dakota............	680,845	4,516	0.7	10,708	1.6
Ohio...................	6,646,697	69,241	1.0	183,463	2.8
Oklahoma...............	2,396,040	1,645	b	6,068	0.3
Oregon.................	953,786	11,640	1.2	31,178	3.3
Pennsylvania............	9,631,350	87,856	0.9	348,015	3.6
Rhode Island............	687,497	11,646	1.7	57,879	8.4
South Carolina..........	1,738,765	381	b	1,042	0.1
South Dakota...........	692,849	3,175	0.5	6,155	0.9
Tennessee..............	2,616,556	751	b	2,680	0.1
Texas..................	5,824,715	10,794	0.2	245,187	4.2
Utah...................	507,847	3,479	0.7	12,946	2.5
Vermont................	359,611	3,094	0.9	17,938	5.0
Virginia................	2,421,851	1,682	0.1	5,047	0.2
Washington.............	1,563,396	27,368	1.8	64,778	4.1
West Virginia...........	1,729,205	5,137	0.3	21,266	1.2
Wisconsin..............	2,939,006	35,568	1.2	69,977	2.4
Wyoming...............	225,565	1,481	0.7	7,221	3.2
Total..............	122,288,177	1,264,037	1.0	4,511,648	3.7

[a] Population figures in this column include Indians not taxed; for apportionment population by states see App. C. Figures by districts for Indians not taxed are not available.
[b] Less than one-tenth of 1 per cent.

CHAPTER VII

VOTING AND APPORTIONMENT

At present the number of votes cast or the number of qualified electors bears no relation to the apportionment of representatives, as apportionment is based solely on population. However, voting is a factor that should be given consideration. In the proportion of votes to population the states fall into two well-defined groups. In the northern and western states the ratio of votes to population is materially higher than in the South, the ratio being least in the southernmost states.

In 1938 the percentage of votes for representatives to population was 29.6 for the entire country, 36.6 for the northern and western states, and 6.8 for the southern states.[1] In 1938 it took only 35,439 votes to elect seven representatives in Mississippi, but it required 730,024 votes to elect the same number of representatives in Kansas. In other words, each voter in Mississippi exerted 20 times the power of a voter in Kansas.

In the separate districts in 1936 and 1938 the highest percentage was 66.9 in the fifth Missouri district, which includes Kansas City, in 1936, and the lowest was 0.5 in the third Mississippi, in 1938. The percentage for the fifth Missouri is much above any other district in the country. The fourth and fifth districts of Missouri include all of Jackson County, and no part of any other county. In 1930 the county had 470,454 inhabitants, of whom 399,746 were in Kansas City and 42,652 in Blue Township immediately adjacent to Kansas City.

In 1930 the native and naturalized population of Jackson County 21 years of age and over totaled 315,705, which was the maximum number entitled to vote. As 293,241 votes were cast, the percentage of votes to persons entitled to vote was 92.9.

[1] The percentages for the states included in this group were as follows: Alabama, 4.7; Arkansas, 7.8; Florida, 10.4; Georgia, 2.3; Louisiana, 7.3; Mississippi, 1.8; North Carolina, 15.1; South Carolina, 2.7; Tennessee, 10.1; Texas, 6.3; Virginia, 5.2. The percentages are based on the entire population, including Indians not taxed, in 1930. The percentages for each state in 1936 and 1938 are given on pp. 98-106.

To obtain the actual voting population there must be deducted from 315,705 the persons who had not the required statutory period of residence or who had neglected to register. It is true that the population figures are for 1930, and the election figures for 1936. But during the intervening six years there was no great trend toward the cities. By 1940 the population of the county had increased 6,112, or 1.3 per cent, and that of Kansas City had increased 429, or 0.1 per cent. More detailed figures for 1940 are not available. The high ratio of votes to population may be an index to a high degree of civic interest or it may indicate something very different.

In sharp contrast to the fifth district of Missouri is the third district in Mississippi, where in 1938 only 2,172 voters, or 0.5 per cent of the total population, took part in the election. In 1930 the persons over 21 years of age numbered 55,571 for the native and naturalized white, and 168,452 for the negro. The voters comprised only 1 per cent of those entitled to vote. Incidentally, this district, which is one of seven in Mississippi, contains 30.9 per cent of the negroes. The total population of the district is 46.6 per cent in excess of the average for the state.

If the discrepancy in the number of votes cast was confined to its effect on the membership of the House of Representatives the situation would be bad enough, but it extends to the electoral vote for President, as the electoral vote of each state is the number of representatives plus two. Mississippi and Kansas each have nine presidential electors who in 1936 were chosen by 162,090 voters in Mississippi and 865,013 voters in Kansas. Thus a voter in Mississippi had five times the weight of a voter in Kansas. If a constitutional amendment providing for the election of the President by popular vote were adopted, the inequality would be removed as far as the election of the President is concerned, but it would still remain as regards representation in the House.

At this point it may be well to review briefly the power of the United States over voting. The Constitution confers no right to vote; it merely prohibits its denial in certain cases. For representatives in Congress the Constitution originally provided that the electors in each state must have the qualifications "requisite for electors of the most numerous branch of the State legislature" (Art. I, sec. 2, clause 1). The same qualifications were prescribed for electors of senators when the direct election of senators was provided for in 1913 (Seventeenth Amendment).

After the Civil War the Fourteenth Amendment declared that all persons born or naturalized in the United States are citizens thereof, and the Fifteenth Amendment laid down the rule that the right of a citizen to vote shall not be denied or abridged on account of race, color, or previous condition of servitude. The Nineteenth Amendment, adopted in 1920, provided that the right to vote shall not be denied or abridged on account of sex.

Presidential electors are appointed by each state "in such manner as the legislature thereof may direct" (Art. II, sec. 1, clause 2), but Congress may determine the time of choosing the electors (Art. II, sec. 1, clause 4).

With the exception of the limitations prescribed above, the qualifications for suffrage are entirely matters of state law.

Notwithstanding the constitutional provision that the right of citizens to vote shall not be abridged by reason of race or color, it is well known that in the South the voting privileges of the negro are much curtailed. Existing laws governing voting have met the constitutional test, but it is likely that there are general qualifications for suffrage which bear more heavily on the negroes than on the whites. Probably more effective than these is the social pressure which discourages the negro from voting.

It is therefore pertinent to raise the question whether the population basis of representation should not be abandoned, and the number of votes be substituted as the criterion. Such action would require a constitutional amendment, although attempts have been made to amend apportionment acts with this end in view.

The defenders of the existing system of representation in the one-party states will probably say that the interest of the voters is manifested in the primaries and not in the election.

Statistics of voting in the primaries are buried in local newspapers and are not generally available, but even if the primary vote is much greater than the vote in the election the fact remains that a large proportion of the voters is practically disfranchised.

It will also be contended that minors do not vote but are counted in the apportionment population, as a member of the House theoretically represents every person in his district, regardless of voting privilege. But as a rule minors bear a more or less constant ratio to the total population, and it is doubtful whether the quota of any state would be changed if the minors were excluded from the apportionment population. The question is quite different when a group of the population is allowed to vote in one section and denied the suffrage in another.

Perhaps the present system in the one-party states is the best that can be devised to meet the prevailing social, economic, and political conditions. It is not suggested that any attempt be made to interfere with the internal affairs of any state. But as has been shown on previous pages the apportionment of representatives is a matter that transcends state lines, and is one of national concern. If a state elects to limit the suffrage, through legislation that affects a particular group, through social pressure, or through extra-legal action, it has no valid ground for objecting to a reduction in its federal apportionment quota.

The second sentence of section 2 of the Fourteenth Amendment was designed to curtail representation if the suffrage was limited by reason of race or color. The pertinent sentence reads as follows:

But when the right to vote at any election for the choice of electors for President and Vice President of the United States, Representatives in Congress, the Executive and Judicial Officers of a State, or the members of the Legislature thereof, is denied to any of the male inhabitants of such state, being twenty-one years of age, and citizens of the United States, or in any way abridged, except for participation in rebellion, or other crime, the basis of representation therein shall be reduced in the proportion which the number of such male citizens shall bear to the whole number of male citizens twenty-one years of age in such State.

On July 28, 1868, the Fourteenth Amendment was certified by the Secretary of State as being a part of the Constitution. In reporting the bill providing for the next census, that of 1870, James A. Garfield made the following clear statement of the difficulties involved in attempting to apply the amendment:

The census is our only constitutional means of determining the political or representative population. The fourteenth amendment has made that work a difficult one. At the time of its adoption it was generally understood that the exclusion applied only to colored people who should be denied the ballot by the laws of their State. But the language of the article excludes all who are denied the ballot on any and all grounds other than the two specified. This has made it necessary to ascertain what are in fact the grounds of such exclusion, and the Census Committee have compiled a record from the constitutions and laws of the several States from which exclusion from the privilege of voting (otherwise than on account of rebellion or other crime) may be stated in nine general classes as follows:

1. On account of race or color.................... 16 States
2. On account of residence on lands of United States.. 2 States
   On account of residence less than required time in United States............................. 2 States
   On account of residence in State less than required time, (six different specifications)............. 36 States
   On account of residence in county, city, town, district, etc., (eighteen different specifications).... 37 States
3. Wanting property qualifications or nonpayment of taxes, (eight specifications).................. 8 States
4. Wanting literary qualifications, (two specifications).. 2 States
5. On account of character or behavior, (two specifications)..................................... 2 States
6. On account of services in army or navy......... 2 States
7. On account of pauperism, idiocy, and insanity, (seven specifications)...................... 24 States
8. Requiring certain oaths as preliminary to voting, (two specifications)......................... 5 States
9. Other causes of exclusion, (two specifications)..... 2 States

After much reflection the committee could devise no better way than to add to the family schedule a column for recording those who are voters, and another with this heading, copied substantially from the amendment: "Citizens of the United States, being twenty-one years of age, whose right to vote is denied or abridged on other grounds than rebellion or crime." It may be objected that this will allow the citizen to be a judge of the law as well as the fact, and that it will be difficult to get true and accurate answers. I can only say this is the best method that has been suggested.[2]

The misgivings of the committee were confirmed by the returns, which showed only 40,380 persons whose right to vote was abridged out of a total of 8,314,805. In South Carolina out of 146,979 males over 21 years of age, only 516 were reported as having their voting rights denied. The Secretary of the Interior was undoubtedly correct when, in a letter to the Speaker of the House, he made the following statement:

It is necessary to state, in transmitting these tables, that the Department is disposed to give but little credit to the returns made by assistant marshals in regard to the denial or abridgment of suffrage. The unfavorable opinion of the Department in respect to this single class of statistics is formed, first, from the application of certain statistical tests, and second, from a consideration of the agencies employed which are not deemed adequate to the determination of the numerous questions of difficulty and nicety which are involved.[3]

The statement by the Secretary was conservative. That the questions utterly failed in achieving their purpose is shown by the fact that they showed the largest disfranchisement, 6.4 per cent, in Rhode Island, doubtless due to the high property qualification. The next highest was Missouri, with 2.4 per cent. For five states the percentage was between 1 and 2 per cent. All the other states showed less than 1 per cent. For all the southern states except Texas the disfranchised voters amounted to only 0.5 per cent or less.

No attempt has been made at any later census to collect figures that will meet either the exact requirements of section 2 of the Fourteenth Amendment, or the underlying reasons for its adoption. It is obvious that no such information can be obtained by census enumerators or from any other source. That

[2] 41 Cong. 2 sess., H. Rept. 3, pp. 52–53. Extracts from the state constitutions are given in the report cited, on pp. 71–93.

[3] 42 Cong. 2 sess., *Cong. Globe*, Pt. 1, p. 66. The figures for each state are given on the same page.

portion of the amendment cannot be enforced, and the sooner it is repealed or superseded by a workable plan the better.

An apportionment fixed on the basis of votes cast would not involve the delay necessarily caused by using census figures. The official returns would be available immediately after the election. A census question "Did you vote at the last presidential election?" is a simple one of fact, but nevertheless the returns might be subject to some error. It is well known that the census enumerator generally obtains the information concerning all persons in a household from one member of the family, and the member interviewed might not give a correct answer. It is not unlikely that in many cases the individual would not remember whether he voted or not. Such errors as these would tend to counterbalance one another, but it would not be necessary to use the census in view of the fact that correct figures are easily obtained from other sources.

It is therefore recommended that there be adopted a constitutional amendment providing that apportionment be based on votes cast. If the apportionment is to be made every ten years, as at present, the amendment should provide that the votes to be taken into account should be those cast at the presidential election preceding the apportionment. The direct effect of such an amendment would be to reduce the representation of states where a large proportion of the electorate is deprived of the suffrage by either legal or extra-legal means. An indirect effect would be that persons who are entitled to vote would find an incentive to exercise the suffrage if they could thereby contribute to preventing a decrease in the representation of the state. In view of the fact that an amendment requires a two-thirds vote in both houses and approval by three-fourths of the states, it is doubtful if there is immediate prospect of the adoption of one such as is suggested. It is unfortunate that the states which acquire an undue influence should be able to prevent rectification of conditions.

The following table shows the population of each congressional district in 1930 and the votes cast in the congressional elections of 1936 and 1938.

POPULATION AND VOTING IN CONGRESSIONAL DISTRICTS

State and District	Population[a] 1930	Votes Cast 1936 Number	Votes Cast 1936 Percentage of Population	Votes Cast 1938 Number	Votes Cast 1938 Percentage of Population
Alabama.................	2,646,248	255,052	9.6	123,838	4.7
1st district.............	272,633	23,423	8.6	9,853	3.6
2d district.............	330,677	32,750	9.9	15,569	4.7
3d district.............	297,574	22,535	7.6	10,090	3.4
4th district.............	264,658	26,171	9.9	12,603	4.8
5th district.............	273,763	29,891	10.9	16,636	6.1
6th district.............	236,412	18,325	7.8	10.246	4.3
7th district.............	256,797	34,437	13.4	25,110	9.8
8th district.............	282,241	27,874	9.9	10,226	3.6
9th district.............	431,493	39,646	9.2	13,505	3.1
Arizona[b].................	435,573	108,750	25.0	104,058	23.9
Arkansas.................	1,854,482	173,557	9.4	144,056	7.8
1st district.............	385,965	20,555	5.3	23,274	6.0
2d district.............	218,596	22,262	10.2	18,613	8.5
3d district.............	170,576	28,070	16.5	22,141	13.0
4th district.............	230,259	26,249	11.4	22,272	9.7
5th district.............	278,663	29,383	10.5	23,949	8.6
6th district.............	289,250	25,736	8.9	17,662	6.1
7th district.............	281,173	21,302	7.6	16,145	5.7
California.................	5,677,251	2,242,298	39.5	2,391,108	42.1
1st district.............	263,748	107,941	40.9	117,018	44.4
2d district.............	165,595	51,440	31.1	71,549	43.2
3d district.............	332,314	103,055	31.0	128,684	38.7
4th district.............	335,482	109,579	32.7	105,294	31.4
5th district.............	298,912	87,455	29.3	91,868	30.7
6th district.............	308,897	114,021	36.9	126,116	40.8
7th district.............	244,594	116,110	47.5	113,103	46.2
8th district.............	324,972	136,372	42.0	152,793	47.0
9th district.............	280,317	84,935	30.3	94,745	33.8
10th district.............	309,768	104,252	33.7	126,183	40.7
11th district.............	264,952	137,982	52.1	146,284	55.2
12th district.............	259,287	115,504	44.5	123,482	47.6
13th district.............	349,686	133,400	38.1	146,638	41.9
14th district.............	277,613	103,860	37.4	99,673	35.9
15th district.............	300,133	143,718	47.9	138,132	46.0
16th district.............	296,077	157,787	53.3	155,161	52.4
17th district.............	233,674	94,892	40.6	96,468	41.3
18th district.............	227,070	104,195	45.9	107,620	47.4
19th district.............	333,598	130,747	39.2	142,256	42.6
20th district.............	270,562	105,053	38.8	108,041	39.9
Colorado.................	1,035,791	457,759	44.2	449,537	43.4
1st district.............	287,861	146,026	50.7	127,876	44.4
2d district.............	302,946	124,664	41.2	126,517	41.8
3d district.............	303,442	122,884	40.5	126,743	41.8
4th district.............	141,542	64,185	45.3	68,401	48.3
Connecticut..............	1,606,903	682,933[c]	42.5	623,389[c]	38.8
1st district.............	421,097	175,718	41.7	157,891	37.5
2d district.............	253,099	108,684	42.9	99,679	39.4
3d district.............	304,736	141,547	46.4	128,932	42.3
4th district.............	386,702	161,857	41.9	142,042	36.7
5th district.............	241,269	95,127	39.4	94,845	39.3
At large.................	1,606,903	689,512	42.9	630,132	39.2
Delaware[b].................	238,380	126,663	53.1	108,571	45.5

POPULATION AND VOTING IN CONGRESSIONAL DISTRICTS—*Continued*

State and District	Population[a] 1930	Votes Cast 1936		Votes Cast 1938	
		Number	Percentage of Population	Number	Percentage of Population
Florida..................	1,468,211	284,969	19.4	153,061	10.4
1st district.............	390,965	83,083	21.3	43,837	11.2
2d district.............	325,154	47,521	14.6	24,830	7.6
3d district.............	254,386	34,241	13.5	20,174	7.9
4th district............	254,358	66,380	26.1	36,326	14.3
5th district............	243,348	53,744	22.1	27,894	11.5
Georgia.................	2,908,506	277,073	9.5	68,087	2.3
1st district.............	328,214	25,846	7.9	10,999	3.4
2d district.............	263,606	21,405	8.1	5,137	1.9
3d district.............	339,870	25,613	7.5	5,988	1.8
4th district............	261,234	24,643	9.4	5,413	2.1
5th district............	414,313	39,753	9.6	7,103	1.7
6th district............	281,437	22,966	8.2	4,369	1.6
7th district............	270,112	31,465	11.6	5,623	2.1
8th district............	241,957	26,145	10.8	4,929	2.0
9th district............	218,496	32,090	14.7	8,945	4.1
10th district...........	289,267	27,147	9.4	9,581	3.3
Idaho..................	445,031	193,972	43.6	178,684	40.2
1st district.............	189,576	83,900	44.3	76,958	40.6
2d district.............	255,455	110,072	43.1	101,726	39.8
Illinois.................	7,630,654	3,731,559o	48.9	3,104,444o	40.7
1st district.............	142,916	64,208	44.9	56,603	39.6
2d district.............	577,998	293,395	50.8	239,143	41.4
3d district.............	540,666	264,013	48.8	227,954	42.2
4th district............	237,139	86,522	36.5	80,466	33.9
5th district............	140,481	45,274	32.2	42,946	30.6
6th district............	632,834	312,211	49.3	265,010	41.9
7th district............	889,349	420,714	47.3	354,819	39.9
8th district............	138,216	43,849	31.7	42,263	30.6
9th district............	209,650	101,894	48.6	83,576	39.9
10th district...........	577,261	308,493	53.4	243,932	42.3
11th district...........	363,136	176,966	48.7	143,441	39.5
12th district...........	292,023	135,187	46.3	110,958	38.0
13th district...........	178,198	89,842	50.4	68,885	38.7
14th district...........	199,104	108,059	54.3	85,925	43.2
15th district...........	213,630	110,846	51.9	87,482	41.0
16th district...........	253,713	129,523	51.1	96,093	37.9
17th district...........	175,353	88,717	50.6	74,258	42.3
18th district...........	225,604	113,954	50.5	102,278	45.3
19th district...........	274,137	138,981	50.7	115,402	42.1
20th district...........	158,262	84,862	53.6	67,092	42.4
21st district...........	233,252	121,500	52.1	103,824	44.5
22d district...........	344,666	163,551	47.5	127,261	36.9
23d district...........	213,567	112,398	52.6	92,109	43.1
24th district...........	161,158	88,504	54.9	79,522	49.3
25th district...........	258,341	128,096	49.6	113,202	43.8
At large...............	7,630,654	3,728,783	48.9	3,045,508d	39.9
At large...............	7,630,654	3,692,044	48.4	3,016,812d	39.5
Indiana.................	3,238,503	1,617,839	50.0	1,572,649	48.6
1st district.............	261,310	102,469	39.2	103,073	39.4
2d district.............	260,287	141,390	54.3	137,164	52.7
3d district.............	289,398	123,777	42.8	121,195	41.9
4th district............	275,523	130,729	47.4	124,860	45.3
5th district............	258,037	134,371	52.1	133,745	51.8

POPULATION AND VOTING IN CONGRESSIONAL DISTRICTS—*Continued*

State and District	Population[a] 1930	Votes Cast 1936		Votes Cast 1938	
		Number	Percentage of Population	Number	Percentage of Population
Indiana—*Continued*					
6th district.............	278,685	149,038	53.5	142,011	51.0
7th district.............	283,498	151,829	53.6	152,871	53.9
8th district.............	281,724	140,138	49.7	136,034	48.3
9th district.............	257,311	137,200	53.3	134,778	52.4
10th district............	270,571	139,846	51.7	137,958	51.0
11th district............	264,926	134,657	50.8	127,273	48.0
12th district............	257,233	132,395	51.5	121,687	47.3
Iowa...................	2,470,939	1,052,364	42.6	802,636	32.5
1st district.............	251,084	109,195	43.5	80,796	32.2
2d district.............	302,946	134,357	44.4	95,690	31.6
3d district.............	256,052	103,834	40.6	76,285	29.8
4th district.............	240,282	111,299	46.3	93,761	39.0
5th district.............	271,679	122,895	45.2	94,312	34.7
6th district.............	287,229	120,447	41.9	91,471	31.8
7th district.............	274,168	121,727	44.4	93,165	34.0
8th district.............	278,701	106,909	38.4	83,089	29.8
9th district.............	308,798	121,701	39.4	94,067	30.5
Kansas.................	1,880,999	799,850	42.5	737,024	39.2
1st district.............	273,849	113,461	41.4	109,319	39.9
2d district.............	307,466	135,092	43.9	125,190	40.7
3d district.............	265,319	114,697	43.2	105,478	39.8
4th district.............	229,108	95,001	41.5	87,862	38.3
5th district.............	246,902	104,157	42.2	87,470	35.4
6th district.............	275,301	118,519	43.1	110,455	40.1
7th district.............	283,054	118,923	42.0	111,250	39.3
Kentucky..............	2,614,589	917,647	35.1	533,959	20.4
1st district.............	238,189	81,022	34.0	46,485	19.5
2d district.............	338,117	110,836	32.8	56,736	16.8
3d district.............	355,350	141,010	39.7	93,588	26.3
4th district.............	256,173	92,595	36.1	54,318	21.2
5th district.............	222,614	86,713	39.0	41,478	18.6
6th district.............	317,571	121,102	38.1	58,820	18.5
7th district.............	245,598	72,231	29.4	51,992	21.2
8th district.............	288,108	102,981	35.7	66,314	23.0
9th district.............	352,869	109,157	30.9	64,228	18.2
Louisiana..............	2,101,593	291,963	13.9	152,410	7.3
1st district.............	253,548	61,147	24.1	50,453	19.9
2d district.............	302,893	65,345	21.6	47,746	15.8
3d district.............	230,092	20,605	9.0	5,236	2.3
4th district.............	285,684	26,180	9.2	10,705	3.7
5th district.............	287,585	29,144	10.1	11,644	4.0
6th district.............	294,138	34,908	11.9	12,225	4.2
7th district.............	222,495	27,563	12.4	5,313	2.4
8th district.............	225,158	27,071	12.0	9,088	4.0
Maine.................	797,423	301,050	37.8	281,619	35.3
1st district.............	265,989	104,671	39.4	97,745	36.7
2d district.............	264,434	104,232	39.4	102,618	38.8
3d district.............	267,000	92,147	34.5	81,256	30.4
Maryland..............	1,631,526	543,431	33.3	486,473	29.8
1st district.............	193,658	64,485	33.3	62,026	32.0
2d district.............	461,419	159,718	34.6	137,529	29.8
3d district.............	203,929	61,887	30.3	52,800	25.9

POPULATION AND VOTING IN CONGRESSIONAL DISTRICTS—*Continued*

State and District	Population[a] 1930	Votes Cast 1936		Votes Cast 1938	
		Number	Percentage of Population	Number	Percentage of Population
Maryland—*Continued*					
4th district.............	259,467	89,595	34.5	74,542	28.7
5th district.............	244,519	72,822	29.8	68,642	28.1
6th district.............	268,534	94,924	35.3	90,934	33.9
Massachusetts............	4,249,614	1,785,238	42.0	1,719,677	40.5
1st district.............	274,703	118,919	43.3	110,284	40.1
2d district.............	292,066	117,712	40.3	110,041	37.7
3d district.............	282,230	120,165	42.6	113,158	40.1
4th district.............	288,216	119,753	41.5	116,141	40.3
5th district.............	309,888	144,633	46.7	140,236	45.3
6th district.............	255,879	115,319	45.1	110,401	43.1
7th district.............	312,956	129,596	41.4	131,222	41.9
8th district.............	291,783	114,580	39.3	112,865	38.7
9th district.............	298,398	141,844	47.5	138,317	46.4
10th district............	276,509	124,715	45.1	121,145	43.8
11th district............	242,310	65,326	27.0	56,950	23.5
12th district............	294,272	114,540	38.9	112,297	38.2
13th district............	273,059	131,374	48.1	126,328	46.3
14th district............	278,394	110,239	39.6	108,369	38.9
15th district............	278,951	116,523	41.8	111,923	40.1
Michigan................	4,842,325	1,696,280	35.0	1,547,216	32.0
1st district.............	380,155	89,978	23.7	88,945	23.4
2d district.............	260,168	104,083	40.0	91,454	35.2
3d district.............	261,506	105,767	40.4	88,007	33.7
4th district.............	225,111	98,322	43.7	83,192	37.0
5th district.............	295,369	103,296	35.0	85,464	28.9
6th district.............	347,502	125,696	36.2	121,134	34.9
7th district.............	264,874	91,379	34.5	91,169	34.4
8th district.............	277,224	96,935	35.0	89,008	32.1
9th district.............	214,318	81,085	37.8	70,247	32.8
10th district............	186,738	72,856	39.0	67,549	36.2
11th district............	204,710	84,373	41.2	79,611	38.9
12th district............	204,608	84,579	41.3	84,040	41.1
13th district............	354,135	114,182	32.2	98,992	28.0
14th district............	350,212	119,433	34.1	109,180	31.2
15th district............	378,630	118,803	31.4	106,257	28.1
16th district............	318,919	97,221	30.5	89,117	27.9
17th district............	318,146	108,292	34.0	103,850	32.6
Minnesota................	2,563,953	1,090,795	42.5	1,070,927	41.8
1st district.............	289,887	120,176	41.5	114,833	39.6
2d district.............	281,336	121,324	43.1	122,237	43.4
3d district.............	288,289	125,044	43.4	118,020	40.9
4th district.............	286,721	126,327	44.1	113,429	39.6
5th district.............	297,934	140,796	47.3	123,888	41.6
6th district.............	303,242	120,446	39.7	126,371	41.7
7th district.............	286,125	113,378	39.6	116,038	40.6
8th district.............	276,633	123,702	44.7	131,286	47.5
9th district.............	253,786	99,602	39.2	104,825	41.3
Mississippi................	2,009,821	148,441	7.4	35,439	1.8
1st district.............	241,605	19,600	8.1	4,384	1.8
2d district.............	219,661	13,782	6.3	4,134	1.9
3d district.............	420,969	16,095	3.8	2,172	0.5
4th district.............	184,266	14,446	7.8	3,502	1.9
5th district.............	244,562	26,301	10.8	11,540	4.7
6th district.............	284,457	25,385	8.9	4,873	1.7
7th district.............	414,301	32,832	7.9	4,834	1.2

POPULATION AND VOTING IN CONGRESSIONAL DISTRICTS—*Continued*

State and District	Population[a] 1930	Votes Cast 1936		Votes Cast 1938	
		Number	*Percentage of Population*	Number	*Percentage of Population*
Missouri...............	3,629,367	1,810,995	*49.9*	1,245,032	*34.3*
1st district............	244,369	123,598	*50.6*	79,722	*32.6*
2d district.............	287,820	139,974	*48.6*	88,793	*30.9*
3d district.............	299,490	146,610	*49.0*	91,302	*30.5*
4th district............	239,251	138,668	*58.0*	89,522	*37.4*
5th district............	231,203	154,573	*66.9*	93,620	*40.5*
6th district............	287,786	140,016	*48.7*	104,944	*36.5*
7th district............	293,294	140,806	*48.0*	113,290	*38.6*
8th district............	253,716	116,159	*45.8*	102,181	*40.3*
9th district............	207,068	101,398	*49.0*	67,243	*32.5*
10th district...........	251,817	106,104	*42.1*	75,044	*29.8*
11th district...........	341,538	154,342	*45.2*	102,509	*30.0*
12th district...........	425,481	223,154	*52.4*	151,049	*35.5*
13th district...........	266,534	125,593	*47.1*	85,813	*32.2*
Montana...............	537,606	208,474	*38.8*	208,710	*38.8*
1st district............	211,918	86,444	*40.8*	90,572	*42.7*
2d district.............	325,688	122,030	*37.5*	118,138	*36.3*
Nebraska..............	1,377,963	569,336	*41.3*	477,715	*34.7*
1st district............	269,428	114,645	*42.6*	96,858	*35.9*
2d district.............	255,479	107,765	*42.2*	81,856	*32.0*
3d district.............	291,595	118,600	*40.7*	104,627	*35.9*
4th district............	290,318	120,688	*41.6*	102,751	*35.4*
5th district............	271,143	107,638	*39.7*	91,623	*33.8*
Nevada[b]................	91,058	43,754	*48.1*	45,441	*49.9*
New Hampshire..........	465,293	204,187	*43.9*	181,003	*38.9*
1st district............	228,493	104,260	*45.6*	96,855	*42.4*
2d district.............	236,800	99,927	*42.2*	84,148	*35.5*
New Jersey.............	4,041,334	1,688,241	*41.8*	1,531,121	*37.9*
1st district............	359,948	163,926	*45.5*	155,768	*43.3*
2d district.............	224,204	111,186	*49.6*	112,817	*50.3*
3d district.............	266,337	134,734	*50.6*	127,966	*48.0*
4th district............	280,684	111,346	*39.7*	101,294	*36.1*
5th district............	301,726	128,697	*42.7*	126,497	*41.9*
6th district............	305,209	124,535	*40.8*	103,507	*33.9*
7th district............	259,379	112,412	*43.3*	100,188	*38.6*
8th district............	299,190	113,825	*38.0*	104,685	*35.0*
9th district............	267,663	125,873	*47.0*	109,372	*40.9*
10th district...........	295,297	103,957	*35.2*	91,791	*31.1*
11th district...........	292,284	103,358	*35.4*	86,886	*29.7*
12th district...........	304,935	109,603	*35.9*	88,884	*29.1*
13th district...........	289,795	123,599	*42.7*	111,867	*38.6*
14th district...........	294,683	121,190	*41.1*	109,599	*37.2*
New Mexico[b]............	423,317	168,373	*39.8*	155,157	*36.7*
New York..............	12,588,066	5,307,642[c]	*42.2·*	4,457,958[c]	*35.4*
1st district............	637,022	336,936	*52.9*	292,939	*46.0*
2d district.............	776,425	321,264	*41.4*	258,860	*33.3*
3d district.............	187,953	50,609	*26.9*	43,722	*23.3*
4th district............	211,826	56,537	*26.7*	42,781	*20.2*
5th district............	246,215	98,129	*39.9*	77,814	*31.6*
6th district............	452,275	182,401	*40.3*	150,942	*33.4*
7th district............	205,043	61,103	*29.8*	50,048	*24.4*
8th district............	799,407	301,354	*37.7*	248,722	*31.1*

POPULATION AND VOTING IN CONGRESSIONAL DISTRICTS—*Continued*

State and District	Population[a] 1930	Votes Cast 1936		Votes Cast 1938	
		Number	Percentage of Population	Number	Percentage of Population
New York—*Continued*					
9th district	370,457	139,864	37.8	111,146	30.0
10th district	217,015	69,605	32.1	59,678	27.5
11th district	218,545	84,472	38.7	68,590	31.4
12th district	90,671	22,303	24.6	19,439	21.4
13th district	111,696	25,658	23.0	20,874	18.7
14th district	119,794	41,571	34.7	34,685	29.0
15th district	121,675	41,858	34.4	33,050	27.2
16th district	142,496	55,147	38.7	47,035	33.0
17th district	207,648	93,308	44.9	73,442	35.4
18th district	144,945	49,829	34.4	42,493	29.3
19th district	259,334	106,639	41.1	80,908	31.2
20th district	150,523	36,652	24.3	31,739	21.1
21st district	381,212	155,562	40.8	121,822	32.0
22d district	210,138	63,746	30.3	52,881	25.2
23d district	688,454	272,747	39.6	236,982	34.4
24th district	672,121	281,803	41.9	239,658	35.7
25th district	352,210	173,980	49.4	146,225	41.5
26th district	249,589	123,679	49.6	105,552	42.3
27th district	202,519	108,004	53.3	96,017	47.4
28th district	252,280	145,503	57.7	115,639	45.8
29th district	223,424	121,748	54.5	115,170	51.5
30th district	235,586	111,330	47.3	97,695	41.5
31st district	217,300	92,097	42.4	76,875	35.4
32d district	216,456	99,468	46.0	80,769	37.3
33d district	262,769	118,157	45.0	104,278	39.7
34th district	269,560	124,678	46.3	103,091	38.2
35th district	323,315	157,700	48.8	140,570	43.5
36th district	210,853	103,500	49.1	88,451	41.9
37th district	237,230	113,216	47.7	95,219	40.1
38th district	327,072	160,231	49.0	145,065	44.4
39th district	236,396	114,278	48.3	99,577	42.1
40th district	405,109	180,405	44.5	147,434	36.4
41st district	258,163	110,126	42.7	92,693	35.9
42d district	248,465	98,223	39.5	85,838	34.5
43d district	236,880	102,222	43.2	81,550	34.4
At large	12,588,066	5,714,511	45.4	4,375,030[d]	34.8
At large	12,588,066	5,640,974	44.8	4,342,614[d]	34.5
North Carolina	3,170,276	800,884	25.3	479,267	15.1
1st district	224,768	39,166	17.4	12,083	5.4
2d district	276,795	39,681	14.3	9,955	3.6
3d district	226,465	46,491	20.5	17,507	7.7
4th district	322,346	73,882	22.9	42,141	13.1
5th district	293,779	66,171	22.5	36,559	12.4
6th district	263,517	66,421	25.2	20,918	7.9
7th district	268,579	49,945	18.6	22,676	8.4
8th district	316,614	85,545	27.0	62,944	19.9
9th district	262,213	92,882	35.4	72,114	27.5
10th district	414,808	123,709	29.8	85,950	20.7
11th district	300,392	116,991	38.9	96,420	32.1
North Dakota	680,845	—	—	—	—
At large	680,845	238,273	35.0	208,231[d]	30.6
At large	680,845	210,369	30.9	193,738[d]	28.5
Ohio	6,646,697	2,863,364[c]	43.1	2,313,460[c]	34.8
1st district	296,533	138,017	46.5	108,821	36.7
2d district	292,823	129,759	44.3	104,253	35.6
3d district	410,020	181,024	44.2	131,673	32.1
4th district	236,783	115,279	48.7	94,299	39.8

POPULATION AND VOTING IN CONGRESSIONAL DISTRICTS—*Continued*

State and District	Population[a] 1930	Votes Cast 1936		Votes Cast 1938	
		Number	Percentage of Population	Number	Percentage of Population
Ohio—*Continued*					
5th district.............	159,679	78,568	49.2	65,136	40.8
6th district.............	190,828	100,637	52.7	86,493	45.3
7th district.............	286,374	135,910	47.5	118,348	41.3
8th district.............	182,329	92,233	50.6	74,744	41.0
9th district.............	371,818	134,519	36.2	111,747	30.1
10th district.............	171,054	81,442	47.6	71,234	41.6
11th district.............	168,281	78,213	46.5	64,768	38.5
12th district.............	361,055	152,988	42.4	126,435	35.0
13th district.............	213,825	98,624	46.1	80,953	37.9
14th district.............	525,696	204,396	38.9	163,649	31.1
15th district.............	198,291	95,649	48.2	81,476	41.1
16th district.............	353,727	151,826	42.9	122,558	34.6
17th district.............	237,061	120,334	50.8	97,605	41.2
18th district.............	304,411	137,171	45.1	112,277	36.9
19th district.............	427,566	160,318	37.5	145,482	34.0
20th district.............	301,964	99,820	33.1	76,960	25.5
21st district.............	322,901	94,407	29.2	77,420	24.0
22d district.............	633,678	282,230	44.5	197,129	31.1
At large.............	6,646,697	2,788,153	41.9	2,246,898[d]	33.8
At large.............	6,646,697	2,614,522	39.3	2,116,234[d]	31.8
Oklahoma.............	2,396,040	694,189[c]	29.0	468,257[c]	19.5
1st district.............	404,981	140,878	34.8	87,421	21.6
2d district.............	238,281	72,034	30.2	53,393	22.4
3d district.............	287,397	72,933	25.4	49,902	17.4
4th district.............	360,468	87,048	24.1	61,739	17.1
5th district.............	376,738	112,338	29.8	66,299	17.6
6th district.............	263,164	71,939	27.3	48,634	18.5
7th district.............	240,944	56,336	23.4	32,848	13.6
8th district.............	224,067	80,683	36.0	68,021	30.4
At large.............	2,396,040	672,360	28.1	445,824	18.6
Oregon.............	953,786	389,944	40.9	365,943	38.4
1st district.............	432,572	173,865	40.2	169,638	39.2
2d district.............	182,973	68,225	37.3	60,758	33.2
3d district.............	338,241	147,854	43.7	135,547	40.1
Pennsylvania.............	9,631,350	4,070,241	42.3	3,783,649	39.3
1st district.............	286,462	104,172	36.4	102,511	35.8
2d district.............	247,068	109,967	44.5	98,453	39.8
3d district.............	298,461	124,012	41.6	118,644	39.8
4th district.............	274,376	123,333	45.0	112,474	41.0
5th district.............	269,564	127,443	47.3	121,577	45.1
6th district.............	291,720	138,254	47.4	125,277	42.9
7th district.............	283,310	150,439	53.1	141,840	50.1
8th district.............	280,264	140,407	50.1	124,427	44.4
9th district.............	269,620	110,077	40.8	99,831	37.0
10th district.............	323,511	137,076	42.4	123,164	38.1
11th district.............	310,397	131,925	42.5	126,933	40.9
12th district.............	445,109	184,536	41.5	192,823	43.3
13th district.............	364,009	153,159	42.1	149,285	41.0
14th district.............	231,717	86,755	37.4	74,192	32.0
15th district.............	205,084	101,856	49.7	95,152	46.4
16th district.............	235,574	104,259	44.3	102,907	43.7
17th district.............	265,804	125,815	47.3	105,437	39.7
18th district.............	198,269	91,127	46.0	87,645	44.2
19th district.............	300,570	142,878	47.5	140,540	46.8
20th district.............	277,067	121,378	43.8	107,236	38.7
21st district.............	260,970	99,659	38.2	86,142	33.0

POPULATION AND VOTING IN CONGRESSIONAL DISTRICTS—*Continued*

State and District	Population[a] 1930	Votes Cast 1936		Votes Cast 1938	
		Number	Percentage of Population	Number	Percentage of Population
Pennsylvania—*Continued*					
22d district.............	269,273	121,279	45.0	110,445	41.0
23d district.............	272,861	109,580	40.2	107,457	39.4
24th district............	279,306	102,433	36.7	91,919	32.9
25th district............	246,569	94,651	38.4	82,153	33.3
26th district............	326,800	127,434	39.0	114,081	34.9
27th district............	409,953	155,141	37.8	146,472	35.7
28th district............	294,995	111,495	37.8	96,575	32.7
29th district............	238,257	90,952	38.2	87,130	36.6
30th district............	265,235	110,201	41.5	104,569	39.4
31st district............	312,312	129,481	41.5	113,132	36.2
32d district.............	213,060	75,114	35.3	75,914	35.6
33d district.............	282,119	109,469	38.8	106,315	37.7
34th district............	301,584	124,484	41.3	110,997	36.8
Rhode Island.............	687,497	304,920	44.4	300,220	43.7
1st district.............	341,016	146,697	43.0	145,878	42.8
2d district.............	346,481	158,223	45.7	154,342	44.5
South Carolina...........	1,738,765	115,255	6.6	46,196	2.7
1st district.............	260,439	16,279	6.3	7,788	3.0
2d district.............	338,668	22,036	6.5	7,325	2.2
3d district.............	291,053	19,173	6.6	10,071	3.5
4th district.............	306,346	25,751	8.4	9,053	3.0
5th district.............	235,093	15,881	6.8	6,204	2.6
6th district.............	307,166	16,135	5.3	5,755	1.9
South Dakota.............	692,849	277,449	40.0	274,416	39.6
1st district.............	524,769	210,088	40.0	207,149	39.5
2d district.............	168,080	67,361	40.1	67,267	40.0
Tennessee.................	2,616,556	392,553	15.0	264,404	10.1
1st district.............	333,746	55,474	16.6	40,070	12.0
2d district.............	368,172	79,972	21.7	50,300	13.7
3d district.............	295,760	47,161	15.9	29,532	10.0
4th district.............	292,638	40,536	13.9	25,220	8.6
5th district.............	343,328	36,440	10.6	18,568	5.4
6th district.............	194,915	25,209	12.9	17,421	8.9
7th district.............	240,422	20,432	8.5	19,554	8.1
8th district.............	241,093	28,812	12.0	19,054	7.9
9th district.............	306,482	58,517	19.1	44,685	14.6
Texas....................	5,824,715	819,510	14.1	365,208	6.3
1st district.............	294,426	30,078	10.2	16,270	5.5
2d district.............	304,279	39,487	13.0	12,824	4.2
3d district.............	214,306	30,628	14.3	14,982	7.0
4th district.............	257,879	34,210	13.3	16,877	6.5
5th district.............	325,691	49,467	15.2	10,889	3.3
6th district.............	288,538	30,408	10.5	15,620	5.4
7th district.............	277,601	29,713	10.7	16,478	5.9
8th district.............	359,328	67,140	18.7	37,620	10.5
9th district.............	323,009	39,669	12.3	16,687	5.2
10th district............	264,952	33,814	12.8	14,478	5.5
11th district............	261,147	31,230	12.0	14,874	5.7
12th district............	259,424	42,555	16.4	12,972	5.0
13th district............	292,579	42,986	14.7	20,920	7.2
14th district............	309,516	42,993	13.9	23,438	7.6
15th district............	283,291	35,842	12.7	18,560	6.6
16th district............	210,621	26,358	12.5	9,197	4.4

POPULATION AND VOTING IN CONGRESSIONAL DISTRICTS—*Continued*

State and District	Population[a] 1930	Votes Cast 1936		Votes Cast 1938	
		Number	Percentage of Population	Number	Percentage of Population
Texas—*Continued*					
17th district	238,671	35,395	14.8	17,107	7.2
18th district	254,825	47,440	18.6	19,048	7.5
19th district	254,367	39,059	15.4	16,372	6.4
20th district	292,533	48,183	16.5	16,703	5.7
21st district	257,732	42,855	16.6	23,292	9.0
Utah	507,847	215,786	42.5	182,532	35.9
1st district	241,290	99,494	41.2	88,717	36.8
2d district	266,557	116,292	43.6	93,815	35.2
Vermont[b]	359,611	140,395	39.0	112,552	31.3
Virginia	2,421,851	321,276	13.3	126,043	5.2
1st district	239,757	24,751	10.3	7,210	3.0
2d district	302,715	33,017	10.9	17,512	5.8
3d district	281,064	34,132	12.1	5,578	2.0
4th district	242,204	21,626	8.9	5,814	2.4
5th district	271,794	39,654	14.6	5,782	2.1
6th district	280,708	41,736	14.9	20,596	7.3
7th district	242,778	38,812	16.0	17,848	7.4
8th district	256,511	37,227	14.5	13,852	5.4
9th district	304,320	50,321	16.5	31,851	10.5
Washington	1,563,396	646,858	41.4	586,493	37.5
1st district	396,359	163,196	41.2	147,061	37.1
2d district	236,238	100,993	42.8	94,755	40.1
3d district	235,372	93,305	39.6	86,699	36.8
4th district	209,433	83,402	39.8	76,616	36.6
5th district	250,064	107,462	43.0	92,489	37.0
6th district	235,930	98,500	41.7	88,873	37.7
West Virginia	1,729,205	815,738	47.2	622,821	36.0
1st district	273,185	126,920	46.5	104,094	38.1
2d district	277,001	131,799	47.6	97,611	35.2
3d district	294,334	138,310	47.0	97,129	33.0
4th district	296,484	151,160	51.0	124,714	42.1
5th district	279,342	113,865	40.8	90,490	32.4
6th district	308,859	153,684	49.8	108,783	35.2
Wisconsin	2,939,006	890,207	30.3	912,365	31.0
1st district	280,628	94,089	33.5	92,094	32.8
2d district	284,475	92,439	32.5	93,998	33.0
3d district	274,488	94,839	34.6	86,891	31.7
4th district	353,521	105,594	29.9	106,864	30.2
5th district	371,742	111,182	29.9	109,082	29.3
6th district	268,533	80,592	30.0	85,982	32.0
7th district	276,625	79,192	28.6	85,276	30.8
8th district	300,734	76,859	25.6	92,118	30.6
9th district	283,588	76,295	26.9	80,324	28.3
10th district	244,672	79,126	32.3	79,736	32.6
Wyoming[b]	225,565	97,313	43.1	94,500	41.9

[a] Population figures in this table include Indians not taxed; for apportionment population by states see App. C. Figures by districts for Indians not taxed are not available.
[b] One representative only.
[c] Total for the districts.
[d] Democratic and Republican votes only; does not include other parties.

CHAPTER VIII

HISTORY OF APPORTIONMENT *

This chapter will be devoted to a brief summary of the method of apportionment after each census. As the debates are voluminous, no attempt will be made to state all the proposals advocated. The discussion will be limited to brief statements of what was accomplished. The apportionment after each census is given in Appendix C.

First census, 1790. The Constitution made the first apportionment, which was to remain in effect until the first census was taken. No reliable figures on population were available, and the basis for the constitutional apportionment was little better than a guess.[1] Section 2 of Article 3 of the Constitution required an actual enumeration of the population to be made within three years after the first meeting of Congress. The first session of Congress convened on March 4, 1789, and about a year later the act of March 1, 1790 (1 Stat. L. 101) made provision for the first census.

Provision for the admission of Vermont and Kentucky was made by the act of February 18, 1791 (1 Stat. L. 189), and each of these states was allowed two representatives until the enumeration by the act of February 25, 1791 (1 Stat. L. 191). Vermont was admitted on March 4, 1791 and its representatives took their seats October 31, 1791, but Kentucky was not admitted until June 1, 1792 after the first apportionment act was passed. On November 18, 1791 the House began the debate on the first apportionment bill. The bill was amended in the Senate and after considerable discussion the House agreed to the Senate amendments on March 23, 1792. President Wash-

[1] Estimates used in the Constitutional Convention are given in Max Farrand, *The Records of Federal Convention of 1787*, Vol. 1, pp. 190, 572; Vol. 3, p. 253. Other estimates of the colonial population are given in Carroll D. Wright, *History and Growth of the United States Census*, 1900, pp. 8–11, and in W. S. Rossiter, *A Century of Population Growth, 1790–1900*, pp. 4–15.

ington, after much deliberation, vetoed the bill on April 5, 1792 for the following reasons:[2]

First. The Constitution has prescribed that Representatives shall be apportioned among the several States according to their respective numbers; and there is no one proportion or divisor which, applied to the respective numbers of the States, will yield the number and allotment of Representatives proposed by the bill.

Second. The Constitution has also provided that the number of Representatives shall not exceed 1 for every 30,000, which restriction is, by the context and by fair and obvious construction, to be applied to the separate and respective numbers of the States; and the bill has allotted to eight of the States more than 1 for every 30,000.[3]

This was the first presidential veto. Jefferson made the following notation in his diary: "A few of the hottest friends of the bill expressed passion but the majority were satisfied, and both in and out of doors it gave pleasure to have at length an instance of the negative [veto] being exercised."[4]

A motion to override the veto did not command a majority, much less two-thirds, the vote being 23 for and 33 against. A new bill meeting the objections of the President was introduced April 9, and was approved April 14 (1 Stat. L. 253).[5]

[2] *Annals of Congress*, Vol. 3, p. 539.

[3] In the Constitutional Convention the ratio had been the subject of considerable discussion, which continued after the Constitution was adopted. The first of the twelve amendments to the Constitution proposed by Congress on Sept. 25, 1789 (1 Stat. L. 97) provided as follows:

"After the first enumeration required by the first article of the Constitution, there shall be one representative for every thirty thousand, until the number shall amount to one hundred, after which the proportion shall be so regulated by Congress, that there shall be not less than one hundred Representatives, nor less than one representative for every forty thousand persons, until the number of representatives shall amount to two hundred, after which the proportion shall be so regulated by Congress, that there shall not be less than two hundred Representatives, nor more than one Representative for every fifty thousand persons."

The second proposed amendment was as follows: "No law varying the compensation for the services of the senators and representatives, shall take effect, until an election of representatives shall have intervened."

The two foregoing amendments were not ratified by the states. The proposed amendments 3 to 12 became the first ten amendments, generally known as the Bill of Rights. For an account of the proceedings on the amendment proposing to establish the ratio, see Herman V. Ames, "The Proposed Amendments to the Constitution of the United States during the First Century of Its History," *Annual Report of the American Historical Association for . . . 1896*, Vol. 2, pp. 42–44.

[4] *Works of Thomas Jefferson*, Federal edition, 1904, Vol. 1, p. 218.

[5] A good account of the issues is given in Edmund J. James, "The First Apportion-

The act prescribed a ratio of one member for every 33,000 persons, and fixed the number of representatives from each state. The membership of the House was 105. In fixing the number of representatives, all fractions in the quota were disregarded. This method continued to be used from 1800 to 1830 inclusive.

All the contemporary statements of the population at the first census and most of the statements of the apportionment population at that time seen by the writer contain errors. The population as reported to Congress was as follows:

POPULATION OF STATES AS REPORTED TO CONGRESS
OCTOBER 27, 1791 AND MARCH 5, 1792[a]

Districts	Free White Males of Sixteen Years, and Upwards Including Heads of Families	Free White Males Under Sixteen Years	Free White Females Including Heads of Families	All Other Free Persons	Slaves	Total
Vermont.........	22,435	22,328	40,505	252	16	85,539
New Hampshire...	36,086	34,851	70,160	630	158	141,885
Maine...........	24,384	24,748	46,870	538	None	96,540
Massachusetts....	95,453	87,289	190,582	5,463	None	378,787
Rhode Island.....	16,019	15,799	32,652	3,407	948	68,825
Connecticut......	60,523	54,403	117,448	2,808	2,764	237,946
New York........	83,700	78,122	152,320	4,654	21,324	340,120
New Jersey.......	45,251	41,416	83,287	2,762	11,453	184,139
Pennsylvania.....	110,788	106,948	206,363	6,537	3,737	434,373
Delaware........	11,783	12,143	22,384	3,899	8,887	59,094
Maryland........	55,915	51,339	101,395	8,043	103,036	319,728
Virginia.........	110,936	116,135	215,046	12,866	292,627	747,610
Kentucky........	15,154	17,057	28,922	114	12,430	73,677
North Carolina...	69,988	77,506	140,710	4,975	100,572	393,751
South Carolina....	35,576	37,722	66,880	1,801	107,094	249,073
Georgia..........	13,103	14,044	25,739	398	29,264	82,548

[a] Senate Journal, Oct. 27, 1791 and Mar. 5, 1792; Annals of Congress, Vol. 3, pp. 18, 100.

The figures for Vermont were wrong as the result of errors in the addition of the returns for several towns; there were no slaves in Vermont, and the 16 persons reported as slaves should be added to the "all other free persons." The correct total population of Vermont was 85,425. The original returns show 255 "all other free persons," and not 252 as given in the report quoted.

The number of slaves in New Jersey is given as 11,453; the

correct number is 11,423. If 11,423 is used the several classes add to the total of 184,139, as given above, which is correct.

The correct population of Delaware was 59,096 instead of 59,094; the several classes add to this total.

Jefferson's figures for the apportionment population, taken from the manuscript of his memorandum of April 4, 1792 to the President, on file in the Library of Congress, are as follows:

APPORTIONMENT POPULATION AS GIVEN BY JEFFERSON
IN MEMORANDUM OF APRIL 4, 1792,
TO THE PRESIDENT

Vermont	85,532
New Hampshire	141,823
Massachusetts	475,327
Rhode Island	68,444
Connecticut	235,941
New York	352,915
New Jersey	179,556
Pennsylvania	432,880
Delaware	55,538
Maryland	278,513
Virginia	630,558
Kentucky	68,705
North Carolina	353,521
South Carolina	206,236
Georgia	70,843
	3,636,312

The total given above is that shown in the memorandum; the correct total is 3,636,332. The list is given three times in the memorandum, and the figures are the same in each one. In the third list the last item in the first column reads Virginia instead of Georgia, but it is clear that Georgia is meant, as the figures check with those for that state.

Apparently the earliest available publication containing these figures was House Document 234, 22d Congress, 1st Session, printed in 1832 by order of the House of Representatives. The papers in this document were furnished by Jared Sparks from the Washington papers which were in his possession. All the figures in the Sparks transcript were the same as in the original Jefferson manuscript. In some of the compilations of Jefferson's works published during recent years all the figures are not reported correctly.

Jefferson made one peculiar mistake. He gave 352,915 as the apportionment population in New York. This is manifestly impossible, as the total population of New York was only 340,120. He evidently added three-fifths of the slaves to the total population which included the slaves. His computation was evidently as follows:

Population (total, including slaves)		340,120
Slaves	21,324	
Three-fifths of slaves		12,795
Jefferson's figure for apportionment population		352,915

As far as is known the above is the first explanation of this error in Jefferson's figures.

There is also a small error in the apportionment population of New Jersey. Jefferson gives 179,556; the correct figure is 179,570. This error probably arose from the mistake in the original return regarding the number of slaves, which were reported to be 11,453 instead of 11,423. If 11,453 is used for the slave population, Jefferson's computation would be as follows:

Total population		184,139
Slaves		11,453
Population except slaves		172,686
Slaves	11,453	
Three fifths of slaves		6,872
Correct figure		179,558
Jefferson's figure		179,556

Second census, 1800. In the intercensal period between 1790 and 1800 Tennessee was admitted by the act of June 1, 1796 (1 Stat. L. 491), its representation being fixed at one member until the next apportionment. A new apportionment bill was introduced in the House December 16, 1801, passed the House

June 6, 1802, passed the Senate without amendment January 11, and was approved January 14 (2 Stat. L.'128), the law being the first one enacted by the 7th Congress.

The apportionment act of 1802 continued the ratio of 33,000, which provided a House of 141 members. As in the first census all fractions in the quota were disregarded.

Third census, 1810. Only one state—Ohio—was admitted (in 1802) in the intercensal period between 1800 and 1810. Its representation was fixed at one member until the next apportionment (2 Stat. L. 173). Debate on the third apportionment bill began in the House on November 22, 1811, and the bill was approved on December 21 (2 Stat. L. 669). The ratio was fixed at 35,000. While the total membership was not specified in the act, the sum of the quotas for the several states gave a House of 181 members.

Fourth census, 1820. Seven states were admitted between the third and fourth apportionments, namely, Louisiana in 1812 (2 Stat. L. 701), Indiana in 1816 (3 Stat. L. 289, 399), Mississippi in 1817 (3 Stat. L. 348, 472), Illinois in 1818 (3 Stat. L. 428, 536), Alabama in 1819 (3 Stat. L. 489, 608), and Maine and Missouri in 1820 (3 Stat. L. 348, 547, 645). Each of these except Maine was allowed one representative until the next apportionment. As Maine had been a part of Massachusetts, the act of April 7, 1820 (3 Stat. L. 555) provided that the Massachusetts delegation should be reduced from 20 to 13 and that Maine should be entitled to 7 representatives.

An apportionment bill was introduced in the House on January 7, 1822 and approved on March 7 (3 Stat L. 651). It provided a ratio of 40,000, all fractions in the quota being disregarded. The total membership was not specified, but the sum of the quotas gave a House of 213 members.

Fifth census, 1830. No new states were admitted between the apportionments after the census of 1820 and 1830. The act of May 22, 1832 (4 Stat. L. 516) fixed the ratio at 47,700, all fractions in the quota being disregarded. This resulted in a House of 240 members. The debate in 1832 was marked by

Daniel Webster's emphatic protest against the inequalities resulting from the method used.[6] Webster's views did not prevail, but they resulted in a change ten years later.[7]

Sixth census, 1840. In the intercensal period between 1830 and 1840 two states were admitted—Arkansas in 1836 (5 Stat. L. 50) and Michigan in 1837 (5 Stat. L. 49, 144). The enabling act for Arkansas specified that the state should have one representative; there seems to have been no legislation on the representation from Michigan, but one representative was elected and seated.

The act of 1842 made a definite change in the method of apportionment, putting into effect part of Webster's proposal of a decade earlier. This act specified a ratio of 76,680 for each member with "one additional member for each state having a fraction greater than one moiety of the said ratio." This is a true method of major fractions. The act specified the number of representatives from each state computed according to the method described, the total being 223, a reduction of 17 from the total established in 1832. As two new states with four members were included, the reduction in members from the other states was 21.

A new feature in the act of 1842 was the second section requiring members to be elected from districts "composed of contiguous territory equal in number to the number of representatives to which said state may be entitled, no one district electing more than one representative." When he signed the act President Tyler appended to it a memorandum expressing his doubt as to the constitutionality of this provision, thereby arousing the ire of John Quincy Adams. For an account of this incident, see page 133.

Seventh census, 1850. Five states were admitted between the apportionment act after the sixth census and that after the seventh. These were: in 1845, Texas (5 Stat. L. 497; 9 Stat. L. 108) and Florida (5 Stat. L. 742); in 1846, Iowa (5 Stat. L. 742;

---

[6] See *Report of Select Committee*, 22 Cong. 1 sess., S. Doc. 119, 22 pp.
[7] For a discussion of the defects in the Webster method, see p. 78.

9 Stat. L. 52, 117); in 1848, Wisconsin (9 Stat. L. 56, 223); and in 1850, California (9 Stat. L. 452). One representative was assigned to Florida and two to each of the other states.

The method which was used in 1850, and which continued to be used to 1900, is generally known as the Vinton method, from Samuel F. Vinton, a representative from Ohio, who proposed it. The method prescribed by the act was as follows:

> . . . it shall be the duty of the Secretary of the Interior to ascertain the aggregate representative population . . . ; which aggregate population he shall divide by the number two hundred and thirty-three, and the product of such division, rejecting any fraction of an unit, if any such happen to remain, shall be the ratio, or rule of apportionment, of representatives among the several States under such enumeration; and the said Secretary of the Department of the Interior shall then proceed, in the same manner, to ascertain the representative population of each State, and to divide the whole number of the representative population of each State by the ratio already determined by him as above directed; and the product of this last division shall be the number of representatives apportioned to such State under the then last enumeration: *Provided*, That the loss in the number of members caused by the fractions remaining in the several States, on the division of the population thereof, shall be compensated for by assigning to so many States having the largest fractions, one additional member each for its fraction as may be necessary to make the whole number of representatives two hundred and thirty-three. *And provided, also*, That if, after the apportionment of the representatives under the next, or any subsequent census, a new State or States shall be admitted into the Union, the representative or representatives assigned to such new State or States shall be in addition to the number of representatives herein above limited; which excess of representatives over two hundred and thirty-three shall only continue until the next succeeding apportionment of representatives under the next succeeding census.

A simpler statement is that the population of the country is divided by the number of members of the House to give the ratio or number of persons for each district. This ratio is then divided into the population of each state to give the exact quota for each state. After assigning one representative to each state whose quota is less than one, in order to meet the constitutional requirement that each state is entitled to one representative, each of the other states receives a representative for each whole number in its exact quota. The remaining representatives are then assigned in order to the states having the highest fractions. The highest fractions used to complete the membership of the House may not include all the major fractions; likewise they may include some minor fractions. The Vinton method is subject to the Alabama paradox, as a state may lose a member if the size of the House is increased. This is shown in the example on page 7.

The size of the House was fixed at 233 members; the number could be increased by the admission of new states, but the increased number was to continue only until the next succeeding apportionment. An amendatory act of July 30, 1852 (10 Stat. L. 25) increased the size of the House to 234 until the next apportionment, when it would revert to 233.

Certification of the apportionment was made by the Secretary of the Interior on August 2, 1852.[8] As the apportionment was made by the Secretary as the agent of Congress, it is not printed in the Statutes at Large. The act of 1850 contained no provision regarding election of members by districts.

In 1850 the census act (9 Stat. L. 432) contained three provisions not included in any previous law, as follows: (1) it provided not only for the census of 1850, but for all subsequent censuses; (2) it fixed permanently the size of the House;[9] and (3) it provided in advance for an automatic apportionment to be made by the Secretary of Interior according to the method prescribed in the act (9 Stat. L. 432, secs. 23–26).

A new census act has been passed prior to the taking of every census after 1850, but each of those acts provided for the current and subsequent censuses, so that there would be authority for each census in case a new law was not passed. The freezing of the size of the House and the permanent provision for automatic apportionment did not last, as both the membership and apportionment were changed in 1862. However, both were revived in 1929.

Representative Vinton ably discussed their desirability in a

[8] *Apportionment of Members*, 32 Cong. 1 sess., H. Ex. Doc. 129; *Apportionment among the Several States*, 56 Cong. 2 sess., H. Rept. 2130, p. 11.

[9] Several resolutions amending the Constitution in order to limit the size of the House were introduced between 1821 and 1888, but none was submitted to the states. See Ames, *Proposed Amendments*, pp. 54–55.

speech in the House on April 30, 1850. Regarding the size of the House and the automatic apportionment Representative Vinton spoke in part as follows:

Now, this arrangement [fixing the size of the House] would be attended with many and great advantages. The first and greatest of all is, it completes the organization of the Government, and puts it beyond the reach of accident or faction from this cause. Next, it obviates the necessity of future legislation in respect to the organization of the House; and if in future it should be thought by any that the number of the body was too large or too small, the burden of showing the necessity of the change would devolve on its advocates. This is the footing on which all laws, certainly those which are organic, should stand. Next, if a permanent number is established, it will be likely to be fixed with reference chiefly, if not solely, to those general considerations of public expediency and convenience, which ought to be alone regarded in the adoption of such a measure. Next, it will do away with the necessity of passing an apportionment law, after the census shall have been taken, and thus save Congress from the waste of much time and from a disreputable contest about the unrepresented fractions. These which, in the view of a real statesman, are entitled to no consideration, have unfortunately had more influence in fixing the apportionment, and with it the number of the House, than all other motives besides. A great waste of time, for weeks, has been lost in a disreputable scramble to throw the fractions from one State or section upon another. The consequence has been, that a large part of the House has been deeply dissatisfied. The work has been usually accomplished by a combination of the large States, who could best afford to bear the loss of the fractions, hitting upon some ratio that would leave them with small fractions, and then, with the aid of such small States as happened to have small fractions also under the proposed ratio, voting it through without much regard to the number of the House, and to the injustice done to the small States. This will be likely to occur again two years hence, if no provision be now made to organize the House.

The proposed measure will save the future waste of time on this subject, as well as future complaints of injustice or unfair dealing. As one of the members of a large State, which can afford as well as any other to bear the loss of a fraction, I am willing to waive the advantage Ohio would have over a small State in the adjustment of an apportionment bill, and that she shall take her equal chance only with her smaller sisters. I know no reason why the large States, such as Ohio or Virginia, shall have any advantage over New Hampshire or Arkansas. The next advantage from fixing the number of the members now is, that it would save the States much expense and inconvenience. The census cannot be taken and returned to Congress before the first session of the next Congress, in December, 1851. There is not the remotest probability that Congress would pass a bill to fix the number of the House under that census, and apportion the members among the States till long after the sessions of the State legislatures for that year had closed. The consequence will be, as I believe it was under the last apportionment, that a special session of every State legislature throughout the Union must be called for the special purpose of dividing the States into Congressional districts. To get five or six thousand members of the State legislatures together for this purpose, alone, is a burden and inconvenience that ought not to be unnecessarily imposed on the States.

Eighth census, 1860. In the intercensal period following 1850, two states were admitted—Minnesota in 1858 (11 Stat. L. 285) and Oregon in 1859 (11 Stat. L. 383). The acts admitting them assigned two representatives to Minnesota and one to Oregon until the next apportionment.

No general apportionment act was passed after the census of 1860, as the permanent apportionment act of May 23, 1850 (9 Stat. L. 432) continued in effect. The Secretary of the Interior certified the apportionment of 233 members on July 5, 1861.[10] However, on March 4, 1862 (12 Stat. L. 353) an act fixed the number of representatives at 241 and assigned one additional representative each to Pennsylvania, Ohio, Kentucky, Illinois, Iowa, Minnesota, Vermont, and Rhode Island.[11]

A supplemental act of July 14, 1862 (12 Stat. L. 572) revived the provisions of the act of 1842 requiring districts to be composed of contiguous territory.

Ninth census, 1870. During the decade following the Civil War three states were admitted—West Virginia in 1863 (12 Stat. L. 633; 13 Stat. L. 731); Nevada in 1864 (13 Stat. L. 30, 749); and Nebraska in 1867 (13 Stat. L. 47; 14 Stat. L. 391,

---

[10] *Apportionment of Representatives of the Several States, in the House of Representatives, under the Eighth Census,* 37 Cong. 1 sess., H. Ex. Doc. 2; *Apportionment among the Several States,* 56 Cong. 2 sess., H. Rept. 2130, p. 12.

[11] This act is confusing. While it supersedes the act of May 23, 1850 (9 Stat. L. 432) as regards the size of the House, the increased representation for the states mentioned is not in addition to that specified by statute, but is amendatory to the apportionment made by the Secretary of the Interior on July 5, 1861.

820). Three representatives were assigned to West Virginia and one each to Nevada and Nebraska.

The act of February 2, 1872 (17 Stat. L. 28) fixed the size of the House at 283, with the proviso that the number should be increased if new states were admitted. The act specified the number of members from each state, the apportionment having been made by the Vinton method.

A supplemental act of May 30, 1872 (17 Stat. L. 192) assigned one additional representative each to New Hampshire, Vermont, New York, Pennsylvania, Indiana, Tennessee, Louisiana, Alabama, and Florida.

The act of 1872 again enacted the earlier provision requiring districts to be composed of contiguous territory, and added a new requirement that the districts should contain "as nearly as practicable an equal number of inhabitants."

Two provisions that could not be enforced were included in the act. Section 5 provided that no state should thereafter be admitted "without having the necessary population to entitle it to at least one representative according to the ratio of representation fixed by this bill." This law could not be enforced, as no Congress can bind a succeeding Congress. Moreover, no ratio was fixed by the act, although the basis on which the representatives were assigned was 131,425. In 1890, Idaho was admitted with a population of 84,385 and Wyoming with a population of 60,705. The population of Wyoming did not exceed the 1872 ratio until 1900.

The second unenforceable provision was section 6, which repeated the language of section 2 of the Fourteenth Amendment, which required reduction in representation if the right of male citizens to vote was abridged, except for rebellion or other crime. The effect of this provision is discussed on page 94.

Tenth census, 1880. Only one state—Colorado—was admitted in the decade between 1870 and 1880. The enabling act assigned one representative (18 Stat. L. 474).

The apportionment act of February 25, 1882 (22 Stat. L. 5) provided for a House of 325 members, with additional members if new states should be admitted. The act specified the number assigned to each state; it contained no formula for the apportionment, which was made by the Vinton method. This act again enacted the provisions of the 1872 act requiring districts to be compact, and to contain equal population.

Eleventh census, 1890. Between the apportionments under the tenth and eleventh censuses, six states were admitted as follows: in 1889, Montana (25 Stat. L. 676; 26 Stat. L. 1551), North Dakota (25 Stat. L. 676; 26 Stat. L. 1548), South Dakota (25 Stat. L. 676; 26 Stat. L. 1549), and Washington (25 Stat. L. 676; 26 Stat. L. 1553); in 1890, Idaho (26 Stat. L. 215) and Wyoming (26 Stat. L. 222).

The act of February 7, 1891 (26 Stat. L. 735) fixed the size of the House at 356 with additional members if other states should be admitted. The apportionment was made by the Vinton method, the number of representatives assigned to each state being given in the act. This law also continued the previous provisions requiring districts to be composed of contiguous territory and to have an equal number of inhabitants.

Twelfth census, 1900. Only one state—Utah—was admitted during the intercensal period between 1890 and 1900. Its enabling act provided for one representative (28 Stat. L. 107).

Apportionment was provided by the act of January 16, 1901 (31 Stat. L. 733), which fixed the House at 386 members, with the usual provision for additional members if new states were admitted. This apportionment was the last one made by the Vinton method. The number of representatives from each state was specified in the act.

The apportionment act of 1901 again contained the provisions regarding contiguous territory and equal population, and added another requirement, namely, that the territory should be compact.

Thirteenth census, 1910. Oklahoma was admitted in the intercensal period preceding 1910 with five representatives until a new apportionment was made (34 Stat. L. 271).

The apportionment act of August 8, 1911 (37 Stat. L. 13) fixed the size of the House at 433 members with the proviso that if either Arizona or New Mexico became a state before the next apportionment, it should have one representative. Both became states in 1912 and the membership was thus increased to 435, which figure has continued to the present time.

A new method of apportionment, that of major fractions, was adopted in assigning representatives under the act of 1911. The computation by this method at that time was not as simple as at present, as the table of multipliers and the priority list had not been developed.[12] The 1911 act repeated the previous provisions that districts should be composed of compact and contiguous territory and should have an equal number of inhabitants.

Fourteenth census, 1920. The census of 1920 showed the usual increase in population of the entire country, a considerable shifting of population from the rural districts to the urban centers, and a marked increase in certain states. There was, however, considerable criticism of the census figures. The enumeration was made in January, and it was claimed that owing to the bad weather many rural inhabitants were not counted.

Generally, each previous apportionment had provided for an increase in the size of the House so that no state would lose a member. In line with this precedent the House Committee on the Census in 1921 reported a bill in the third session of the 66th Congress (H.R. 14498) fixing the size of the House at 483 members.[13] This bill was amended in the House to provide for 435 members, the existing size, but the Senate took no action.

In the first session of the 67th Congress, in 1921, the House Committee on the Census reported a bill (H.R. 7882) fixing the size of the House at 460.[14] Under this bill Maine and Missouri would each have lost a member, but the representation of no other state would have been reduced. A motion to amend the

[12] See Chap. III for description of method of computation.

[13] *Apportionment of Representatives*, 66 Cong. 3 sess., H. Rept. 1173, 30 pp. See also House Committee on Census, *Apportionment of Representatives*, Hearings on H.R. 14498, 15021, 15158, and 15217, Dec. 28, 1920–Jan. 6, 1921, 222 pp.; also *Apportionment of Each Number of Representatives*, 66 Cong. 3 sess., H. Doc. 918.

[14] *Apportionment of Representatives*, 67 Cong. 1 sess., H. Rept. 312, 41 pp.; see also House Committee on Census, *Apportionment of Representatives*, Hearings, June 27–29, 1921, 94 pp.

bill to read 435 members failed. A motion to recommit was agreed to by four votes. This killed the bill.

No further action was attempted until 1926, when a motion to take up a pending reapportionment bill (H.R. 111, 69th Congress) as a privileged matter was lost by a vote of 87 to 265. A year later, at the end of the 67th Congress, a motion was made to suspend the rules and pass H.R. 17378, a bill providing a House of 435 members. The motion was defeated by a vote of 187 to 199.

Seven years had passed since the census was taken, and 42 bills for reapportionment had been introduced in the House, but no bill had passed. After every preceding census an apportionment bill had been enacted soon after the population figures were available. As the "long honored tradition, therefore, has been broken for the first time, and creates a precedent which is fraught with serious consequences"[15] the House Committee on the Census in 1928 reported a new bill (H.R. 11725) in the first session of the 70th Congress to provide an automatic system of apportionment. This bill was recommitted on May 18, 1928 by a vote of 186 to 164. The provisions of this bill were in the main similar to those of the act of 1929 and will not be discussed at this point.

As was stated by the committee in the report cited above, Congress after the census of 1920 for the first time failed to pass an apportionment act after a new census had been taken. The result of a failure to act is that apportionment becomes more difficult with the lapse of time, particularly if the representation of any state is decreased. Two successive reductions of one member at each ten-year period are not as likely to excite resentment as one reduction of two members at the end of the twenty-year period.

All the bills reported up to this time had provided for the computation of the apportionment by the method of major fractions, which had been used in 1910. But new methods had been developed, particularly that of equal proportions, which had been recommended by committees of the National Academy of

[15] *Apportionment of Representatives*, 70 Cong. 1 sess., H. Rept. 1137, p. 2.

Sciences and the American Statistical Association. There had been considerable debate in the House over the relative merits of the methods of major fractions and equal proportions, but as the House took no final action on any of the bills, no new method was prescribed.

Section 22 of the act of June 18, 1929 (46 Stat. L. 26) finally broke the long.deadlock. This act broadly resembled the apportionment of 1850 (9 Stat. L. 428) in that the provision for apportionment was made in advance in the act for the taking of the census, the method of making the apportionment was prescribed, and the computation of the result was made by an officer of the executive branch acting as the agent of Congress. Neither the automatic apportionment nor the fixing of the size of the House was new. Both had been provided by sections 24 to 26 of the act of May 23, 1850 (9 Stat. L. 432),[16] which has never been repealed, but which has been superseded by later legislation. Constitutional limitations on the size of the House had been proposed as early as 1821.[17]

The act of 1929 provided that within one week of the assembling of the second regular session of the 71st Congress (December 1930) and of each fifth Congress thereafter, the President should transmit to Congress a statement of the apportionment population of each state, together with an apportionment of representatives to each state according to the then existing membership of the House. The apportionment so reported was to be according to each of the following methods: (1) method of last preceding apportionment; (2) method of major fractions; and (3) method of equal proportions.

If the Congress to which the statement was submitted failed to pass a new apportionment act, each state became entitled in the second succeeding Congress, and in each Congress thereafter, to the number of representatives shown by the method used in the last preceding census. When the act of 1929 was passed, the second regular session convened on the first Monday in December of each even-numbered year, and ended by limita-

16 See p. 115.
17 See p. 115.

tion on March 4. This gave Congress three months in which to take action.

The main objections to this legislation were that it froze the size of the House, that it took away from Congress its power to apportion, and that it conferred legislative duties on the executive branch of the government. None of these objections is tenable. No power lodged in Congress can be taken away except by an amendment to the Constitution, and no Congress can bind a succeeding Congress. Congress may at any time change the size of the House or prescribe a method of apportionment other than the ones specified in the act. While a new apportionment goes into effect at the end of the waiting period, Congress can at any subsequent session change the apportionment in any way it sees fit.

As to the delegation of legislative power, the executive branch merely acts as a clerical agency of Congress. The census, on which the apportionment is based, has always been taken by the executive branch, and it has never been suggested that Congress should take the census. When Congress specifies the method by which the apportionment should be made, the computation of the result is a simple mathematical problem to which there is only one solution for any one method of apportionment.

Representative Robert Luce, an experienced member of the House and an authority on legislative practices and procedure, made the following concise answer to some of the objections to the bill.[18]

It has been argued against this bill that the task contemplated will be put into the hands of somebody in another branch of the Government. That is simply a ministerial duty, and is no more a delegation of power than would be intrusting the adding up of a column of figures to a clerk in the auditing department or of turning over to any other official any other of the mechanical operations of the Government.

It has been argued that a Congress may not bind its successor. That is perfectly true. But if the application of that principle should be carried to extreme, yet logical conclusions, it would be necessary for the first session of the next Congress to reenact the whole code of

[18] *Cong. Record*, 70 Cong. 2 sess., Vol. 70, Pt. 2, p. 1493.

statute law on the ground that our authority does not extend beyond the period of our life here as a Congress.

It is also objected that this is not, of itself, an apportionment bill. Granting that such a quibble over words should have any attention, nevertheless, the fact is that this bill is a preliminary step, and is part of the performance of a duty we have long neglected.

These three things are pretexts, not reasons. Let no man here salve his conscience with a pretext.

The automatic apportionment is desirable because the method is specified in advance, and no one knows whether any state or group of states will be favored. It avoids log-rolling and controversy, and prevents a stalemate such as occurred after the census of 1920. However, if one method is deemed better than all others it would be desirable that the act should require the automatic apportionment to be made by that method.

Fifteenth census, 1930. On December 4, 1930, the President transmitted to Congress a statement complying with section 22 of the act of June 18, 1929.[19] This statement gave apportionments by the methods of equal proportions and major fractions. The third method, that of the last preceding apportionment, was not shown separately as the method of major fractions had been used at that time. As it happened, the two methods gave the same results for each state, and there was no choice between them. Congress took no action and the apportionment shown in the report by the President became effective at the expiration of the 72d Congress. Technically the method used was that of major fractions, as that method was used in the last preceding apportionment—that of 1910.

Sixteenth census, 1940. When the act of 1929 was passed, the second regular session of Congress met the first Monday in December of each even-numbered year. As a result of the adoption of the Twentieth Amendment to the Constitution, the second regular session of Congress begins on the third of January in each even-numbered year, or eleven months earlier. The act of 1929 required the apportionment report to be submitted at the beginning of the second session of the 76th Congress, or in January 1940.

[19] *Bureau of the Census, Department of Commerce,* 71 Cong. 3 sess., H. Doc. 664, 2 pp.

As the census had not been taken in January 1940 it was manifestly impossible for the President to submit the report at that time, and the act of 1929 became a dead letter. This situation was remedied by the act of April 25, 1940 (54 Stat. L. 162), which amended the act of 1929 by requiring the report to be submitted within one week of the beginning of the first regular session of the 77th Congress (January 10, 1941), and of each fifth Congress thereafter. This statement will therefore be due in January 1941, and will be available about the time this book is published.[20]

Another amendment made by the act of 1940 is to have the automatic apportionment promulgated within sixty calendar days from the date of transmittal of the report. Thus Congress has less time for consideration as it meets a month later than formerly. The date of promulgation was so fixed because most of the state legislatures are in session during the first three months of each odd-numbered year. The new apportionment will be effective n the next succeeding Congress, or the 78th Congress, which will be elected in 1942, and which will convene in January 1943.

Permanent apportionment act. The permanent apportionment act of June 18, 1929 (46 Stat. L. 26) as amended by the act of April 25, 1940 (54 Stat. L. 162) is as follows:

Sec. 22. (a) On the first day, or within one week thereafter, of the first regular session of the Seventy-seventh Congress and of each fifth Congress thereafter, the President shall transmit to the Congress a statement showing the whole number of persons in each State, excluding Indians not taxed, as ascertained under the sixteenth and each subsequent decennial census of the population, and the number of Representatives to which each State would be entitled under an apportionment of the then existing number of Representatives made in each of the following manners:

(1) By apportioning the then existing number of Representatives among the several States according to the respective numbers of the several States as ascertained under such census, by the method used

---

[20] While this statement had not been formally transmitted to Congress when this book went to press, the basic population figures and apportionments by the methods of major fractions and equal proportions had been made public. All these figures are given in App. C.

in the last preceding apportionment, no State to receive less than one Member;

(2) By apportioning the then existing number of Representatives among the several States according to the respective numbers of the several States as ascertained under such census, by the method known as the method of major fractions, no State to receive less than one Member; and

(3) By apportioning the then existing number of Representatives among the several States according to the respective numbers of the several States as ascertained under such census, by the method known as the method of equal proportions, no State to receive less than one Member.

(b) If the Congress to which the statement required by subdivision (a) of this section is transmitted has not, within sixty calendar days after such statement is transmitted, enacted a law apportioning Representatives among the several States, then each State shall be entitled, in the next Congress and in each Congress thereafter until the taking effect of a reapportionment under this Act or subsequent statute, to the number of Representatives shown in the statement based upon the method used in the last preceding apportionment. It shall be the duty of the Clerk of the last House of Representatives forthwith to send to the executive of each State a certificate of the number of Representatives to which such State is entitled under this section. In case of a vacancy in the office of Clerk, or of his absence or inability to discharge this duty, then such duty shall devolve upon the officer who, under section 32 or 33 of the Revised Statutes, is charged with the preparation of the roll of Representatives-elect.

(c) This section shall have no force and effect in respect of the apportionment to be made under any decennial census unless the statement required by subdivision (a) of this section in respect of such census is transmitted to the Congress within the time prescribed in subdivision (a).

CHAPTER IX

APPORTIONMENT WITHIN THE STATES

Inequalities in the apportionment among the states have never been as extensive and flagrant as the variations in the population of the several districts in many of the states. When three districts in the same city have populations of 90,671, 776,425, and 799,407, as is the case in New York where the state average is 292,746, the situation demands remedial action.

Three states—Arkansas, Illinois, and Maryland—last changed the boundaries of the districts after the census of 1900, and the population is very unevenly distributed over the several districts. The boundaries of the districts in ten states—Connecticut, Idaho, Louisiana, Montana, New York, North Dakota, Ohio, Oklahoma, Oregon, and Utah—date from the census of 1910. One state—Colorado—last rearranged its districts after the census of 1920. The remaining states, except New Hampshire, fixed the boundaries of the districts after the census of 1930.

As a rule the time that has elapsed since the boundaries of the districts were established is a guide to the fairness of the apportionment. There are, however, exceptions. New Hampshire last defined its districts in 1881, but the apportionment has been almost ideal after each succeeding census. Utah established its districts after the census of 1910, but the apportionment was still equitable after the census of 1930. In these states it has not been necessary to redefine the districts. On the other hand, South Dakota and Pennsylvania redistricted after the census of 1930, but in South Dakota the population of the larger district is 212.2 per cent in excess of the smaller and in Pennsylvania that of the largest district is 124.5 per cent in excess of the smallest.

Various factors have combined to cause and perpetuate inequalities. The lack of action may have been due to indifference, but is probably owing to the disinclinations of the political leaders to disturb the status quo. The inequalities in most cases are likely to be due to the exigencies of practical politics. The majority party endeavors to concentrate the minority vote in a few districts, and thus make the remaining districts safe for the majority. The political fortunes of sitting members or aspirants also have considerable effect.

Conflicts between urban and rural areas account for many inequalities; as a rule the urban districts have a greater population than the rural ones, but this is not universally true. Another cause of inequalities is the disinclination to divide a county between two districts. Except in the metropolitan areas the district boundaries generally follow the county lines. Few states have constitutional provisions requiring this, but it is the usual practice.

State districting has been looked upon as a local matter which should be left entirely to the states. But it has a real national significance. The essence of representative government is the existence of a strong and militant minority. Matters of national importance may hinge on a small majority in the House of Representatives. In addition in case no candidate for President receives a majority of the electoral votes the President is elected by the House of Representatives. While the vote in the House is by states, a difference of one vote in a state delegation might throw the election one way or the other. The general situation has been summarized by one commentator as follows:

In the light of these circumstances the constitutional provision for apportionment of representatives among the states according to "the whole number of persons" becomes hopelessly inadequate. Equitable congressional apportionment obviously comes to naught when state legislatures may perpetrate the very injustices prohibited to Congress. Such a provision is comparable to a law which protects an individual from violence committed by citizens of other states while leaving the road clear for such violence by his next door neighbor. Are we so provincial today as to submit to discriminations within our own state while demanding equality as between states? The electorate stands in silence. Popular majorities become increasingly helpless, and the principle for which we once fought and died we now relinquish with ne'er a struggle.[1]

---

[1] Robert B. Stewart, "A Study of Gerrymandering in Kentucky," *Kentucky Law Journal*, Vol. 22, 1934, p. 426.

This chapter will discuss the development of districting, the criteria applicable to state apportionment, proposed remedial measures, and the apportionment situation in the several states. At the end is a table showing the population of each congressional district, and the relative or percentage deviation from the average population of the districts.

CRITERIA APPLICABLE TO DISTRICTS

In an ideal state apportionment each district should have the same population, which would be determined by dividing the population of the state by the number of representatives. This ideal can never be attained, but any apportionment which departs widely from it is inequitable. Several methods may be used for determining the extent of the variation, but it is believed that the best and simplest is the maximum relative departure from the average. This is obtained by dividing the average population into the difference between the average population and the population of the district which shows the greatest departure either above or below the average.

Thus for Wisconsin the total population is 2,939,006; as there are 10 districts the average is 293,901. The district having the greatest departure from the average has a population of 371,742. As the average is 293,901 the district with a population of 371,742 has a population of 77,841 in excess of the average. By dividing 77,841 (the difference) by 293,901 (the average) we obtain 26.5 per cent as the greatest relative departure. For Colorado the population is 1,035,791; as there are 4 districts the average is 258,948. The district having the greatest departure from the average has a population of 141,542. As the average is 258,948 the district with a population of 141,542 has a population 117,406 below the average. By dividing 117,406 (the difference) by 258,948 (the average) we obtain 45.3 per cent as the maximum departure from the average.

A criterion which has been recognized in one bill (H. R. 5099, 76 Congress) is the relative excess of population of the largest district over the smallest. In this case the population of the smallest district is divided into the difference between the smallest and the largest. Thus in New York the population of the largest district is 779,407 and that of the smallest is 90,671. The difference is 708,736. By dividing 90,671 (population of the smallest district) into 708,736 (difference between the smallest and the largest) we get 781.7 per cent.

TESTS OF STATE APPORTIONMENTS BY TWO METHODS

State	Maximum Departure from Average		Excess of Largest over Smallest		State	Maximum Departure from Average		Excess of Largest over Smallest	
	Rank	Per Cent	Rank	Per Cent		Rank	Per Cent	Rank	Per Cent
Illinois........	1	191.4	2	543.3	Connecticut....	20	31.0	20	74.5
New York.....	2	173.1	1	781.7	Texas.........	21	29.5	21	70.6
Ohio..........	3	109.7	3	296.8	Wisconsin......	22	26.5	26	51.9
Maryland......	4	69.7	5	138.3	New Jersey....	23	24.7	23	60.5
Pennsylvania...	5	57.1	9	124.5	Kentucky......	24	22.3	24	59.6
Missouri.......	6	52.4	12	105.5	Montana......	25	21.2	25	53.7
Washington....	7	52.1	15	89.2	South Carolina.	26	18.9	27	44.1
South Dakota..	8	51.5	4	212.2	Louisiana......	27	15.3	28	36.1
Alabama.......	9	46.8	18	82.5	Idaho.........	28	14.8	29	34.8
Mississippi.....	10	46.6	7	128.5	Kansas........	29	14.7	30	34.2
Arkansas......	11	45.7	8	126.3	Massachusetts..	30	14.5	31	29.2
Colorado.......	12	45.3	10	114.4	Virginia.......	31	13.1	33	26.9
North Carolina.	13	43.9	17	84.5	Iowa..........	32	12.5	32	28.5
Oregon ⎰.......	14	{42.4	6	136.4	Minnesota.....	33	10.9	34	19.5
Georgia ⎱		{42.4	14	89.6	West Virginia...	34	7.2	36	13.1
California......	15	41.7	11	111.2	Indiana........	35	7.2	37	12.5
					Nebraska......	36	5.8	35	14.1
Oklahoma.....	16	35.2	19	80.7					
Michigan......	17	34.4	13	103.6	Utah..........	37	5.0	38	10.5
Florida........	18	33.1	22	60.7	New Hampshire	38	1.8	39	3.6
Tennessee......	19	33.0	16	88.9	Rhode Island...	39	0.8	40	1.6
					Maine.........	40	0.5	41	1.0

There will probably be difference of opinion regarding the variation from the average that should be permitted before a state apportionment is characterized as inequitable, but it is believed that a 20 per cent deviation from the average for all districts is a fair and workable tolerance. The census figures for 1940 show that the average population of the districts, with a House of 435 members, will be in the neighborhood of 300,000. A 20 per cent tolerance would be 60,000. This tolerance is large enough to allow a division between congressional districts based on the boundaries of counties and such other subordinate minor civil divisions as may be recognized by the state laws and by the census.[2]

[2] In 1911 an amendment to the apportionment bill proposed that the difference in population of districts should not exceed 20,000. On a division this amendment was rejected by a vote of 69 to 104. Another amendment to fix the difference at 75,000 was rejected without division. *Cong. Record*, 62 Cong. 1 sess., Vol. 47, Pt. 1, p. 695.

The table on page 130 shows for each state the relative maximum departure from the average and the relative excess of the population of the largest over the smallest district. The apportionment in 26 states is defective if 20 per cent is adopted as the maximum permissible departure from the average or if 50 per cent is taken as the maximum permissible excess of the largest over the smallest district.

In the table on page 130, the maximum departure may be above or below the average. In the text describing the apportionment for each state (pages 149–82) the percentages of maximum departures above and below the average are given. In the table showing the population of each district (pages 183–92) the percentage of departure from the average is given for each district.

CONGRESSIONAL CONTROL OVER DISTRICTING

The Constitution provides for the apportionment of representatives among the states, but is silent as to whether the representatives shall be elected by districts or by the state at large. Election by districts was contemplated in at least some states, as Hamilton in his speech before the New York convention on June 21, 1788 made the following statement: "The natural and proper mode of holding elections will be to divide the state into districts, in proportion to the number to be elected. This state will consequently be divided at first into six."[3]

The progress of election by districts is described by Ames as follows:[4]

The variety of methods in use in the different States, both for the choice of electors and Representatives, suggested the attempts made during the early years of this century to provide a uniform system.[5] These resolutions commonly proposed amendments applying both to

[3] *Works of Alexander Hamilton*, edited by Henry Cabot Lodge, Vol. 2, p. 25.

[4] Herman V. Ames, "The Proposed Amendments to the Constitution of the United States during the First Century of Its History," *Annual Report of the American Historical Association for . . . 1896*, Vol. 2, pp. 56–57.

[5] In the early elections the following methods were in use: First, by districts in Massachusetts, Virginia, New York, Maryland, South Carolina. Second, by general ticket in New Hampshire, Pennsylvania, New Jersey, Georgia. Third, in Connecticut a preliminary election was held to nominate a list three times the number to be chosen, from which at a subsequent election the Representatives were selected. [Footnote part of quotation.]

Presidential and Congressional elections. The first resolution of the kind was offered by Mr. Nicholas of Virginia, in the year 1800. It proposed a division of each State into districts, the people in each district to choose one Representative in the manner in which the legislature shall provide.[6] In 1802 the legislatures of Vermont and North Carolina presented resolutions of a similar character. Again, after a lull of a few years, the legislature of North Carolina renewed, in 1813, their resolution. From 1816 to 1826 there were twenty-two resolutions proposing the choice of Representatives by districts. During the years 1816, 1817, and 1818 the legislatures of six of the States applied to Congress for an amendment of this nature.[7] The earlier movement was championed by Mr. Pickens of North Carolina, the later by Senator Dickerson of New Jersey, who offered an amendment regularly almost every year from 1817 to 1826.[8] The Dickerson amendment passed the Senate three different times, namely, in 1819, 1820, and 1822, but each time failed to be brought to a vote in the House. The desire for local representation gradually led to the general adoption by the States of the district system of electing their Congressmen, and caused the introduction of amendments on this question to cease.[9]

By 1842 twenty-two states were electing representatives by districts, and only six states, New Hampshire, New Jersey, Alabama, Georgia, Mississippi, and Missouri, with a representation of 33 of a total of 232, were electing at large; three states had only one representative each, and had no occasion to create districts.[10]

Federal Statutory Provisions for Control of State Apportionment

As the practice of electing by districts had become firmly established, the apportionment act of June 25, 1842 (5 Stat. L.

---

[6] . . . Jefferson favored election by districts and not by general ticket. See letter of January 12, 1800, Works, Vol. IV, p. 308. [Footnote part of quotation.]

[7] Massachusetts, in 1816; New Jersey and North Carolina, in 1817; New York, North Carolina, New Hampshire, New Jersey, and Connecticut, in 1818. [Footnote part of quotation.]

[8] Eight in all. [Footnote part of quotation.]

[9] At the same time the general-ticket system was adopted for Presidential election. . . . In 1828, in the election for the Twenty-Sixth Congress, only New Hampshire, New Jersey, and Georgia adhered to the old method of election by general ticket. [Preceding part of footnote part of quotation.] But in 1842 Missouri also elected its representatives at large (see p. 135).

[10] *Relative to the Right of Members to Their Seats in the House of Representatives*, 28 Cong. 1 sess., H. Rept. 60, Majority Report, p. 2.

491) provided that representatives under that apportionment
"should be elected by districts composed of contiguous territory
equal in number to the representatives to which said state may
be entitled, no one district electing more than one representative."

Both Ames and Woodburn state that the act of 1842 was the
result of a prolonged contest which resulted from a disputed
election in New Jersey in 1839, and which delayed the organization of the House.[11] While that situation may have played some
part in the passage of the act of 1842, there is no reference to it
in the debates, and it seems likely that the act was the result of
the general demand for election by districts.

When President Tyler signed the bill he filed in the State
Department his reasons for so doing.[12] After commenting on the
apportionment he made the following statement regarding the
districting requirement:

One of the prominent features of the bill is that which purports to
be mandatory on the States to form districts for the choice of Representatives to Congress, in single districts. That Congress itself has
power by law to alter State regulations respecting the manner of holding elections for Representatives is clear, but its power to command
the States to make new regulations or alter their existing regulations
is the question upon which I have felt deep and strong doubts. I have
yielded those doubts, however, to the opinion of the Legislature, giving effect to their enactment as far as depends on my approbation,
and leaving questions which may arise hereafter, if unhappily such
should arise, to be settled by full consideration of the several provisions of the Constitution and the laws and the authority of each House
to judge of the elections, returns, and qualifications of its own members.[13]

When the President informed the House that he had filed his
reasons with the State Department, John Quincy Adams "spoke
at great length on the dangerous precedent that must be thus
set."[14] Unfortunately the Globe does not give even a digest of

[11] Ames, *Proposed Amendments*, p. 57; James A. Woodburn, *The American Republic*,
p. 248.
[12] *Cong. Globe*, 27 Cong. 2 sess., p. 688.
[13] James D. Richardson, *Messages and Papers of the Presidents*, Paper of June 25,
1842; 27 Cong. 2 sess., H. Doc. 258.
[14] *Cong. Globe*, 27 Cong. 2 sess., p. 688.

Adams' remarks, but his opinions are doubtless expressed in the 12-page report, made on July 16, 1842, of the select committee appointed on his motion to consider the action of the President. In view of later expressions of presidential opinion the report is particularly interesting. It concludes as follows:

The committee consider the act of the President, notified by him to the House of Representatives in his message of the 25th ultimo, as unauthorized by the Constitution and laws of the United States, pernicious in its immediate operation, and imminently dangerous in its tendencies. They believe it to be the duty of the House to protest against it, and to place upon their journal an earnest remonstrance against its ever being again repeated. They report, therefore, the following resolution:

Resolved, That the House of Representatives consider the act of the President of the United States, notified to them by his message of the 25th ultimo, viz: his causing to be deposited in the office of the Secretary of State, with the act of Congress entitled "An act for an apportionment of Representatives among the several States according to the sixth census," approved and signed by him, an exposition of his reasons for giving to the said act his sanction, as unwarranted by the Constitution and laws of the United States, injurious to the public interest, and of evil example for the future; and this House do hereby solemnly protest against the said act of the President, and against its ever being repeated or adduced as a precedent hereafter.[15]

The House took no action on the resolution, several attempts to call it up under suspension of the rules having failed to receive the necessary two-thirds.

The apportionment act passed after the census of 1850 (9 Stat. L. 433) contained no provision regarding districts. In 1862 an act (12 Stat. L. 572) separate from the apportionment act again revived the provisions of the act of 1842 requiring districts to be composed of contiguous territory, and the act of February 2, 1872 (17 Stat. L. 28) again repeated them and added the further requirement that the districts should contain "as nearly as practicable an equal number of inhabitants." The 1872 act provided that if there were an increase in the quota of any state the additional members might be elected at large.

[15] *Apportionment Bill*, 27 Cong. 2 sess., H. Rept. 909, p. 12. The members of the committee were John Quincy Adams, John Pope, T. M. T. McKennan, R. M. T. Hunter, and George H. Proffit.

After the census of 1880 the provisions of the 1872 act regarding districts were repeated (22 Stat. L. 5). Similar requirements were made in the act of February 7, 1891 (26 Stat. L. 735). In the act of January 16, 1901 (31 Stat. L. 733) the words "compact territory" were added, and the clause read "contiguous and compact territory and containing as nearly as practicable an equal number of inhabitants." The 1901 requirement was repeated in the act of August 8, 1911 (37 Stat. L. 13). There was no apportionment act after the census of 1920 and the permanent act of June 18, 1929 (46 Stat. L. 13) contained no provision for compactness, contiguity, or equality in population, and the Supreme Court held that these requirements "did not outlast the apportionment to which they related,"[16] namely, the one made after the census of 1910. The act of April 25, 1940 (54 Stat. L. 162), which amended the act of 1929, likewise contained no such requirements. Therefore at present there is no federal law applying to the configuration or population of congressional districts.

Results of Congressional Control over State Apportionment

Except in so far as the laws cited on the preceding pages may have had a moral influence, their effect has been nil. The House of Representatives has not attempted to enforce compliance. Some of the district federal courts have declared state apportionment acts unconstitutional, only to have their decisions reversed because the applicable act was held to be no longer in force.

At the election following the passage of the act of 1842, four states—New Hampshire, Georgia, Mississippi, and Missouri—failed to elect by districts. When the House was organized on December 4, 1843 objection was raised to seating the members from these states. As the clerk declined to entertain a motion to exclude them, the members were sworn in. Later a resolution directed the Committee of Elections to report upon whether the several members had been elected in conformity with law.[17]

[16] *Wood* v. *Broom*, 287 U.S. 8 (1932).
[17] Asher C. Hinds, *Precedents of the House of Representatives*, Vol. 1, p. 170.

The majority report, made by Stephen A. Douglas, chairman of the committee, held that the act of 1842 was not binding upon the states and that the members were entitled to their seats; the minority report made by Garrett Davis of Kentucky held that the members from the states in question had not been elected according to the Constitution and the laws, and were not entitled to their seats.[18]

The report was debated in the House from February 6 to 14. An amendment to the majority report in the nature of a substitute omitted all reference to the apportionment law, but declared that the members from the four states were entitled to their seats, having been duly elected.[19] Thus the House did not pass upon the question directly, but in effect overruled it by ignoring it.

The earliest congressional directory at the Public Documents Library—that for the first session of the 30th Congress, 1848—shows that the representatives of the four states concerned in the case cited were elected by districts. Thereafter the practice of electing by districts became universal, except where no redistricting had been done after a state's quota was reduced, as in the case of North Dakota, which after the census of 1930 did not pass a districting act after its quota had been reduced.

The next case involving the power of Congress to regulate districts was that of *Davison* v. *Gilbert* in 1901. It was claimed that a Kentucky act changing the boundaries of districts was contrary to the act of January 16, 1901. A House committee again held that the act giving Congress power over districts was not

---

[18] *Relative to the Rights of Members to Their Seats in the House of Representatives,* 28 Cong. 1 sess., H. Rept. 60; D. W. Bartlett, *Cases of Contested Elections in Congress from 1834 to 1865, Inclusive,* 38 Cong. 2 sess., H. Misc. Doc. 57, pp. 47–69; Chester H. Rowell, *Historical and Legal Digest of Contested Election Cases in the House of Representatives . . . 1789–1901,* 56 Cong. 2 sess., H. Doc. 510, pp. 603–06. Abstracts of the two reports are given in Hinds' *Precedents of the House of Representatives,* Vol. 1, pp. 171–72. The other members signing the minority report were Willoughby Newton of Virginia and Robert C. Schenck of Ohio. The members not signing the minority report, in addition to the chairman, were Lucius Q. C. Elmer of New Jersey, Reuben Chapman of Alabama, Hannibal Hamlin of Maine, Chesselden Ellis of New York, and Aaron V. Brown of Tennessee.

[19] *Cong. Globe,* 28 Cong. 1 sess., pp. 235–36, 241–42, 248–50, 252–60, 264–65, 276–80.

binding on the states, the report concluding as follows:

> Your committee are therefore of opinion that a proper construction of the Constitution does not warrant the conclusion that by that instrument Congress is clothed with power to determine the boundaries of Congressional districts, or to revise the acts of a State Legislature in fixing such boundaries; and your committee is further of opinion that even if such power is to be implied from the language of the Constitution, it would be in the last degree unwise and intolerable that it should exercise it. To do so would be to put into the hands of Congress the ability to disfranchise, in effect, a large body of the electors. It would give Congress the power to apply to all the States, in favor of one party, a general system of gerrymandering. It is true that the same method is to a large degree resorted to by the several States, but the division of political power is so general and diverse that notwithstanding the inherent vice of the system of gerrymandering, some kind of equality of distribution results.[20]

The House took no action, and consequently the sitting member retained his seat.

In 1910 the last case that has claimed the attention of Congress arose in connection with a Virginia act of 1908 which transferred Floyd County from the fifth to the sixth district, making the population of the fifth district 160,191 and of the sixth 196,959. The average for the state was 185,418. Previously the population of the fifth district was 175,579, and that of the sixth was 181,571.

The majority of the committee held that the Virginia act of 1908 was null and void as it did not conform to the act of January 16, 1901 or the constitution of Virginia, and that the district should be regarded as having the counties included in it before the Virginia act of 1908. This gave the contestant a majority of the votes, and the committee recommended that the contestant be seated.[21]

A contrary view was held by the minority of the committee, which made a lengthy report, based in part on *Davison* v. *Gil-*

---

[20] *Davison* v. *Gilbert*, 56 Cong. 2 sess., H. Rept. 3000, p. 4.

[21] *Contested Election Case of Parsons vs. Saunders*, 61 Cong. 2 sess., H. Rept. 1695, 10 pp.; Merrill Moores, *Historical and Legal Digest of . . . Contested Election Cases in the House of Representatives . . . 1901–1917*, 64 Cong. 2 sess., H. Doc. 2052, pp. 43–49.

bert, cited above, and containing a review of the power of Congress over apportionment.[22]

The House took no action on the reports and the contestant was not seated.

In 1932 the state districting acts in Mississippi and Kentucky were held to be invalid by the lower federal courts on the ground that they were contrary to the provisions of the act of August 8, 1911.[23] Both decisions were reversed by the Supreme Court on the ground that the act of August 8, 1911 was no longer in force.[24]

EXISTING FEDERAL LAW ON STATE DISTRICTING

If the doctrine of *stare decisis* has any validity the following principles seem to be established at the present time.

If there is no change in the quota of a state the existing districts continue until new ones are created by the legislature.[25]

If the quota is increased and there is no redistricting the existing districts remain the same, and the additional members are elected at large.[25]

If the quota is reduced and there is no redistricting, all members are elected at large.[25]

If a state constitution confers the veto power on the governor as regards ordinary legislation, a districting act must be approved by the governor or passed over his veto in the manner provided by the state constitution.[26]

If the state constitution provides for a referendum on legislation, a districting act may be repealed by a referendum in the same manner as other laws.[27]

The requirements of section 3 of the act of August 8, 1911 (37

[22] *Parsons* vs. *Saunders*, 61 Cong. 2 sess., H. Rept. 1695, Pt. 2, 24 pp. For testimony, much of which does not relate to apportionment but applies to irregularities, see House of Representatives, *Contested Election Case of John U. Parsons* vs. *Edward Saunders . . .* , 1909, 666 pp. The arguments of counsel are given in House of Representatives, Elections Committee No. 2, *Contested Election Case of John U. Parsons v. Edward W. Saunders . . . Arguments of Counsel*, 1910, 224 pp.

[23] Mississippi: *Wood v. Broom*, 1 Fed. Supp. 134; Kentucky: *Mahan v. Hume*, 1 Fed. Supp. 149.

[24] *Wood v. Broom*, 287 U.S. 8; *Mahan v. Hume*, 287 U.S. 575.

[25] *Smiley* v. *Holm*, 285 U.S. 374.

[26] The same, p. 373.

[27] *Davis v. Ohio*, 241 U.S. 568.

Stat. L. 14), requiring districts to be composed of compact and contiguous territory and to contain as nearly as practicable an equal number of inhabitants, are no longer in force, as they expired with the apportionment made under that act.[28]

No categorical answer may be given to the question whether Congress has power to set aside a state districting act or to define the boundaries of districts. This question will be discussed below in the consideration of the remedies for existing unsatisfactory conditions.

PREVENTION OF UNFAIR DISTRICTING IN THE STATES

What can be done to correct the evil of inequitable districting? Obviously the most satisfactory solution is an aggressive public opinion that will force the state legislatures to take proper action. In addition to the exigencies of practical politics one of the impediments to fair districting is the tradition in most states that district boundaries must follow county lines. The tradition has been recognized by the Supreme Court of Appeals of Virginia, which has stated:

These variations [in population of districts] will necessarily be augmented where, as in Virginia, it has been the unbroken custom to refrain from dividing any county or city into separate districts. From the early history of Virginia, even in Colonial days, the community of interest in the respective counties has been recognized, and in no division of the state for any governmental purpose has any county line been broken.[29]

In the metropolitan districts the counties have necessarily been divided among several districts. The boundaries of districts in Maine and Massachusetts did not follow county lines as early as 1848. In Massachusetts, Connecticut, and New Hampshire, at present the district boundaries do not follow county lines, even outside the metropolitan districts. In Maine the exterior limits of the districts are coterminous with county lines, but the apportionment made after the census of 1930 was an equitable one. While the Virginia court, in the decision quoted above, was undoubtedly correct in speaking of the "unbroken custom to re-

[28] *Wood* v. *Broom*, 287 U. S. 6.
[29] *Brown* v. *Saunders*, 166 S.E. 107.

frain from dividing any city or county," it is not believed that a county presents any such unity or that areas in separate counties have such divergencies as to warrant the inequalities in population that exist.

It should not be assumed that all bad apportionments are due to adherence to county lines, and that all good ones disregard county boundaries. A Virginia districting act of 1932 was declared unconstitutional by the Supreme Court of Appeals of Virginia because of inequalities in population,[30] but the succeeding act of 1934, in which the boundaries of districts also followed county lines, is an equitable one, as the maximum departure from the average is only 13.1 per cent. On the other hand, in Michigan, where the city of Detroit is divided among several districts, the population of one is 32.9 per cent above the average.

Another factor which has had a potent influence in promoting inequalities is the custom of confining the election of a representative to residents of the several districts. A redistricting act seldom fixes the boundaries of districts so that a sitting member will have his residence in a district adjoining the one he previously represented. Residence in the district is not required by the Constitution, the only constitutional requirement being residence within the state. Occasionally a representative is not a resident of the district he represents, but such instances are few and far between.

Obviously no federal legislation can require states to ignore county lines or to elect a member who is not a resident of the district he represents. Both of these things may be done now, and are done occasionally. The extension of these practices depends on vigorous and enlightened public opinion in the states.

If the states will not act to correct the inequalities, what legal steps may be taken? After the census of 1840 and after each census from 1870 to 1910 the apportionment acts provided for equalization of population, and in some cases for compact and contiguous territory. Under none of these acts has there been a final test of validity. In one case the House of Representatives

[30] See p. 180.

voted to ignore the act without passing directly on the question; in two cases the House took no action; and in one case taken to the Supreme Court the court held that the law was no longer in effect.[31]

With any statute requiring equalization there arises the question of enforcement. Manifestly the legislature of a state cannot be forced to pass a districting act by mandamus or other court proceedings.

None of the equalization statutes heretofore in effect contained any provision for enforcement. Two methods were available, and both have been made use of, but, as shown, without effect. One is to challenge the right of the returned members to their seats; the other is court action to have the state districting act declared invalid. If the matter is thrown into the House the question will probably be decided by a party vote. In either event the unseating of the returned representatives creates vacancies and leaves the state without representation for the time being.

Paragraph (c) of the bill introduced in 1939 (H. R. 5099, 76 Cong.) provides that if the population of the largest district exceeds that of the smallest by more than 50 per cent, "all members of Congress [representatives] from that state shall be elected at large until new districts conforming to the above requirement shall be established." The proposed statute is silent as to method of enforcement, and as to who shall institute proceedings.

When the districting is made the census figures will show whether it conforms to the congressional mandate, but how can it be challenged, and if the districting is upset when will the election of representatives at large take effect?

It has been suggested that any citizen of a state can sue, but this right is by no means clear. In the Mississippi case of *Wood* v. *Broom*, involving compliance with the act of August 8, 1911, and decided in 1932, the complainant was a citizen of the state, a qualified elector, and qualified to be a candidate for the House of Representatives. The defendant moved to dismiss for want

[31] See p. 162.

of equity, but the Supreme Court held that in view of the fact that the act under which relief was sought was no longer in effect, it was unnecessary to consider the question of equity or the justiciability of the controversy. "Upon these questions the court expresses no opinion." However, four of the justices were of the opinion that the decree should be reversed and the bill dismissed for want of equity.[32]

Of course the question may be raised in the House of Representatives, but it is desirable to make the controversy a justiciable one, and the right to sue should be specifically conferred.

If a districting act is declared invalid either by the courts or by the House of Representatives, the state involved will be without representation until the next election. In order to avoid the expense of a special primary and a special election, or prevent vacancies in the House, it may be desirable to provide that the returned members shall hold their seats until a date not later than that of the next regular election.

A more vital objection to paragraph (c) of H. R. 5099 is the provision that if the state apportionment does not meet the requirement, all members from the state concerned shall be elected at large until new districts conforming to the requirement are established. This wipes out all representation by a minority in one section of the state, and resurrects the evils that the districting act of 1842 sought to eradicate. If the proposed rule were applied to New York, which has 45 representatives, it would involve the placing of at least 90 names on the ballot, with additional names for any third party candidates. Such a large number of names would probably preclude the use of voting machines, and with a printed ballot even the most intelligent voter would have difficulty.

Would the threat of election at large be an incentive to the states to district equitably? In some states the local machine might welcome the election at large. If one party has secure control of the state as a whole, with only a few districts represented by the minority party, the election at large would ensure a solid delegation. Even in states where the outcome of state-

---

[32] *Wood* v. *Broom*, 287 U.S. 8.

wide voting is in doubt, the politicians of both parties might be tempted to gamble on the result. The stake would be high, but the winnings would be correspondingly great.

If a state will not meet the requirements of federal law, and if the election of members at large is not a desirable remedy, what other methods are available? In 1921 it was proposed that if a state failed to redistrict, the governor, the secretary of state, and the attorney general should fix the boundaries.[33] But districting is not an executive function, and there is no assurance that the specified officers would act or make an equitable distribution. The task certainly cannot be assigned to the courts; their duty begins when the validity of an act is questioned, and it ends when a decision on that question is reached.

The most satisfactory remedy in case of lack of action or compliance by the state seems to be to have the districting done by Congress. The reports and files of the Bureau of the Census contain all the statistical and geographical material necessary for districting. This material and the personnel of the Bureau are available to assist Congress and its committees in the work. Any additional data may be obtained by public hearings.

Congress, of course, is swayed by political considerations, and it might be said that if Congress did the districting the gerrymandering would be simply transferred from the states to Washington. There is this danger, but it seems less imminent in the capital than elsewhere, not necessarily because political ethics are higher, but by reason of the greater publicity and better printed recording of proceedings and the arguments of proponents. As a rule state legislatures operate under a veil. Neither the hearings nor the debates are published, and it is only through the newspapers that the public may ascertain what is going on. What appears in the papers depends on the alertness and industry of the reporters and on the amount of other news competing for space. In Congress the debates in the Congressional Record and the published hearings indicate the supporters of proposed legislation.

It may be said that Congress might not act. This is a possi-

[33] *Cong. Record*, 67 Cong. 1 sess., Vol. 61, Pt. 6, p. 6340.

bility, as there is no way to compel a legislative body to take action. Even if this happened the conditions would not be any worse than at present.

It is not proposed that Congress should define the districts in the first instance, but should act only when the states do not, or when the state law does not meet the federal requirement. If Congress should prescribe the districts the state should be allowed to revise the boundaries of the districts, and the later state law should prevail, provided it meets the requirements. This will prevent federal domination, as the state will always have the last word if it districts fairly and equitably.

Wherever power is lodged to declare a state districting act invalid, care should be taken that the state is not left entirely without representation until a new act becomes effective. As stated above, provision should be made that the returned members should retain their seats until a new act is passed.

Has Congress power over the districting in the states? If it has it does not arise from clause 3 of section 2 of Article 1 of the Constitution relating to apportionment, but from clause 1 of section 4 of Article 1, which reads as follows:

The time, places and manner of holding elections for Senators and Representatives, shall be prescribed in each state by the Legislature thereof; but the Congress may at any time by law make or alter such regulations, except as to the places of chusing Senators.

Does the power to make regulations regarding "manner of holding elections" include the power to make rules regarding a state apportionment or to define the districts if the states do not conform to the rules? The authorities are not in agreement; the Supreme Court has not ruled directly on the subject, and it is difficult to draw conclusions from cases indirectly bearing on it.

Congress has never attempted to district a state and has never invalidated a state districting act, although it has at various times prescribed that the districts must be approximately equal in population. The authorities differ as to the power of Congress. President Tyler, when he signed the act of 1842 requiring districting, expressed doubts as to its constitutionality.[34] Committees of which Stephen A. Douglas and Daniel Webster were chairmen emphatically denied any such power to Congress.[35] These reports are generally ascribed to Douglas and Webster, and probably correctly so. The Webster report, which is often quoted, includes the following statement:

Whether the subdivision of the representative power within any State, if there be a subdivision, be equal or unequal, or fairly or unfairly made, Congress can not know, and has no authority to inquire. It is enough that the State presents her own representation on the floor of Congress in the mode she chooses to present it. If a State were to give to one portion of her territory, a representative for every twenty-five thousand persons, and to the rest a representative only for every fifty thousand, it would be an act of unjust legislation, doubtless, but it would be wholly beyond redress by any power in Congress; because the Constitution has left all this to the State itself.[36]

House committees have both upheld and denied the power, but in each case there has been a minority report maintaining the opposing premise.[37] In considering the conclusions of the committees, weight must be given to the political background in each case, but the reports state the reasons for the conclusions.

The Supreme Court has never ruled on the power of Congress in this matter. Two cases from the district courts in Mississippi and Kentucky, holding the state districting acts invalid as being contrary to the act of August 8, 1911, were reversed on the

[34] See p. 133.

[35] The Douglas report was entitled "Relative to the Rights of Members to Their Seats in the House of Representatives," and was issued as House Report 60, 28 Cong. 1 sess. The Webster report was entitled "Report of Select Committee," and was issued as Senate Document 119, 22 Cong. 1 sess.

[36] *Report of Select Committee,* 22 Cong. 1 sess., S. Doc. 119, p. 9. The members of the committee, in addition to Webster, were John M. Clayton, John Forsyth, Willie P. Mangum, and Robert Y. Hayne.

[37] For reports of committees, see the following: In 1844—[*Report*] *Relative to the Rights of Members to Their Seats in the House of Representatives,* 28 Cong. 1 sess., H. Rept. 60; D. W. Bartlett, *Cases of Contested Election in Congress from 1834 to 1865, Inclusive,* 38 Cong. 2 sess., pp. 47–49; Chester H. Rowell, *Historical and Legal Digest of Contested Election Cases in the House of Representatives . . . 1789–1901,* 56 Cong. 2 sess., H. Doc. 510, pp. 603–06; Hinds' *Precedents of the House of Representatives,* Vol. 1, pp. 171–72. In 1901—*Davison vs. Gilbert,* 56 Cong. 2 sess., H. Rept. 3000. In 1910—[*Contested Election case of*] *Parsons vs. Saunders,* 61 Cong. 2 sess., H. Rept. 1695; Merrill Moores, *Historical and Legal Digest of Contested Election Cases in the House of Representatives, 1901–1917,* 64 Cong. 2 sess., H. Doc. 2052, pp. 43–49.

ground that the act was no longer in effect.[38]

In 1884 in considering the power of Congress over elections the Supreme Court said:

> This section [the fourth of the first article] declares that: "The times, places, and manner of holding elections for senators and representatives shall be prescribed in each state by the legislature thereof; but the Congress may at any time make or alter such regulations, except as to the place of choosing senators."

> It was not until 1842 that Congress took any action under the power here conferred, when conceiving that the system of electing all the members of the House of Representatives from a state by general ticket, as it was called, that is, every elector voting for as many names as the state was entitled to representatives in that house, worked injustice to other states which did not adopt that system, and gave an undue preponderance of power to the political party which had a majority of the votes in the state, however small, enacted that each member should be elected by a separate district, composed of contiguous territory. 5 Stat. 49.[39]

There was no intimation that the act of 1842 or later acts were unconstitutional.

It was held in 1921 that the federal corrupt practices did not extend to primary elections. In an opinion concurring in part, Justice Pitney, who was joined by Justices Brandeis and Clarke, made the following statement:

> It is said that section 4 of Article 1 does not confer a general power to regulate elections, but only to regulate "the manner of holding" them. But this can mean nothing less than the entire mode of procedure—the essence, not merely the form, of conducting elections. The only specific grant of power over the subject contained in the Constitution is contained in that section; and the power is conferred primarily upon the legislatures of the several states, but subject to revision and modification by Congress.

> . . . .

> For if this section of the Constitution is to be strictly construed with respect to the power granted to Congress thereunder, it must be construed with equal strictness with respect to the power conferred upon the states. . . . For the election of Senators and Representatives in Congress is a federal function; whatever the states do in the matter

---

[38] *Wood* v. *Broom,* 287 U.S. 8; *Mahan* v. *Hume,* 287 U.S. 575.
[39] *Ex parte Yarbrough,* 110 U.S. 660.

they do under authority derived from the Constitution of the United States.[40]

On the implied powers of Congress, the Supreme Court has spoken in no uncertain terms. In 1884, it said:

The proposition that it [the United States] has no such power is supported by the old argument often heard, often repeated, and in this court never assented to, that when a question of the power of Congress arises, the advocate of the power must be able to place his finger on words which expressly grant it. The brief of counsel before us, though directed to the authority of that body to pass criminal laws, uses the same language. Because there is no *express* power to provide for violence exercised on the voter as a means of controlling his vote, no such law can be enacted. It destroys at one blow, in construing the Constitution, the doctrine universally applied to all instruments of writing, that what is implied is as much a part of the instrument as what is expressed. This principle, in its application to the Constitution of the United States, more than to almost any other writing, is a necessity, by reason of inherent inability to put into words all derivative powers—a difficulty which the instrument itself recognizes by conferring on Congress the authority to pass all laws necessary and proper to carry into execution the powers expressly granted and all other powers vested in the government or any branch of it by the Constitution. Article 1, sec. 8, clause 18.[41]

Again in 1921 we find the court spoke as follows:

As an incident to the grant [of the power to regulate the manner of holding elections] there is, of course, power to make all laws which shall be necessary and proper for carrying it into effect. Art. 1, sec. 8, cl. 18.[42]

This summary of the powers of Congress may be closed by a quotation from a discussion by Professor Bowman:[43]

. . . So, today it is clear that the Constitution contemplates representation of the states according to population. It would not be very fanciful to deduce from this a principle of representation among the districts into which the states are divided.

. . . .

[40] *Newberry v. United States,* 256 U.S. 280.
[41] *Ex parte Yarbrough,* 110 U.S. 658.
[42] *Newberry v. United States,* 256 U.S. 256.
[43] Harold M. Bowman, "Congressional Redistricting and the Constitution," *Michigan Law Review,* Vol. 31, pp. 170–74, 176, 177, 178.

State courts, construing and applying state constitutional provisions, have spoken in no uncertain terms. . . .[44]

. . . .

It is not necessary to elaborate this point. Courts have described the rights as "sacred" and the duty of officers to apportion so as to confer equality of representation as no less "sacred."[45]

Nor would it be at all unreasonable to spell out of the Fourteenth Amendment in like manner a duty of state authorities to apportion so as to confer equality of representation.

. . . .

In the case of *Ex Parte Siebold*[46] . . . [decided in 1879] the Supreme Court had said: "Congress has partially regulated the subject heretofore. In 1842, it passed a law for the election of representatives by separate districts; and, subsequently, other laws fixing the time of election, and directing that the elections shall be by ballot. *No one will pretend, at least at the present day, that these laws are unconstitutional because they only partially cover the subject.*"[47]

Today it is possible to say with confidence that the source of whatever power Congress has in this regard is to be found in Article I, section 4, and to say with hardly less confidence that the provisions of the Act of 1911 and preceding acts concerning districting were all of them constitutional. The decision in *Davis* v. *Ohio*,[48] rendered in 1916, seems conclusive on these points, a conclusion strongly reinforced by the decision in *Smiley* v. *Holm*.[49]

But what is the extent of the power of Congress? How much farther might it go than it has gone in control of redistricting? May Congress itself redistrict the State, and, if it attempts to do so, must it, for example, create districts that are equal in population as far as is practicable?

. . . .

Finally we again refer to *Smiley* v. *Holm*,[50] the latest expression of the Supreme Court on this subject:

. . . .

"In exercising this power the Congress may supplement these state

---

[44] Cases quoted: *Attorney General* v. *Suffolk County Commissioners*, 113 N.E. 584; *Giddings* v. *Blacker*, 52 N.W. 946.

[45] *State* v. *Cunningham*, 51 N.W. 729, quoted with approval in the state ex rel. *Lamb* v. *Cunningham*, 53 N.W. 55 [footnote part of quotation].

[46] 100 U.S. 371 at 384, 25 L. ed. 717 at 722 (1880). [Footnote part of quotation.]

[47] The italics are the present writer's. [Footnote part of quotation.]

[48] 241 U.S. 565, 36 Sup. Ct. 708, 60 L. ed. 1172 (1916). [Footnote part of quotation.]

[49] 285 U.S. 355, 52 Sup. Ct. 397 (1932). [Footnote part of quotation.]

[50] 285 U.S. 355, 52 Sup. Ct. 397 (1932). [Footnote part of quotation.]

regulations or may substitute its own. It may impose additional penalties for the violation of the state laws or provide independent sanctions. It 'has a general supervisory power over the whole subject.'"

It may be said that these statements of the Supreme Court fall short of a direct declaration that Congress itself may create congressional districts within a State. But the broad statements made in *Ex parte Yarbrough*, *Davis* v. *Ohio*, and *Smiley* v. *Holm*, are made in connection with the very subject of districting or redistricting. Do the words, found in several of these cases, that it has a "general supervisory power" in the premises, import any limitations? It seems not; especially as it is expressly declared that Congress may "substitute its own" regulations for those of the State if it sees fit to do so.

Conclusions drawn from previous decisions of the Supreme Court are now more precarious than when the statement above was written in 1932, but if Congress does not have the power to correct the districting made by the states, the matter is of sufficient importance to warrant a constitutional amendment.

CONDITIONS IN THE SEVERAL STATES

The following pages contain brief reviews of the apportionment situation in the several states. Figures are given for the maximum deviations above and below the average population of the districts. The average in each case is the total population divided by the number of districts. If members are elected at large, the average is the population divided by the number of representatives elected by districts, as the voters in each district have a share in the representative at large. If the total number of representatives were taken as the divisor the average would be smaller; the deviation above the average would be more than indicated and the deviation below would be less. The population of each district and its departure from the average for the state are given in the table on pages 183–92.

Quotas of the several states are those in effect in 1940, and apply to the districting after the census of 1930. Population figures are those of the census of 1930, unless figures for earlier censuses are indicated. Preliminary population figures for 1940 are given on pages 183–92, for all districts comprising complete counties. As this volume goes to press figures for districts since

civil divisions smaller than the counties are not available. All population figures are for the total population, and take no account of Indians not taxed, as these figures are not available for districts. The terms "largest" and "smallest" as applied to districts indicate population, and not area.

Comments on the factors which have affected the districting are included if they are available. Persons familiar with conditions in a particular state will probably recognize the political considerations which have been potent in determining the configuration of districts. A detailed discussion of such factors would unduly extend the present volume even if the information were readily available. Studies of apportionment conditions in each state since 1789 would be desirable additions to the literature on the subject.

Maps showing the boundaries of the districts in each state have been printed at the end of each issue of the Congressional Directory during recent years. The boundaries of the several districts are given in detail in the biographical section at the beginning of the Congressional Directory.

Alabama. The quota of Alabama was reduced from 10 to 9 members by the apportionment after the census of 1930, and the new districts were established by the act of February 25, 1931.[51] The population of six of the nine districts is below the average for the state, the percentages ranging from 4.0 to 19.6. Three districts are above the average, the percentages being 1.2, 12.5, and 46.8. The most populous district—the ninth— consists of only Jefferson County, which includes Birmingham, the largest city. This district has a population of 431,493, the city alone having a population of 259,678, which is larger than one other district—the seventh. The second largest district, with a population 12.5 per cent above the average, is the second, which includes the city of Montgomery, the third largest city, with a population of 66,079. The second largest city, Mobile, with a population of 68,202, is in the first district, which has a population 7.3 per cent below the average.

---

[51] General Laws . . . of Alabama, 1931, p. 98; 1936 Cumulative Supplement to the Alabama Code of 1928, p. 30.

Arizona. As Arizona has been entitled to only one representative there has been no problem of districting. However, Arizona will be entitled to two representatives under the census of 1940.

Arkansas. The last change in the quota of Arkansas was made after the census of 1900, and the act of May 23, 1901 is the latest prescribing the boundaries of districts.[52] The population of the several districts ranges from 35.6 per cent less than the average to 45.7 per cent more than the average.

Unlike many states, the district having the greatest excess in population is not the one containing the largest city. Little Rock, with a population of 81,679, is in the fifth district, which has a population only 5.2 per cent larger than the average for the state.

The existing apportionment was an equitable one when it was made in 1901. At that time the population of the largest district was only 4.8 per cent in excess of the average and that of the smallest 5.3 per cent below. The excess of the largest district over the average was 29.7 per cent in 1910, 32.0 per cent in 1920, and 45.7 per cent in 1930. The population of the smallest district was 11.6 per cent below the average in 1910, 28.0 per cent below in 1920, and 35.6 per cent in 1930. The population of the several districts at the censuses since the districts were established is shown in the accompanying table.

POPULATION OF DISTRICTS IN ARKANSAS, CENSUSES OF 1900 TO 1930

District	1900	1910	1920	1930
Average.....	187,366	196,806	250,315	264,926
1.......	180,790	255,301	330,292	385,965
2.......	184,492	208,890	220,544	218,596
3.......	177,396	174,019	180,348	170,576
4.......	191,752	225,774	238,685	230,259
5.......	190,333	233,776	262,862	278,663
6.......	196,292	243,649	273,850	289,250
7.......	190,509	233,040	245,623	281,173
Total.......	1,311,564	1,574,449	1,752,204	1,854,482

California. The constitutional provision governing apportionment in California is as follows:

Sec. 27. When a congressional district shall be composed of two or

---

[52] Acts . . . of Arkansas, 1901, pp. 274–75. Digest of the Statutes of Arkansas; Vol. 1, 1937, by Walter L. Pope, pp. 699–700.

more counties, it shall not be separated by any county belonging to
another district. No county, or city and county, shall be divided in
forming a congressional district so as to attach one portion of a county,
or city and county, to another county, or city and county, except in
cases where one county, or city and county, has more population than
the ratio required for one or more congressmen; but the Legislature
may divide any county, or city and county, into as many congressional districts as it may be entitled to by law. Any county, or city and
county, containing a population greater than the number required for
one congressional district shall be formed into one or more congressional districts, according to the population thereof, and any residue,
after forming such district or districts, shall be attached by compact
adjoining Assembly districts, to a contiguous county or counties, and
form a congressional district. In dividing a county, or city and county, into congressional districts no Assembly district shall be divided
so as to form a part of more than one congressional district, and every
such congressional district shall be composed of compact contiguous
Assembly districts.[53]

The present apportionment was fixed by the act of April 22,
1931.[54] The districts range in population from 23.2 per cent
above the average to 41.7 per cent below. The district having
the smallest population—the second—has the greatest area,
extending about 700 miles along the Nevada boundary with a
varying width. The district with the largest population—the
thirteenth—forms part of Los Angeles County.

There is likewise considerable variation in the population of
adjacent districts. In Los Angeles County the population of the
largest district is 54.0 per cent more than that of the smallest
district.

Colorado. The constitution of Colorado, adopted when the
state had only one representative, contains the following provision: "When a new apportionment shall be made by Congress
the General Assembly shall divide the State into congressional
districts accordingly."[55]

While there was no new apportionment after the census of
1920, the boundaries of the Colorado districts were changed by

---

[53] Const. (1879), Art. IV, sec. 27.
[54] Statutes of California, 1931, pp. 297–98; Deering's Political Code of the State of
California, 1937, sec. 117, p. 49.
[55] Const. (1876), Art. V, sec. 44.

the act of April 7, 1921.[56] No later changes have been made. The population of the largest district is 17.2 per cent above the average, and that of the smallest is 45.3 per cent below. Colorado has had four representatives beginning with the apportionment made after the census of 1910, and under each act, the fourth district, which at present includes—roughly speaking—the portion of the state west of the Rocky Mountains and which comprises 41 per cent of the area of the state, has had a materially lower population.

The population of the districts at the last three censuses is indicated in the accompanying table.

POPULATION OF DISTRICTS IN COLORADO, CENSUSES OF 1910 TO 1930

District	1910	1920	1930
Average.......	194,756	234,907	258,948
1.........	213,381	256,491	287,861
2.........	222,730	261,436	302,946
3.........	228,444	281,170	303,442
4.........	134,469	140,532	141,542
Total.........	799,024	939,629	1,035,791

Connecticut. The apportionment in Connecticut really harks back to the act of September 19, 1911,[57] which fixed the boundaries of the existing five districts, but which is superseded by an act of 1931,[58] which provided that the additional representative to which the state was entitled after the census of 1930 should be elected at large. The 1931 act then proceeded to define the five districts as they were before. This was unnecessary legislation as the additional member would have been elected at large if the act had not been passed.

The population of the districts ranges from 24.9 per cent below the average to 31.0 per cent above. When the apportionment was made in 1911, the population of the largest district was 12.2 per cent above the average and that of the smallest was 14.6 per cent below. By 1920 the population of the largest district was 21.7 per cent above the average and that of the smallest was 18.7 per cent below. The population of the several

[56] Laws, 1921, p. 170; 1935 Colorado Statutes, Annotated, Vol. 2, sec. 9, p. 56.
[57] Public Acts ... Connecticut, 1911, p. 1570.
[58] Public Acts ... Connecticut, 1931, p. 28.

the apportionment has been applicable is shown in the accompanying table.

POPULATION OF DISTRICTS IN CONNECTICUT, CENSUSES OF 1910 TO 1930

District	1910	1920	1930
Average.......	222,951	276,126	321,381
1.........	250,182	336,027	421,097
2.........	211,710	232,192	253,099
3.........	217,139	267,050	304,736
4.........	245,322	320,936	386,702
5.........	190,403	224,426	241,269
Total.........	1,114,756	1,380,631	1,606,903

Delaware. There are no districts in Delaware as that state is entitled to only one representative.

Florida. The boundaries of congressional districts in Florida were last established by the act of May 28, 1935.[59] The population of the districts ranges from 17.1 per cent below the average to 33.1 per cent above.

Georgia. The latest districting act of Georgia is that of August 25, 1931.[60] The population of the districts ranges from 42.4 per cent above the average to 24.9 per cent below. The district with the largest population (414,313) is the fifth, which includes the city of Atlanta with a population of 270,366; it includes two counties in addition to the one in which Atlanta is located. The average population per district is 290,851.

Idaho. The present boundaries of the districts in Idaho were fixed by the act of March 13, 1917.[61] The state has only two districts, the variation from the average being 14.8 per cent.

Due to the shifting of population the districting is more equitable than it was in 1920; at that time the variation from the average was 17.4 per cent. No figures are available on the population when the districts were established in 1917. The population of the districts in 1920 and 1930 is shown in the accompanying table.

[59] General Acts . . . of Florida, 1935, Vol. 1, p. 314; Permanent Cumulative Supplement to Compiled General Laws of Florida [1936], Vol. 1, secs. 80–86, p. 31.
[60] Acts . . . of Georgia, 1931, p. 46; Code of Georgia of 1933, Chap. 34-2301, p. 1018.
[61] General Laws of . . . Idaho, 1917, p. 408; Idaho Code, 1932, Vol. 2, Chap. 33-1601–1603, p. 812.

POPULATION OF DISTRICTS IN IDAHO,
CENSUSES OF 1920 AND 1930

District	1920	1930
Average.....	215,943	225,516
1........	178,324	189,576
2........	253,542	255,455
Total.......	431,866	445,031

Illinois. Illinois elects 25 representatives by districts and two at large. As the boundaries of the districts were fixed by the act of May 13, 1901[62] the apportionment is extremely inequitable. The most populous district is 191.4 per cent above the average and the least populous is 54.7 per cent below.

The districts having the extremes in population are either entirely or partly in Chicago. Of the ten districts in the city, three have a population 53 per cent or more below the average for the state, and five have a population 77 per cent or more above; of the five above 77 per cent, two are between 100 and 200 per cent. The districts entirely outside Chicago, with the exception of two near the city and one including East St. Louis, have populations ranging from 4.3 to 48.1 per cent below the average. Outside Chicago the boundaries of the districts follow county lines.

In 1931 the legislature redistricted the state,[63] but the law was held unconstitutional by the Supreme Court of Illinois, which said in part:

An apportionment cannot be sustained when the result is to give the voter in one district vastly more power than is given to a voter in another district, especially where such an inequality extends to a considerable number of districts.[64]

The population of the districts as fixed in the invalid act of 1931 is shown in the table on page 156.

By this proposed apportionment the population of the largest district would have been 91.7 per cent above the average, and that of the smallest district 43.8 per cent below. While the court

[62] Laws of . . . Illinois, 1901, p. 3; Illinois Revised Statutes, 1939, Chap. 46, sec. 154, p. 1433.
[63] Act of July 2, 1931, Laws, 1931, p. 545.
[64] *Moran* v. *Bowley*, 179 N.E. 531.

prevented the application of an inequitable apportionment, the legislature took no further action and an even more inequitable apportionment remained in effect.

POPULATION OF DISTRICTS IN ILLINOIS ACCORDING TO INVALID ACT OF 1931[a]

District	Population	District	Population	District	Population
1........	269,989	10.......	205,074	19.......	268,656
2........	329,759	11.......	322,319	20.......	229,384
3........	311,814	12.......	308,516	21.......	261,408
4.......	232,261	13.......	285,499	22.......	213,154
5.......	541,785	14.......	211,948	23.......	276,521
6.......	273,679	15.......	343,293	24.......	301,605
7.......	311,021	16.......	199,104	25.......	280,854
8.......	285,891	17.......	158,738	26.......	227,827
9.......	309,785	18.......	272,505	27.......	308,365

[a] *Moran* v. *Bowley*, 179 N.E.257. The figures given in the decision add to 7,540,754; the population was 7,630,654.

The apportionment of 1901 was not a good one at that time; the population of the largest district was 48.6 per cent above the average, and that of the smallest was 11.4 per cent below. By 1910 the population of the largest district was 55.1 per cent

POPULATION OF DISTRICTS IN ILLINOIS, CENSUSES OF 1900 TO 1930

District	1900	1910	1920	1930
Average......	192,862	225,544	259,411	305,226
1........	237,701	169,828	167,220	142,916
2........	181,936	279,646	401,585	577,998
3........	186,140	250,328	359,018	540,666
4........	201,870	229,963	240,970	237,139
5........	212,978	192,411	158,092	140,481
6........	196,610	283,148	458,175	632,834
7........	268,163	349,883	560,434	889,349
8........	286,643	236,481	183,031	138,216
9........	220,766	187,013	190,307	209,650
10........	189,552	281,590	408,470	577,261
11........	211,502	242,174	267,694	363,136
12........	218,771	237,162	259,169	292,023
13........	171,622	167,634	170,013	178,198
14........	170,820	180,689	197,952	199,104
15........	213,059	216,884	215,525	213,630
16........	194,243	211,595	224,930	253,713
17........	178,739	176,291	174,545	175,353
18........	209,253	219,425	225,735	225,604
19........	228,896	241,728	256,252	274,137
20........	184,593	175,978	169,292	158,262
21........	177,475	211,614	237,397	233,252
22........	200,470	259,059	290,334	344,666
23........	211,830	233,149	222,960	213,567
24........	190,438	187,279	179,836	161,158
25........	185,721	217,639	266,344	258,341
Total........	4,821,550[a]	5,638,591	6,485,280	7,630,654

[a] This is the correct population, but the figures as reported for the several districts add to 5,129,791.

above the average, and that of the smallest was 25.7 per cent below. After 1920 conditions became progressively worse, the population of the largest district being 116.0 per cent above the average and that of the smallest 39.1 per cent below. The situation after 1930 is described above. The population of the several districts at each census from 1900 to 1930 is shown in the table on page 156.

Indiana. The Indiana apportionment was made by the act of March 10, 1931, as amended by the acts of March 8, 1933 and March 12, 1935.[65] The apportionment is good, the inequities of the act of 1931 being removed by the amendatory acts of 1933 and 1935, both of which applied only to the eleventh and twelfth districts, which include Indianapolis and the surrounding area, the 1935 act superseding the 1933 act. The effect of the amendments is shown in the accompanying table.

POPULATION CHANGES IN DISTRICTS IN INDIANA, 1931–35
(Average population of districts, 269,875)

Act	Eleventh District	Twelfth District
Act of March 10, 1931		
Population..........................	193,671	237.155
Departure from average, per cent.....	−28.6	−12.1
Act of March 8, 1933		
Population..........................	255,898	266,261
Departure from average, per cent.....	−5.2	−1.3
Act of March 12, 1935		
Population..........................	264,926	257,233
Departure from average, per cent......	−1.8	−4.7

At present no district has a population more than 7.2 per cent above the average, or 4.7 per cent below.

Iowa. The constitutional provision governing districts in Iowa is as follows:

Sec. 37. When a congressional, senatorial, or representative district shall be composed of two or more counties, it shall not be entirely separated by any county belonging to another district; and no county shall be divided in forming a congressional, senatorial, or representative district.[66]

---

[65] Laws . . . Indiana . . . , 1931, p. 447; the same, 1933, p. 920; the same, 1935, p. 1256; Baldwin's Indiana Statutes, Annotated, 1934, secs. 4800–4813, p. 1054; Baldwin's Indiana Statutes Service . . . May 1935, secs. 4812–4813, p. 185.

[66] Const. (1857), Art. III, sec. 37.

The boundaries of the districts in Iowa were established by the act of April 10, 1931.[67] The largest district has a population 12.5 per cent above the average, while the smallest district is 12.5 per cent below.

Kansas. The apportionment in Kansas was fixed by the act of March 16, 1931.[68] The population of the districts ranges from 14.4 per cent above the average to 14.7 per cent below.

Kentucky. The present districts in Kentucky were established by an act of 1932 as amended by an act of 1934,[69] neither of which was approved or disapproved by the governor. Kentucky is one of the states whose quota was reduced after the census of 1930, the number of representatives being decreased from 11 to 9. This necessitated redistricting unless the entire delegation was to be elected at large. The 1934 act was confined to the transfer of Shelby County from the fifth to the fourth district.

The population of the largest district is 22.3 per cent above the average, while that of the smallest is 23.4 per cent below. The amendment of 1934 did not improve the districting. It decreased the departure from the average for the fourth district from 17.9 to 11.8 per cent, but increased that for the fifth district from 17.3 to 23.4 per cent.

POPULATION OF DISTRICTS IN KENTUCKY, CENSUSES OF 1920 AND 1930

District	1920	1930	District	1920	1930
Average....	219,694	290,510	7......	205,328	245,598
			8......	168,067	288,108
1......	211,298	238,189	9......	272,725	352,869
2......	196,607	338,117			
3......	192,971	355,350	10......	199,710	—
			11......	289,766	—
4......	207,721	256,173			
5......	286,369	222,614	Total......	2,416,630	2,614,589
6......	186,068	317,571			

The former districting after the census of 1920 was not an equitable one, as the population in the largest district was 31.9 per cent above the average, and that of the smallest was 23.5 per cent below. The population of the several districts after the last two censuses is shown in the table above.

[67] Acts . . . Regular Session . . . , 1931, p. 9; Code of Iowa, 1939, sec. 526.1, p. 134.

[68] Session Laws, 1931, p. 31; General Statutes of Kansas, 1935, secs. 4-105 to 4-112, p. 37.

[69] Acts of . . . Kentucky, 1932, p. 675; the same, 1934, p. 175; Carroll's Kentucky Statutes, Annotated, Baldwin's 1936 Revision, sec. 418a, p. 238.

The political implications of the new apportionment in 1930 have been described as follows:[70]

The recent redistricting [in 1932], it should be observed, has failed to improve the situation. Louisville and Jefferson County, formerly the fifth but now composing the new third district, is again the largest of the State with its population of 355,350. The new ninth district, made from the old Republican eleventh district simply by adding Jackson and Owsley counties from the old tenth, has a population of 352,869. On the other extreme the first district has a population of only 238,189, the fourth district 238,494, and the fifth district 240,-293.[71] It has been called an interesting commentary upon the 1932 Redistricting Act that "the six new districts of Democratic hue have an average of 276,794, while the three districts with Republican leanings have an average of 317,939."

The geographic aspects of the apportionment of 1932 were described by the United States District Court for the Eastern District of Kentucky as follows:[72]

In dividing the state into congressional districts under the provisions of section 3 of the Act of August 8, 1911, the state Legislature undoubtedly has a wide discretion, and its good-faith exercise should not be disturbed by the court. But where the result leaves no escape from the conclusion that there was no good-faith attempt to comply with the national statutory requirement of practical equality of population and/or of contiguous and compact territory, the court should not hesitate to declare the legislative act void. A study of the redistricting act here involved satisfies me that the General Assembly made absolutely no effort to comply with the federal statutory requirement of practical equality of population and no good-faith effort to meet the requirement of compactness of territory. Indeed, it is difficult to contemplate the result without concluding that the act was framed in deliberate disregard of the federal statute.

The population of the state, according to the 1930 census, is 2,614,589. Under the Congressional Reapportionment Act (2 US CA Sec. 2a), this population entitled Kentucky to nine Representatives in Congress, instead of eleven as formerly allowed. Under an ideal re-

---

[70] Robert B. Stewart, "A Study of Gerrymandering in Kentucky," *Kentucky Law Journal*, Vol. 22, 1934, p. 425. See also C. O. Sauer, "Geography and the Gerrymander," *American Political Science Review*, Vol. 12, 1918, pp. 417–21.

[71] The fourth district now has a population of 256,173 and the fifth district of only 222,614, as the result of the transfer of Shelby County from the fifth district to the fourth district after the article quoted from was written.

[72] 1 Fed. Supp. 149–50.

districting act each of these nine districts would contain in round numbers 290,500 inhabitants. Owing to the fact that Jefferson County, in which the city of Louisville is located, has a population of 355,350, which is in excess of this number but not enough to make two districts, and owing to the practical consideration against throwing a part of this county into another congressional district, the action of the Legislature in erecting this county into a single district cannot be regarded as a violation of the spirit of the federal act.

After the creation of Jefferson County as a congressional district, there were left one hundred and nineteen counties, with a total population of 2,259,239, out of which to erect the remaining eight congressional districts apportioned to the state. Under an ideal redistricting act each of these eight districts would have in round numbers a population of 282,400. None of these counties has a population of as much as 100,000. One, Kenton County, has in round numbers 93,500; one, Campbell County, has 73,391; and only three others, Fayette, Harlan, and Pike, have in excess of 60,000. The average population of the one hundred and nineteen counties outside of Jefferson is slightly less than 19,000, and the average, eliminating the counties of Jefferson, Kenton, Campbell, Fayette, Harlan, and Pike, is less than 17,000, and each of seventy-five of the counties has a population of less than this average, and each of twenty-eight of the counties has less than 10,000 population.

In view of this situation, the Legislature was confronted with no difficulty whatever in dividing these one hundred and nineteen counties into eight congressional districts of substantially equal population, and this without the necessity of dividing any county; and the topography of the state presents no obstacle to carving these districts out of contiguous and compact territory. As an example of the ease with which these one hundred and nineteen counties can be erected into eight congressional districts, composed of contiguous and compact territory and with substantially equal population, the court during the argument called upon counsel for the plaintiff to file a map showing if and how this could be done. Such map was prepared and filed as an exhibit in the case. This map shows that these counties could have been laid off into eight congressional districts with no greater difference in population between them than approximately 4,000 people, and this without doing violence to the requirement that the districts must be composed of compact and contiguous territory. Of course, I do not mean to intimate that the legislative act should be declared void because it is not in substantial compliance with the tentative districting shown by the map referred to. I simply mean to hold that this tentative districting of the state, as disclosed by the map referred to, clearly shows no real difficulty confronted the Legislature in substantially complying with the federal law.

Instead of doing so, however, the Legislature, without any reason whatever so far as I can discover other than the exigencies of practical politics, in redistricting the state worked out a gross inequality in population between the respective districts. To the First district, beginning at the Mississippi river and extending eastwardly between the Ohio river on the north and the Tennessee line on the south, were allotted counties containing a population of 238,189. The Second district, which is the very next district to the east from the First district and which extends from the Ohio river to the Tennessee line, was given a population of 338,117, or substantially 100,000 more population than was assigned to the First district, and substantially 100,000 more population than the Fourth district, which is the district to the east of and adjoining the Second. To the east of the Fourth is the Sixth, containing a population of 317,591, or approximately 80,000 more than either the Fourth or the First. To the south of the Fourth and the Sixth lies the new Ninth with a population of 352,869, or approximately 114,000 more than the population of either the First or the Fourth, and with a population of approximately 107,000 in excess of the new Seventh which adjoins the Ninth on the north and east and has a population of 245,598. The Ninth has a population of approximately 65,000 in excess of the new Eighth, which lies along the eastern boundary line of the state and between the Ohio river and the Seventh, and more than 112,000 in excess of the new Fifth district, which lies along the Ohio river and north of the central part of the state. The discrimination in population against the Second and the Sixth districts, and in favor of the Fifth, Seventh, and Eighth, is only slightly less than glaring. In view of the ease with which these discriminations could have been avoided, we are forced to the conclusion that no attempt was made to avoid them, but that other considerations than the securing of equality of population dictated the laying out of these districts.

Not only did the Legislature disregard the requirement of substantial equality of population, but the new Fifth district, especially, outrageously violates the requirement of compactness of territory. Its shape very much resembles a French style telephone, with the counties of Oldham, Trimble, Carroll, Gallatin, Boone, Kenton, and Campbell strung along the river forming the handle of the telephone, and the county of Shelby on one end and the counties of Grant and Pendleton on the other end forming the mouthpiece and receiver respectively. Henry and Oldham [Owen] and the northern parts of Franklin and Scott counties project, appendix-like, between the eastern and western ends of the district. In any good-faith attempt to make the Fifth district a compact one, as required by the federal statute, Owen and Henry counties, with a population of 10,710 and 12,564, respectively, certainly would have been included. Irrespective of the inequality of population between the districts, a visual examination of the outlines upon the map of the new Fifth district is sufficient to repel any presumption of a good-faith attempt on the part of the Legislature to comply with section 3 of the Act of August 8, 1911.

A three-judge district court declared the state districting act of 1932 invalid as being contrary to the provisions of section 3 of the act of congress of August 8, 1911 (37 Stat. L. 14), which required districts to be composed of contiguous and compact territory and containing as nearly as practicable an equal number of inhabitants.[73] On appeal the Supreme Court reversed the ruling of the lower court on the ground that section 3 of the act of August 8, 1911 was no longer in force.[74] There was no detailed decision as reference was made to *Wood* v. *Broom*,[75] a Mississippi case decided earlier in the same term.[76]

Louisiana. The present districts in Louisiana were established by the act of July 11, 1912.[77] The largest district has a population 15.3 per cent above the average, while the smallest district is 15.3 per cent below. With the exception of the district including New Orleans the boundaries follow parish lines.

POPULATION OF DISTRICTS IN LOUISIANA, CENSUSES OF 1910 TO 1930

District	1910	1920	1930	District	1910	1920	1930
Average...	207,048	224,814	262,699	5.....	204,036	221,715	287,585
				6.....	247,612	255,372	294,138
1.....	203,120	220,478	253,548	7.....	165,563	204,909	222,495
2.....	220,557	245,176	302,893	8.....	196,077	214,930	225,158
3.....	234,382	212,152	230,092				
4.....	185,041	223,777	285,684	Total...	1,656,388	1,798,509	2,101,593

When the districts were established in 1911 the population of the largest district was 19.6 per cent above the average, and that of the smallest was 20.0 per cent below. By reason of shifting of population by 1920 the largest district was only 13.6 per cent above the average, and the smallest 8.9 per cent below. The population of the several districts at the last three censuses is shown in the table above.

[73] *Hume* v. *Mahan*, 1 Fed. Supp. 149–50.
[74] *Mahan* v. *Hume*, 287 U.S. 575.
[75] 287 U.S. 8.
[76] See p. 167.
[77] Acts . . . of Louisiana, 1912, p. 294; General Statutes of the State of Louisiana, 1939, Vol. 2, sec. 2703, p. 272.

The boundaries of the congressional districts in Louisiana at each apportionment are given on pages 41–47 of Judicial and Congressional District Boundary Law in Louisiana (mimeographed 1939), prepared by the Historical Records Survey of the Works Projects Administration and published by the Department of Archives of Louisiana State University.

Maine. The apportionment in Maine, as fixed by the act of April 3, 1931,[78] is as nearly perfect as is possible. The departures from the average are plus 0.5 per cent for one district, and minus 0.1 and 0.4 per cent for the other two districts. The counties comprising the districts are contiguous, and the boundaries of the districts are almost parallel, extending south from the northwest boundary to the sea.

Maryland. Maryland is one of the three states whose apportionment goes back to the beginning of the century, the present districts having been established by the act of April 8, 1902.[79] Amendments of April 13, 1922,[80] following the enlargement of the city of Baltimore, did not change the boundaries of the districts, but merely adjusted the descriptions to fit the names of the new minor civil divisions.

Owing to changes in population the present apportionment is extremely inequitable. One of the districts—the second—has a population 69.7 per cent in excess of the average; while all the other districts are below the average, the deficiency in two districts is not appreciable.

The most populous district—the second—includes only 5 wards (and a part of another) out of 28 wards in the city of Baltimore, but within it is the thickly settled suburban area in Baltimore County north of the city. Two districts completely within the city and one partly within the city have populations less than the average. The smallest district, with a population 28.8 per cent less than the average, comprises the counties east of Chesapeake Bay, generally known as the Eastern Shore.

[78] Acts and Resolves . . . of Maine, 1931, p. 277.

[79] Laws of . . . Maryland, 1902, p. 211; Annotated Code of Public General Laws of Maryland, 1939, Vol. I, Art. 33, secs. 204–10, p. 1503.

[80] Laws of . . . Maryland . . . , 1922, p. 372; Annotated Code of Public General Laws of Maryland, 1939, Vol. I, Art. 33, secs. 206–09, p. 1503.

This area has had a constantly decreasing population during recent years.

When made in 1902 the apportionment was an excellent one. The largest district was only 2 per cent above the average, and the smallest only 1.7 per cent below.

In 1910 the departure from the average was 11.1 per cent for the largest district and 7.3 per cent for the smallest. After the census of 1920 the largest district was 28.9 per cent above the average, and the smallest district was 19.4 per cent below. From 1900 to 1930 inclusive the first district has shown a progressive decline in population at each census; the second district has shown a progressive increase greater than that for the state as a whole; the sixth district, in the western part of the state, has had almost the same rate of increase as the entire state, and its population has varied little from the average for the six districts.

The accompanying table shows the population of the several districts after each census.

POPULATION OF DISTRICTS IN MARYLAND, CENSUSES OF 1900 TO 1930

District	1900	1910	1920	1930
Average....	198,007	215,891	241,610	271,921
1.......	196,004	200,171	194,568	193,658
2.......	196,878	239,891	311,413	461,419
3.......	194,606	215,914	228,168	203,929
4.......	201,882	218,416	255,084	259,467
5.......	199,775	204,059	223,656	244,519
6.......	198,899	216,895	236,772	268,534
Total......	1,188,044	1,295,346	1,449,661	1,631,526

Massachusetts. The apportionment in Massachusetts was last fixed by the act of June 10, 1931.[81] The population of the largest district is 10.5 per cent above the average and that of the smallest is 14.5 per cent below. In all the other districts the variation is less than 10 per cent, and in ten of the fifteen districts it is less than 5 per cent. The most populous district—the seventh— is immediately northeast of Boston, while the smallest district —the eleventh—includes parts of Boston, Cambridge, and Chelsea.

[81] Acts and Resolves ... of Massachusetts ..., 1931, p. 667; Annotated Laws [1933], Vol. 2, Chap. 57, sec. 1, p. 158.

Michigan. The last apportionment act of Michigan is that of April 15, 1931.[82] The population of the largest district is 33.5 per cent above the average and that of the smallest district is 34.4 per cent below. Three of the districts in the two counties including and adjacent to Detroit have populations more than 20 per cent above the average.

The Michigan apportionment of 1931 has been described as follows:

> The Michigan reapportionment deserves the admiring inspection of politicians. The Anti-Saloon League had a share in working out its artifices. These include taking so much Wet territory from the districts of two Wet representatives, and adding so many dry votes, that the anti-prohibitionists have little chance of reelection. The boundaries of no safely dry district were changed. And very thoughtfully the measure gives a representative to every 250,000 inhabitants outside Detroit, while 350,000 residents of that great city are required to select a Congressman. Legislators from Detroit supported the bill because they considered it the best that could be obtained from a body dominated by "up-staters."[83]

Minnesota. The apportionment in Minnesota was fixed by the act of April 8, 1933.[84] The population of the largest district is only 6.4 per cent greater than the average and that of the smallest district is 10.9 per cent less.

Apportionment legislation in Minnesota has definitely established the principle that the legislature cannot act independently of the governor in apportioning the state if the governor has the veto power. In April 1931 the governor vetoed an apportionment bill, but the house of representatives ordered the bill deposited with the secretary of state as a legislative enactment. The apportionment was upheld by the state supreme court, but it was declared invalid by the United States Supreme Court, which said in part as follows:[85]

. . . We find no suggestion in the Federal constitutional provision of

---

[82] Public Acts . . . of Michigan . . . , 1931, p. 30; Michigan Statutes Annotated, 1936, Vol. 2, sec. 4.21, p. 269.

[83] Editorial, *New York Times,* Apr. 20, 1931, p. 18.

[84] Session Laws of . . . Minnesota . . . , 1933, p. 227; 1940 Supplement to Mason's Minnesota Statutes, 1927, sec. 22, p. 36.

[85] *Smiley* v. *Holm,* 285 U.S. 361.

an attempt to endow the legislature of the state with power to enact laws in any manner other than that in which the constitution of the state has provided that laws shall be enacted. . . .

. . . That [established] practice is eloquent of the conviction of the people of the states, and of their representatives in state legislatures and executive office, that in providing for congressional elections, and for the districts in which they were to be held, these legislatures were exercising the law-making power and thus were subject, where the state constitution so provided, to the veto of the Governor as a part of the legislative process.[86]

Neither court passed upon the equity of the apportionment, but the political and geographic aspects of the proposed redistricting in 1931 have been described as follows:[87]

There can be little question that the bill was a gerrymander. The population of the proposed districts ranged from 228,596 to 344,500, and they were not composed of "compact, contiguous territory."[88] The seventh district, for example, almost cut the state in half. Beginning on the South Dakota boundary, it embraced a large farming territory in the western part of the state, and then extended a long finger to the eastward a distance of nearly 175 miles, to include a single ward of the city of Minneapolis. Hennepin County—the county in which Minneapolis is situated—with a population of 517,785, was divided among three districts. The major portion of the county was constricted into one large district containing 344,500 inhabitants, and the remainder was divided between two districts that were largely rural. The result probably would have been to give the county a single representative.

The legislature which effected this gerrymander was predominantly rural and Republican. The obvious purpose was to increase the representation of the rural part of the state over that of the urban, and to favor the Republican party at the expense of the Farmer-Labor party. . . .

. . . .

An unprecedented scramble for nominations followed the Court's decision. In all, eighty-eight candidates entered the lists.[89] The primaries, of course, eliminated all but nine of each party. Three Communist candidates were then nominated by petition. Thus, thirty

---

[86] The same, pp. 367, 369.

[87] Roger V. Shumate, "Minnesota's Congressional Election at Large," *American Political Science Review*, Vol. 27, pp. 58, 60.

[88] See map, Minn. Yearbook, 1931, p. 19. [Footnote part of quotation.]

[89] For lists, with bibliographical sketches, see Minn. Journal, June 12, 1932. [Footnote part of quotation.]

aspirants were presented to the voter, on the office-column type of ballot, and he was asked to choose nine of them. The results were not entirely what might have been expected from election at large. It is often assumed that the great majority of voters will vote a straight ticket, which would have the effect of giving all of the seats to the dominant party but such was not the case here. When the smoke cleared, it was found that the three leading parties had polled a total of 7,746,319 votes,[90] divided as follows: Farmer-Labor, 2,939,373; Republican, 2,859,558; Democratic, 1,947,388. The Farmer-Laborites with 38 per cent of the votes, had captured five of the nine seats, while the Republicans, with 37 per cent, secured only three seats, and the Democrats, with 25 per cent, got the remaining place. Thus, in a very crude way, something approaching proportional representation was achieved. It probably would have been more nearly proportional but for the fact that one of the Republicans who was defeated in the primaries appeared again in the general election as a "sticker" candidate; hence the Republican vote was divided between ten candidates instead of nine.

Mississippi. The boundaries of the existing districts in Mississippi were fixed by the act of May 18, 1932.[91] The apportionment is very inequitable. The population of the third and seventh districts, in the western part of the state along the Mississippi River, is 46.6 and 44.3 per cent above the average; all the other districts are below the average, the smallest having a deficiency of 35.8 per cent.

The apportionment was challenged on the ground that it was contrary to the provisions of section 3 of the act of August 8, 1911 (37 Stat. L. 13), which provides that each district shall be composed of compact and contiguous territory and, as nearly as practicable, an equal number of inhabitants.

A three-judge district court (one member dissenting) held the act invalid,[92] but on appeal the Supreme Court held that the 1911 act was no longer in force, the decision reading in part as follows:

There is thus no ground for the conclusion that the act of 1929 reenacted or made applicable to new districts the requirements of

<hr/>

[90] The three Communist candidates received a total of 34,799 votes. [Footnote part of quotation.]

[91] Laws of . . . Mississippi . . . Regular Session . . . , 1932, p. 416; 1938 Supplement to the Mississippi Code of 1930, sec. 2277, p. 1444.

[92] 1 Fed. Supp. 134.

[sec. 3 of] the act of 1911. That act in this respect was left as it had stood, and the requirements it had contained as to compactness, contiguity and equality in population of districts, did not outlast the apportionment to which they related.[93]

Missouri. State apportionment in Missouri followed to a certain extent the same course as in Minnesota. As the representation of the state was reduced by the apportionment after the census of 1930, it was necessary to redistrict the state or elect the representatives at large. The legislature in 1931 passed an apportionment bill which was vetoed by the governor.[94] Thereafter one John J. Carroll attempted to mandamus the secretary of state to receive his declaration of candidacy on the ground that the redistricting of the state was complete without the governor's approval. The Supreme Court of Missouri held that as the bill had been vetoed by the governor it had not become law.[95] The Supreme Court affirmed the decision of the lower court by reference to the Minnesota case of *Smiley* v. *Holm*.[96]

An act of April 17, 1933 established the districts with their present boundaries.[97] The population of the districts ranges from 52.4 per cent above the average to 25.8 per cent below. The largest district includes St. Louis County and a part of the city of St. Louis. On the other hand, both of the districts comprising Kansas City are less than the average in population, the percentages below the average being 14.3 for the fourth district and 17.2 for the fifth district.

Montana. The constitution of Montana, adopted when the state had only one representative, contains the following provision: "When a new apportionment shall be made by Congress the Legislative Assembly shall divide the State into Congressional Districts accordingly."[98]

[93] *Wood* v. *Broom*, 287 U.S. 8 (1932).

[94] For an account of redistricting in Missouri from 1901 to the passage of the vetoed bill in 1931, and of the attitude of Missouri representatives on federal legislation, see Lloyd M. Short, "Congressional Redistricting in Missouri," *American Political Science Review*, Vol. 25, 1918, pp. 634–49. See also C. O. Sauer, "Geography and the Gerrymander," *American Political Science Review*, Vol. 25, 1918, pp. 407–17.

[95] *State ex rel. Carroll* v. *Becker, Secretary of State*, 45 S.W. (2d), 533.

[96] *Carroll* v. *Becker*, 285 U.S. 380 (1932).

[97] Laws of Missouri . . . , 1933, p. 250; Missouri Statutes Annotated, Vol. 5, 1939 Cumulative Annual Pocket Part, secs. 10712–10725.

[98] Const. (1889), Art. VI, sec. 1.

Under the act of August 8, 1911 (37 Stat. L. 13) Montana became entitled to two representatives, but the state was not divided into districts until the act of February 9, 1917,[99] representatives being elected at large to the 63d, 64th, and 65th Congresses.

The two districts in Montana are separated by the main range of the Rocky Mountains. The departure from the average population is 21.2 per cent. The equity of the apportionment was little different in 1930 than at the previous census. In 1920 the departure from the average was 21.5 per cent. The population in 1920 and 1930 is given in the accompanying table.

POPULATION OF DISTRICTS IN MONTANA,
CENSUSES OF 1920 AND 1930

District	1920	1930
Average.....	274,444	268,803
1........	215,413	211,918
2........	333,476	325,688
Total.......	548,889	537,606

Nebraska. The apportionment is fixed by the act of May 7, 1931.[100] The largest district is 5.8 per cent above the average and the smallest is 7.3 per cent below.

Nevada. There is only one representative from Nevada, and the state therefore presents no problem of districting.

New Hampshire. Two representatives have been assigned to New Hampshire at each apportionment beginning with the one after the census of 1880. The boundaries of the present districts were fixed by the act of August 19, 1881,[101] and there has been no material shifting of population up to 1930 to affect the equity of the apportionment. The departure from the average is only 1.8 per cent.

The population of each district at each census beginning with 1880 is shown in the table on the following page.

[99] Laws . . . of Montana . . . , 1917, p. 47; Revised Codes of Montana of 1935, Vol. 1, sec. 48, p. 306.

[100] Session Laws . . . of Nebraska . . . , 1931, p. 88; 1939 Cumulative Supplement to the Compiled Statutes of Nebraska, 1929, sec. 5–101, p. 62.

[101] Laws of . . . New Hampshire . . . , 1881, p. 500; Public Laws of New Hampshire 1926, Vol. 1, Chap. 29, sec. 5, p. 143.

POPULATION OF DISTRICTS IN NEW HAMPSHIRE,
CENSUSES OF 1880 TO 1930

Census	Average	First District	Second District
1880............	173,496	172,662	174,329
1890............	188,265	190,532	185,998
1900............	205,794	204,002	207,586
1910............	215,286	218,572	212,000
1920............	221,541	224,842	218,241
1930............	232,647	228,493	236,800

New Jersey. The present apportionment in New Jersey dates from the act of December 15, 1931.[102] The population of the districts ranges from 24.7 per cent above the average to 22.3 per cent below. Both the largest and the smallest districts—the first and second—are in the southern part of the state between the Atlantic Ocean and the Delaware River. The population of districts in the metropolitan area adjacent to New York does not depart materially from the average, but the boundaries are unique, the eleventh district being almost entirely surrounded by the twelfth.

New Mexico. As New Mexico has had only one representative there have been no districts, but the state will be entitled to two representatives under the census of 1940.

New York. The present districts in New York were established by the act of October 18, 1911, as amended by the acts of April 20, 1915 (affecting the ninth and tenth districts), acts of June 9, 1917 (affecting third to tenth, fifteenth to eighteenth, and twenty-first to twenty-third districts), act of April 17, 1918 (affecting forty-first and forty-second districts), and act of April 13, 1922 (affecting eleventh to fourteenth districts).[103] All the districts whose boundaries were changed during the intercensal period were in New York City with the exception of the forty-first and forty-second, which include parts of Erie County and the city of Buffalo.

[102] Acts of . . . New Jersey . . . , 1932, additional laws of 1931, p. 1476 (the additional laws of 1931, pp. 1451–1522, precede the laws of 1932); New Jersey Statutes, Annotated, Title 19, Chap. 46, sec. 1, 1940, p. 403.

[103] Laws of . . . New York, 1911 . . . , Vol. 3, p. 2621; the same, 1915, Vol. 2, p. 1009; the same, 1917, Vol. 3, pp. 2631, 2652; the same, 1918, Vol. 2, p. 896; the same, 1922, Vol. 2, p. 1745; Thompson's Laws of New York, 1939, Pt. 2, Unconsolidated Laws, sec. 1051, p. 1152.

Notwithstanding the fact that New York has amended the districting act more than any other state and that it had the advantage of a state census in 1915 and 1925, it has the most inequitable distribution of any state. The excess of the most populous district (the eighth) over the least populous (the twelfth) is 708,736, or 781.7 per cent. The variations from the average range from 173.1 per cent above to 69.0 per cent below. Five districts have populations more than 100 per cent above the average; these are all in or adjacent to New York City. The districts with the smallest population are also in New York City, seven being more than 40 per cent below the average.

In 1931 the legislature attempted to make an apportionment by means of a concurrent resolution which was not submitted to the governor. This resolution was declared invalid by the Supreme Court of the United States for the reasons given in the Minnesota case of *Smiley* v. *Holm* (see page 165).[104]

The following comment on the resolution was made by the *New York Times:*

. . . One example of the politics of redistricting is the joining of Suffolk and Richmond, wholly dissimilar communities, separated by many miles of sea. If Suffolk's Republican majority prevails, the Representative will be as much out of touch with the feeling of the urban folk of Staten Island as a Staten Island Democrat would be with the sentiments of the people tributary to Riverhead. But it is all in the game of politics . . . As yet, however, all that the Legislature can be said to have enacted is a lawsuit.[105]

In the apportionment made in 1911 the population of many districts was close to the average, but one district was much out of line, with a population 41.5 per cent above the average. By 1920 the population of the largest district was 61.9 per cent above the average, and that of the smallest was 32.4 per cent below. The variations after 1930 are given above. The population of the several districts after the censuses of 1910, 1920, and 1930 are given on the following page.

[104] *Koenig* v. *Flynn*, 285 U.S. 379.
[105] Editorial, *New York Times*, Apr. 13, 1931, p. 18. The boundaries of the districts are given in the *Times* of Apr. 11, 1931, p. 10.

POPULATION OF DISTRICTS IN NEW YORK, CENSUSES OF 1910 TO 1930

District	1910	1920	1930	District	1910	1920	1930
Average...	211,945	241,517	279,735	23......	300,000	391,050	688,454
				24......	212,676	355,754	672,121
1......	207,443	279,813	637,022	25......	209,786	232,515	352,210
2......	221,206	355,737	776,425				
3......	212,840	240,290	187,953	26......	218,327	222,393	249,589
4......	205,593	247,873	211,826	27......	223,304	194,171	202,519
				28......	221,711	228,556	252,280
5......	197,344	231,807	246,215				
6......	214,661	258,770	452,275	29......	216,149	207,269	223,424
7......	204,731	266,592	205,043	30......	194,709	216,188	235,586
8......	212,264	298,968	799,407	31......	216,410	207,431	217,300
9......	214,913	291,851	370,457	32......	216,184	216,534	216,456
10......	207,465	252,062	217,015	33......	210,513	247,795	262,769
11......	214,760	217,371	218,545	34......	207,175	237,553	269,560
12......	218,428	165,123	90,671				
				35......	229,547	271,090	323,315
13......	210,852	163,292	111,696	36......	215,185	208,076	210,853
14......	210,289	179,572	119,794	37......	211,299	219,094	237,230
15......	213,514	191,645	121,675				
16......	208,400	200,072	142,496	38......	220,355	283,556	327,072
				39......	202,389	202,217	236,396
17......	219,772	217,882	207,648	40......	209,587	287,050	405,109
18......	206,947	203,677	144,945				
19......	212,235	258,139	259,334	41......	207,335	239,401	258,163
				42......	204,099	226,942	248,465
20......	204,498	195,814	150,523	43......	212,457	223,513	236,880
21......	209,700	317,803	381,212				
22......	213,436	232,926	210,138	Total....	9,113,614[a]	10,385,227	12,588,066

[a] This is the correct population but the figures as reported for the several districts add to 9,200,488.

North Carolina. The present apportionment in North Carolina was made by the act of March 30, 1931.[106] The population of the largest district is 43.9 per cent above the average and that of the smallest is 22.0 per cent below.

Within the most populous district (the tenth) is the city of Charlotte (population 82,675), the largest city in the state, and a rapidly developing industrial region in the Piedmont area as well as several counties in the mountains along the Tennessee line. The smallest district (the first) is in the tidewater region in the northeastern corner of the state, and is almost entirely rural.

North Dakota. The constitutional provision regarding apportionment in North Dakota is as follows: "Until otherwise provided by law, the member of the House of Representatives of the United States apportioned to this State shall be elected at large."[107] This is a futile provision, as a single member must necessarily be elected at large.

---

[106] ... North Carolina ... Public Laws, 1931, p. 269; North Carolina Code of 1939, sec. 6004, p. 2166.

[107] Const. (1889), Art. XVIII, sec. 214.

The latest act defining the districts in North Dakota was that of March 17, 1911,[108] which provided for the three districts to which the state was entitled at that time. After the census of 1930 the state was entitled to only two representatives, and as the legislature could not agree on the boundaries of the districts, the two members have been elected at large.

The districting was moderately good when it was made, and it became better with the readjustment of population shown by the census of 1920. After the census of 1910 the population of the largest district was 6.8 per cent above the average, and that of the smallest was 13.6 per cent below. After the census of 1920 the population of the largest district was 2.0 per cent above the average, and that of the smallest was 2.3 per cent below.

The population of the districts after the censuses of 1910 and 1920 is given in the accompanying table.

POPULATION OF DISTRICTS IN NORTH DAKOTA,
CENSUSES OF 1910 AND 1920

District	1910	1920
Average.......	192,352	215,227
1..........	205,391	215,969
2..........	202,287	219,508
3..........	169,378	210,203
Total........	577,056	645,680

Ohio. The boundaries of the districts in Ohio were established by the act of May 6, 1913.[109] An act of June 2, 1915[110] making a new apportionment was defeated in a referendum on November 2, 1915 by a vote of 291,986 to 329,095.[111] This referendum was attacked on the ground that it was not part of the legislative power. The Supreme Court of the United States held in substance that the legislative power under the constitution of the state was vested in both the legislature and the people, and that

[108] Laws . . . of North Dakota, 1911, p. 181; Compiled Laws of the State of North Dakota, 1913, Vol. 1, secs. 22–25, p. 6.
[109] State of Ohio, Legislative Acts . . . , 1913, Vol. 103, p. 568; Page's Ohio General Code, Annotated [1938], Vol. 4, sec. 4828–1, p. 162.
[110] Legislative Acts . . . , 1915, Vol. 106, p. 474.
[111] Throckmorton's Ohio Code, Annotated, Baldwin's, 1936, p. 1729, note.

the referendum was not contrary to the act of August 8, 1911 (37 Stat. L. 13).[112]

The quota of Ohio was increased from 22 to 24 by the apportionment of 1930, but as the legislature did not create two new districts two members are elected at large.

In Ohio the districts vary widely in population, 11 of the 22 districts being more than 30 per cent above or below the average. The largest district is 109.7 per cent above the average, and the smallest is 47.1 per cent below.

Districts with a material excess population contain the large cities with the exception of the two in Cincinnati (the first and second) and two districts in Cleveland. In these four districts the departure from the average ranges from 1.9 to 6.9 per cent. The population of the other districts containing large cities is given in the accompanying table.

DISTRICTS WITH EXCESS POPULATION IN OHIO, CENSUS OF 1930
(Average population per district, 302,123)

District		City or Other Area	
Number	Population	Name	Population
3......	410,020	Dayton	200,982
9......	371,818	Toledo	290,718
12......	361,055	Columbus	290,564
14......	525,696	Akron	255,040
19......	427,566	Youngstown	170,002
22......	633,678	Portions of Cuyahoga County outside Cleveland	301,026

The apportionment made in 1913 was not particularly good. The population of the largest district was 22.0 per cent above the average, and that of the smallest was 24.1 per cent below. By 1920 the population of the largest district was 67.7 per cent above the average and that of the smallest was 36.1 per cent below. The range after 1930 is given above.

The population of the several districts after each census from 1910 to 1930 is given in the table on page 175.

Oklahoma. An additional representative was assigned to Oklahoma under the apportionment of 1930, but as the state was not redistricted the present boundaries are those established by

---

[112] *Davis* v. *Ohio,* 241 U.S. 565.

the act of July 5, 1913.[113] There are eight districts and one member is elected at large.

POPULATION OF DISTRICTS IN OHIO, CENSUSES OF 1910 TO 1930

District	1910	1920	1930	District	1910	1920	1930
Average...	216,687	261,791	302,123	12......	221,567	283,951	361,055
				13......	196,455	197,390	213,825
1......	234,422	246,594	296,533	14......	238,195	439,013	525,696
2......	234,254	247,084	292,823	15......	204,568	199,445	198,291
3......	257,868	319,795	410,020				
4......	228,005	241,884	236,783	16......	235,984	299,107	353,727
				17......	213,716	221,419	237,061
5......	180,550	170,680	159,679	18......	253,735	289,471	304,411
6......	172,035	177,926	190,828	19......	228,464	335,775	427,566
7......	264,297	277,974	286,374				
8......	173,849	180,670	182,329	20......	224,357	314,174	301,964
				21......	181,371	302,243	322,901
9......	215,088	297,914	371,818	22......	223,148	370,781	633,678
10......	182,512	178,887	171,054				
11......	164,474	167,217	168,281	Total....	4,767,121[a]	5,759,394	6,646,697

[a] This is the correct population, but the figures as reported for the several districts add to 4,728,914.

The districts range in population from 35.2 per cent above the average to 25.2 per cent below.

The two largest cities in the state, Oklahoma City and Tulsa, are in the districts having the largest population. Since the districts were established the population of Oklahoma City has increased from 64,205, to 185,389, and that of Tulsa from 18,182 to 141,258.

When the apportionment was made in 1913 it was equitable. The largest district was only 11.8 per cent above the average and the smallest district 13.1 per cent below. By 1920, as a result of the shifting of population, the largest district was 24.7 per cent above the average, and the smallest district 25.2 per cent below. The population of the several districts at the last three censuses is given in the accompanying table.

POPULATION OF DISTRICTS IN OKLAHOMA, CENSUSES OF 1910 TO 1930

District	1910	1920	1930	District	1910	1920	1930
Average...	207,144	253,535	299,505	5......	214,498	258,312	376,738
				6......	207,451	207,648	263,164
1......	180,053	316,156	404,981	7......	208,022	189,472	240,944
2......	188,098	244,315	238,281	8......	201,921	200,402	224,067
3......	231,634	325,680	287,397				
4......	225,478	286,298	360,468	Total....	1,657,155	2,028,283	2,396,040

Oregon. The latest Oregon apportionment, which was made

[113] Session Laws, 1913, p. 655; Oklahoma Statutes, Annotated (1937), Title 14, sec. 1, p. 100.

by the act of February 23, 1911,[114] placed all the state east of the Cascade Mountains in the second district; Multnomah County, which includes the city of Portland, in the third district; and the remainder of the state in the first district. As regards the first and second districts the apportionment was inequitable when made in 1911, and has become slightly more so with each succeeding census. The third district shows only a slight deviation from the average at each census. The population of the three districts from 1910 to 1930 is given in the following table.

POPULATION OF DISTRICTS IN OREGON, CENSUSES OF 1910 TO 1930

District	1910	1920	1930
Average.......	224,255	261,130	317,929
1.........	303,634	346,989	432,572
2.........	142,870	160,502	182,973
3.........	226,261	275,898	338,241
Total.........	672,765	783,389	953,786

According to the 1930 census the population of the first district is 36.1 per cent above the average, and that of the second district is 42.4 per cent below.

Pennsylvania. Existing districts in Pennsylvania were established by the act of June 27, 1931.[115] The Pennsylvania districts show a striking mixture of good and bad apportionment. Of the 34 districts, 12 deviate less than 5 per cent from the average, but the largest district is 57.1 per cent above the average, and the smallest is 30 per cent below.

Contrary to the usual practice, five of the six districts having the largest departures from the average are not in the two largest cities—Philadelphia and Pittsburgh. When the governor signed the apportionment act in 1931 he attached thereto the following comment:

The passage of this Bill compels me to choose between signing it, and thereby enacting into law a vicious apportionment, or vetoing it, and thereby bringing upon the Commonwealth an unworkable and

---

[114] Oregon General Laws, 1911, p. 290; Oregon Code 1930, Vol. 2, sec. 24–101, p. 2090.
[115] Laws of . . . Pennsylvania, 1931, p. 1416; Purdon's Pennsylvania Statutes, Annotated (1938), Title 25, sec. 2189, p. 261.

unfair election, in which the use of voting machines would be impossible.

This Bill was drawn not to be passed, but to be killed. The purpose behind it was to force the election of Representatives in Congress and Delegates to the National Convention in the State at large instead of by Districts as at present.

To this end there were written into the Bill provisions so unjust yet so easily corrected that the intention of the Senate majority (with the Republican State machine behind it) to force an election at large upon the Commonwealth was beyond all doubt.

Under this Bill the Twelfth Congressional District, for example, has a population of 444,409; the Fifteenth District, which surrounds it on two sides, has a population of 205,084, or less than half. Berks, a Democratic County, with a population of only 231,717, is made into a separate district, while Schuylkill and Northumberland, both Republican, are made into a district with a population of 364,009.

The Twenty-seventh District is given 409,953 people, while the Twenty-fifth, with 246,569, and the Twenty-ninth, with 238,257, have between them but 75,000 more than the Twenty-seventh alone.

It is, of course, impossible to prevent differences between districts. But to insist on discrepancies like these against the vehement protests of the House and the Governor can mean only one thing—the intention to bring on an election at large by killing the Bill.

By this raw deal the votes of some citizens of our Commonwealth in electing Congressmen are worth, under the Bill, only half or less than half the votes of other citizens. . . .

So much for the injustice the Bill would work if it were approved.

But if the Bill were not approved the result at the Statewide Primary Election in 1932 would be to put so large a number of candidates upon the ballot that the average voter would be deprived of any reasonable chance to express his will. Indeed, in most if not all the districts of the State, a veto of this bill would make it utterly impossible for the full vote to be cast because of the unconscionable length of time needed to mark the ballot.

The Bureau of Elections certifies that the following officers would be chosen at large on a State-wide ticket if this Bill were vetoed: 1 United States Senator, 1 Judge of the Superior Court, 1 State Treasurer, 1 Auditor General, 34 Representatives in Congress, 79 Delegates to National Convention, 79 Alternate Delegates, making a total of 196 places to be filled and squares to be marked by each voter.

If on the average there were only three candidates for each place on the State-wide ticket, a total of 588 names would appear on the State-wide ballot. There is also, of course, the possibility that this number would be greatly increased.

But that is not all. In addition to this bedlam of State-wide names on the ballot, candidates for the entire House of Representatives would be voted for, as well as one Senator from each even numbered district throughout the State. Add to that candidates for the State Committee in each Senatorial District and members of the County Committees in every political unit, and I have no language to describe the result.

Such a condition would nullify all chance of a fair and free election. A ballot like this could not be marked and voted by the honest voters of the State. But it could be counted by dishonest election officials. No voting machine could be used, for none has space for such a flood of candidates.

This would amount to a heavy and intentional handicap against those portions of the State where elections are honest, and in favor of those machine-controlled portions where they are not. By the sheer impossibility of recording the upstate vote it would throw the election into the hands of machine-controlled cities.

This discrimination will continue for the next ten years, and those who will suffer from it must put the blame where it belongs. I regret profoundly that I cannot prevent the bitter injustice committed in this Bill against the people of individual counties. That could be done only by yielding to the greater injustice of disfranchising the uncontrolled voters of this Commonwealth.

I refuse to be a party to the practical disfranchisement of the honest voters of Pennsylvania through a political trick. Therefore I sign the Bill.[116]

Rhode Island. Rhode Island has two districts of almost equal population, the departure from the average being only 0.8 per cent. More than a third of the population is in the city of Providence, which is divided between the two districts. The present act was approved March 5, 1932.[117]

South Carolina. Existing districts in South Carolina were established by the act of April 1, 1932.[118] The population of the largest district is 16.9 per cent above the average, and that of the smallest is 18.9 per cent below.

South Dakota. By the apportionment after the census of 1930 the quota of South Dakota was reduced from three to two mem-

[116] Laws . . . of Pennsylvania, 1931, pp. 1421–22.

[117] Acts and Resolves . . . Rhode Island . . . 1932, p. 10; Rhode Island General Laws of 1938 (annotated), Chap. 322, p. 688.

[118] Acts . . . South Carolina, 1932, p. 1355; 1934 Supplement to the Code of Laws of South Carolina 1932, sec. 2333, p. 87.

bers. The state met this situation by the simple but inequitable method of combining the former first and second districts into a new first district, and making the former third district the second district.[119] As a result one district has a population 51.5 per cent above the average, and the other 51.5 per cent below. The Missouri River forms the boundary between the two districts.

Tennessee. The boundaries of the districts in Tennessee were established by the act of March 20, 1931, as amended by the act of April 21, 1933.[120] The population of the districts ranges from 26.6 per cent above the average to 33.0 per cent below.

The amendatory act of 1933 was of little importance, as the only provision was to transfer Cumberland County, with a population of 11,440, from the second to the fourth district.

For an account of districting in Tennessee prior to 1920 see C. O. Sauer, "Geography and the Gerrymander."[121]

Texas. Existing districts in Texas were defined by the act of May 16, 1933.[122] The population of the largest district is 29.5 per cent above the average, and that of the smallest is 24.1 per cent below.

Five cities have a population over 100,000. The districts including two of these—Dallas in the fifth district and Houston in the eighth district—have populations 17.4 and 29.5 per cent above the average. The population of the district including El Paso—the sixteenth—is 24.1 per cent below the average. The population of the district including Fort Worth—the twelfth —is 6.5 per cent below the average, and that including San Antonio—the twentieth—is 5.5 per cent above the average. The variations in the size of the districts seem to arise not from discrimination against the cities, but from adherence to county lines as district boundaries.

Utah. Prior to the census of 1910 Utah was entitled to only

[119] Act of March 6, 1931, Laws . . . of South Dakota 1931, p. 299; South Dakota Code of 1939, Vol. 3, Chap. 55.03, p. 657.
[120] Public Acts of . . . Tennessee, 1931, p. 48; the same, 1933, p. 387; Michie's Tennessee Code of 1938, sec. 138, p. 15.
[121] *American Political Science Review*, Vol. 12, 1918, pp. 421–26.
[122] General Laws of . . . Texas . . . , 1933, p. 344; Vernon's Texas Statutes 1936, Art. 197, p. 52.

one representative. After it became entitled to two representatives, the state was districted by the act of March 19, 1913,[123] and the boundaries of the districts have not been changed since, as there has been no necessity for such action.

Departure from the average in the two districts is 5.0 per cent. The population of the districts in Utah after the censuses of 1910, 1920, and 1930 is shown in the table below.

POPULATION OF DISTRICTS IN UTAH, CENSUSES OF 1910 TO 1930

District	1910	1920	1930
Average.......	186,675	224,698	253,924
1..........	185,868	229,907	241,290
2..........	187,483	219,489	266,557
Total.........	373,351	449,396	507,847

Vermont. Under the apportionment of 1930 only one representative is assigned to Vermont, but by the act of March 30, 1931 the legislature established the boundaries of two districts, if that number should be authorized.[124] That act is still in force and would be effective if the quota of Vermont should be increased to two. The proposed districting is equitable on the basis of the census of 1930. The population at that time was 359,611; that of one of the proposed districts was 179,214 and of the other 180,397.

Virginia. The boundaries of districts in Virginia are fixed by the act of February 15, 1934.[125] The population of the districts ranges from 13.1 per cent above the average to 10.0 per cent below.

The apportionment of 1930 reduced the quota of Virginia from 10 to 9, and the first act to meet the new apportionment became law on February 16, 1932 without the approval of the governor.[126]

The act of 1932 was declared unconstitutional by the Su-

---

[123] Laws of . . . Utah, 1913, p. 72; Revised Statutes of Utah, 1933, 25-9-4, p. 419.

[124] Acts and Resolves . . . Vermont . . . , 1931, p. 1; Public Laws of Vermont, 1933, sec. 79, p. 82.

[125] Acts of . . . Virginia, 1934, p. 17 (extra session of 1933 and regular session of 1934 bound in one volume with separate pagination); Virginia Code of 1936, sec. 70, p. 28.

[126] Acts of . . . Virginia, 1932, p. 19.

preme Court of Appeals of Virginia because the state constitution provides that districts "shall be formed of contiguous counties, cities, and towns, be compact, and include as nearly as may be, an equal number of inhabitants."[127]

The accompanying table gives the population of the several districts and the variations from the average, as stated in the decision.[128]

POPULATION OF DISTRICTS IN VIRGINIA UNDER INVALID ACT OF 1932

District	Population	Variation
1	239,835	−19,257
2	302,715	+33,623
3	288,939	+19,847
4	212,952	−56,140
5	251,090	−18.002
6	280,708	+11,616
7	336,654	+67,562
8	183,934	−85,158
9	325,024	+55,932

Washington. The present districts in Washington were established by the act of March 9, 1931.[129] One district—the first—has a population 52.1 per cent above the average, and all the other districts range from 4.0 per cent to 19.6 per cent below.

The largest district includes the city of Seattle and Kitsap County. The city of Seattle alone had a population of 365,583, which is 105,017, or 40.3 per cent above the average.

West Virginia. The boundaries of the districts in West Virginia were established by the act of March 13, 1934.[130] The apportionment is an equitable one, the population of the largest district being only 7.2 per cent above the average, and that of the smallest being 5.2 per cent below.

Wisconsin. The present Wisconsin districts date from the act of February 6, 1932.[131] The population of the largest district

[127] *Brown* v. *Saunders,* 166 S.E. 111.

[128] The same, p. 106. The population of each district and the departure from the average at each apportionment from 1868 to 1910 are given in a footnote on page 110 of the decision cited.

[129] Session Laws of . . . Washington, 1931, p. 95; Remington's Revised Statutes of Washington, Annotated, 1932, Vol. 5, secs. 3792–3796–1, p. 548.

[130] Acts of . . . West Virginia, Second Extraordinary Session 1933, p. 98; West Virginia Code of 1937, sec. 7, p. 3.

[131] Wisconsin Session Laws . . . Special Session 1931–32 . . . Biennial Session . . . 1933, p. 102; Wisconsin Statutes, 1939, Chap. 3, p. 78.

is 26.5 per cent above the average and that of the smallest is 16.8 per cent below.

The two districts which have the largest populations, the fifth (20.3 per cent above the average) and the sixth (26.5 per cent above the average), comprise Milwaukee County. The smallest district, the tenth (16.8 per cent below the average), includes a group of counties in the northern part of the state.

Wyoming. As Wyoming has had only one representative no problem of districting has arisen.

VARIATIONS IN THE DISTRICTS

The table on pages 183–92 shows the population of each district in 1930 and its departure from the average for each state. Similar figures are given for 1940 if the data are available. When this table was prepared the only final population figures available were for the states. For counties and cities only preliminary figures were available. No figures have been announced for other minor civil divisions, so that if a county or city is divided among several districts it is not possible at present to give the population of the districts. The state totals as given in this table do not agree with the state totals in Appendix C, page 233, which give the final figures. It has been deemed desirable to retain in this table the preliminary figures for the state population, as the figures given for the districts add to this total if all the districts in a state follow county lines. The difference between the state populations as given in this table and in Appendix C must be distributed over the several districts. It was not possible to make this distribution when this table was prepared.

As regards the figures for 1940 it should be borne in mind that they apply to the districts as now constituted. No legislature has met since the 1940 figures have been available, and consequently there has been no opportunity to change the boundaries. The population will be the same at the next congressional election only if the several legislatures take no action.

POPULATION OF DISTRICTS

State and District	Census of 1930		Census of 1940	
	Population[a]	Departure from State Average (Per cent)	Population[b]	Departure from State Average (Per cent)
Alabama.................	2,646,248	—	2,830,285	—
Average per district........	294,028	—	314,476	—
1st district...............	272,633	− 7.3	297,197	− 5.5
2d district...............	330,677	+12.5	356,453	+13.3
3d district...............	297,574	+ 1.2	303,818	− 3.4
4th district..............	264,658	−10.0	282,635	−10.1
5th district..............	273,763	− 6.9	295,047	− 6.2
6th district..............	236,412	−19.6	252,410	−19.7
7th district..............	256,797	−12.7	284,922	− 9.4
8th district..............	282,241	− 4.0	298,847	− 5.0
9th district..............	431,493	+46.8	458,956	+45.9
Arizona[c].................	435,573	—	497,789	—
Arkansas..................	1,854,482	—	1,948,268	—
Average per district........	264,926	—	278,324	—
1st district...............	385,965	+45.7	422,340	+51.7
2d district...............	218,596	−17.5	222,964	−19.9
3d district...............	170,576	−35.6	177,188	−36.3
4th district..............	230,259	−13.1	241,744	−13.1
5th district..............	278,663	+ 5.2	293,978	+ 5.6
6th district..............	289,250	+ 9.2	302,941	+ 8.8
7th district..............	281,173	+ 6.1	287,113	+ 3.2
California.................	5,677,251	—	6,873,688	—
Average per district........	283,863	—	343,684	—
1st district...............	263,748	− 7.1	307,709	−10.5
2d district...............	165,595	−41.7	216,649	−37.0
3d district...............	332,314	+17.1	408,372	+18.8
4th district..............	335,482	+18.2	—	—
5th district..............	298,912	+ 5.3	—	—
6th district..............	308,897	+ 8.8	—	—
7th district..............	244,594	−13.8	—	—
8th district..............	324,972	+14.5	412,879	+20.1
9th district...............	280,317	− 1.2	360,174	+ 4.8
10th district..............	309,768	+ 9.1	410,001	+19.3
11th district..............	264,952	− 6.7	—	—
12th district..............	259,287	− 8.7	—	—
13th district..............	349,686	+23.2	—	—
14th district..............	277,613	− 2.2	—	—
15th district..............	300,133	+ 5.7	—	—
16th district..............	296,077	+ 4.3	—	—
17th district..............	233,674	−17.7	—	—
18th district..............	227,070	−20.0	—	—
19th district..............	333,598	+17.5	398,020	+15.8
20th district..............	270,562	− 4.7	349,124	+ 1.6
Colorado..................	1,035,791	—	1,118,820	—
Average per district........	258,948	—	279,705	—
1st district...............	287,861	+11.2	318,415	+13.8
2d district...............	302,946	+17.0	320,535	+14.6
3d district...............	303,442	+17.2	308,146	+10.2
4th district..............	141,542	−45.3	171,724	−38.6

[a] Population figures in this table include Indians not taxed; for apportionment population by states see p. 233. Figures by districts for Indians not taxed are not available.
[b] Preliminary figures; final figures for states only are given on p. 233.
[c] One representative only.

POPULATION OF DISTRICTS—*Continued*

State and District	Census of 1930		Census of 1940	
	Population	Departure from State Average (Per cent)	Population	Departure from State Average (Per cent)
Connecticut................	1,606,903	—	1,710,112	—
Average per district........	321,381	—	342,022	—
1st district...............	421,097	+31.0	449,653	+31.5
2d district................	253,099	−21.2	268,417	−21.5
3d district................	304,736	− 5.2	—	—
4th district...............	386,702	+20.3	422,003	+23.4
5th district...............	241,269	−24.9	—	—
At large..................	—	—	—	—
Delaware°.................	238,380	—	264,603	—
Florida...................	1,468,211	—	1,887,804	—
Average per district........	293,642	—	377,561	—
1st district...............	390,965	+33.1	472,729	+25.2
2d district................	325,154	+10.7	388,092	+ 2.8
3d district................	254,386	−13.4	305,544	−19.1
4th district...............	254,358	−13.4	433,465	+14.8
5th district...............	243,348	−17.1	287,974	−23.7
Georgia...................	2,908,506	—	3,119,953	—
Average per district........	290,851	—	311,995	—
1st district...............	328,214	+12.8	334,242	+ 7.1
2d district................	263,606	− 9.4	275,135	−11.8
3d district................	339,870	+16.9	356,566	+14.3
4th district...............	261,234	−10.2	280,473	−10.1
5th district...............	414,313	+42.4	486,015	+55.8
6th district...............	281,437	− 3.2	289,042	− 7.4
7th district...............	270,112	− 7.1	307,250	− 1.5
8th district...............	241,957	−16.8	254,949	−18.3
9th district...............	218,496	−24.9	235,570	−24.5
10th district..............	289,267	− 0.5	300,711	− 3.6
Idaho.....................	445,031	—	523,440	—
Average per district........	222,516	—	261,720	—
1st district...............	189,576	−14.8	223,891	−14.5
2d district................	255,455	+14.8	299,549	+14.5
Illinois...................	7,630,654	—	7,877,167	—
Average per district........	305,226	—	315,087	—
1st district...............	142,916	−53.2	—	—
2d district................	577,998	+89.4	—	—
3d district................	540,666	+77.1	—	—
4th district...............	237,139	−22.3	—	—
5th district...............	140,481	−54.0	—	—
6th district...............	632,834	+107.3	—	—
7th district...............	889,349	+191.4	—	—
8th district...............	138,216	−54.7	—	—
9th district...............	209,650	−31.3	—	—
10th district..............	577,261	+89.1	—	—
11th district..............	363,136	+19.0	381,985	+21.2
12th district..............	292,023	− 4.3	297,713	− 5.5
13th district..............	178,198	−41.6	186,394	−40.8
14th district..............	199,104	−34.8	214,303	−32.0
15th district..............	213,630	−30.0	217,113	−31.1
16th district..............	253,713	−16.9	276,174	−12.3
17th district..............	175,353	−42.5	176,087	−44.1
18th district..............	225,604	−26.1	234,864	−25.5
19th district..............	274,137	−10.2	283,640	−10.0

POPULATION OF DISTRICTS—*Continued*

State and District	Census of 1930		Census of 1940	
	Population	*Departure from State Average (Per cent)*	Population	*Departure from State Average (Per cent)*
Illinois—*Continued*				
20th district..............	158,262	−48.1	162,384	−48.5
21st district..............	233,252	−23.6	236,938	−24.8
22d district..............	344,666	+12.9	357,907	+13.6
23d district..............	213,567	−30.0	242,880	−22.9
24th district..............	161,158	−47.2	173,497	−44.9
25th district..............	258,341	−15.4	261,229	−17.1
At large.................	—	—	—	—
At large.................	—	—	—	—
Indiana...................	3,238,503	—	3,416,152	—
Average per district.......	269,875	—	284,679	—
1st district..............	261,310	− 3.2	288,283	+ 1.3
2d district..............	260,287	− 3.6	281,810	− 1.0
3d district..............	289,398	+ 7.2	298,113	+ 4.7
4th district..............	275,523	+ 2.1	287,603	+ 1.0
5th district..............	258,037	− 4.4	267,422	− 6.1
6th district..............	278,685	+ 3.3	280,798	− 1.4
7th district..............	283,498	+ 5.0	284,900	+ 0.1
8th district..............	281,724	+ 4.4	305,145	+ 7.2
9th district..............	257,311	− 4.7	271,285	− 4.7
10th district..............	270,571	+ 0.3	288,790	+ 1.4
11th district..............	264,926	− 1.8	—	—
12th district..............	257,233	− 4.7	—	—
Iowa.....................	2,470,939	—	2,535,430	—
Average per district.......	274,549	—	281,714	—
1st district..............	251,084	− 8.5	253,281	−10.1
2d district..............	302,946	+10.3	321,080	+14.0
3d district..............	256,052	− 6.7	268,578	− 4.7
4th district..............	240,282	−12.5	250,673	−11.0
5th district..............	271,679	− 1.0	268,720	− 4.6
6th district..............	287,229	+ 4.6	312,392	+10.9
7th district..............	274,168	− 0.1	261,620	− 7.1
8th district..............	278,701	+ 1.5	283,773	+ 0.7
9th district..............	308,798	+12.5	315,313	+11.9
Kansas...................	1,880,999	—	1,799,137	—
Average per district.......	268,714	—	257,020	—
1st district..............	273,849	+ 1.9	263,171	+ 2.4
2d district..............	307,466	+14.4	307,894	+19.8
3d district..............	265,319	− 1.3	249,167	− 3.1
4th district..............	229,108	−14.7	208,947	−18.7
5th district..............	246,902	− 8.1	247,803	− 3.6
6th district..............	275,301	+ 2.5	252,562	− 1.7
7th district..............	283,054	+ 5.3	269,593	+ 4.9
Kentucky.................	2,614,589	—	2,839,927	—
Average per district.......	290,510	—	315,547	—
1st district..............	238,189	−18.0	251,773	−20.2
2d district..............	338,117	+16.4	353,992	+12.2
3d district..............	355,350	+22.3	385,256	+22.1
4th district..............	256,173	−11.8	277,052	−12.2
5th district..............	222,614	−23.4	224,358	−28.9
6th district..............	317,571	+ 9.3	339,249	+ 7.5
7th district..............	245,598	−15.5	287,001	− 9.0
8th district..............	288,108	− 0.8	307,655	− 2.5
9th district..............	352,869	+21.5	413,591	+31.1

Population of Districts—*Continued*

State and District	Census of 1930		Census of 1940	
	Population	Departure from State Average (Per cent)	Population	Departure from State Average (Per cent)
Louisiana................	2,101,593	—	2,360,661	—
Average per district........	262,699	—	295,083	—
1st district...............	253,548	− 3.5	—	—
2d district...............	302,893	+15.3	—	—
3d district...............	230,092	−12.4	269,745	− 8.6
4th district..............	285,684	+ 8.7	317,915	+ 7.7
5th district..............	287,585	+ 9.5	325,192	+10.2
6th district..............	294,138	+12.0	333,282	+12.9
7th district..............	222,495	−15.3	268,192	− 9.1
8th district..............	225,158	−14.3	240,563	−18.5
Maine....................	797,423	—	845,139	—
Average per district........	265,808	—	281,713	—
1st district...............	265,989	+ 0.1	289,544	+ 2.8
2d district...............	264,434	− 0.5	276,466	− 1.9
3d district...............	267,000	+ 0.4	279,129	− 0.9
Maryland.................	1,631,526	—	1,811,546	—
Average per district........	271,921	—	301,924	—
1st district...............	193,658	−28.8	194,993	−35.4
2d district...............	461,419	+69.7	—	—
3d district...............	203,929	−25.0	—	—
4th district..............	259,467	− 4.6	—	—
5th district..............	244,519	−10.1	—	—
6th district..............	268,534	− 1.2	317,881	+ 5.3
Massachusetts..............	4,249,614	—	4,312,332	—
Average per district........	283,308	—	287,489	—
1st district...............	274,703	− 3.0	—	—
2d district...............	292,066	+ 3.1	—	—
3d district...............	282,230	− 0.4	—	—
4th district..............	288,216	+ 1.7	—	—
5th district..............	309,888	+ 9.4	—	—
6th district..............	255,879	− 9.7	—	—
7th district..............	312,956	+10.5	—	—
8th district..............	291,783	+ 3.0	—	—
9th district..............	298,398	+ 5.3	—	—
10th district..............	276,509	− 2.4	—	—
11th district..............	242,310	−14.5	—	—
12th district..............	294,272	+ 3.9	—	—
13th district..............	273,059	− 3.6	—	—
14th district..............	278,394	− 1.7	—	—
15th district..............	278,951	− 1.5	—	—
Michigan..................	4,842,325	—	5,245,012	—
Average per district........	284,843	—	308,530	—
1st district...............	380,155	+33.5	—	—
2d district...............	260,168	− 8.7	284,179	− 7.9
3d district...............	261,506	− 8.2	282,824	− 8.3
4th district..............	225,111	−21.0	242,674	−21.3
5th district..............	295,369	+ 3.7	305,290	− 1.1
6th district..............	347,502	+22.0	378,396	+22.6
7th district..............	264,874	− 7.0	314,209	+ 1.8
8th district..............	277,224	− 2.7	295,012	− 4.4
9th district..............	214,318	−24.8	236,244	−23.4
10th district..............	186,738	−34.4	218,381	−29.2
11th district..............	204,710	−28.1	222,515	−27.9

POPULATION OF DISTRICTS—*Continued*

State and District	Census of 1930		Census of 1940	
	Population	Departure from State Average (Per cent)	Population	Departure from State Average (Per cent)
Michigan—*Continued*				
12th district	204,608	−28.2	199,528	−35.3
13th district	354,135	+24.3	—	—
14th district	350,212	+22.9	—	—
15th district	378,630	+32.9	—	—
16th district	318,919	+12.0	—	—
17th district	318,146	+11.7	—	—
Minnesota	2,563,953	—	2,785,896	—
Average per district	284,884	—	309,544	—
1st district	289,887	+ 1.8	317,460	+ 2.6
2d district	281,336	− 1.2	305,464	− 1.3
3d district	288,289	+ 1.2	—	—
4th district	286,721	+ 0.6	310,431	+ 0.3
5th district	297,934	+ 4.6	—	—
6th district	303,242	+ 6.4	332,799	+ 7.5
7th district	286,125	+ 0.4	304,786	− 1.5
8th district	276,633	− 2.9	290,360	− 6.2
9th district	253,786	−10.9	283,411	− 8.4
Mississippi	2,009,821	—	2,181,763	—
Average per district	287,117	—	311,680	—
1st district	241,605	−15.9	262,887	−15.7
2d district	219,661	−23.5	231,707	−25.7
3d district	420,969	+46.6	434,619	+39.4
4th district	184,266	−35.8	201,588	−35.3
5th district	244,562	−14.8	261,230	−16.2
6th district	284,457	− 0.9	319,287	+ 2.4
7th district	414,301	+44.3	470,445	+50.9
Missouri	3,629,367	—	3,775,737	—
Average per district	279,182	—	290,441	—
1st district	244,369	−12.5	230,709	−20.6
2d district	287,820	+ 3.1	282,448	− 2.8
3d district	299,490	+ 7.3	291,349	+ 0.3
4th district	239,251	−14.3	—	—
5th district	231,203	−17.2	—	—
6th district	287,786	+ 3.1	289,281	− 0.4
7th district	293,294	+ 5.1	312,266	+ 7.5
8th district	253,716	− 9.1	276,290	− 4.9
9th district	207,068	−25.8	214,694	−26.1
10th district	251,817	− 9.8	315,679	+ 8.7
11th district	341,538	+22.3	—	—
12th district	425,481	+52.4	—	—
13th district	266,534	− 4.5	—	—
Montana	537,606	—	554,136	—
Average per district	268,803	—	277,068	—
1st district	211,918	−21.2	231,650	−16.4
2d district	325,688	+21.2	322,486	+16.4
Nebraska	1,377,963	—	1,313,468	—
Average per district	275,593	—	262,694	—
1st district	269,428	− 2.2	260,053	− 1.0
2d district	255,479	− 7.3	269,479	+ 2.6
3d district	291,595	+ 5.8	267,745	+ 1.9
4th district	290,318	+ 5.3	255,738	− 2.6
5th district	271,143	− 1.6	260,453	− 0.9

POPULATION OF DISTRICTS—*Continued*

State and District	Census of 1930		Census of 1940	
	Population	Departure from State Average (Per cent)	Population	Departure from State Average (Per cent)
Nevada°..................	91,058	—	110,247	—
New Hampshire............	465,293	—	489,716	—
Average per district........	232,647	—	244,858	—
1st district................	228,493	− 1.8	—	—
2d district................	236,800	+ 1.8	—	—
New Jersey................	4,041,334	—	4,148,562	—
Average per district........	288,667	—	296,326	—
1st district................	359,948	+24.7	369,499	+24.7
2d district................	224,204	−22.3	225,495	−23.9
3d district................	266,337	− 7.7	—	—
4th district................	280,684	− 2.8	293,960	− 0.8
5th district................	301,726	+ 4.5	—	—
6th district................	305,209	+ 5.7	326,720	+10.3
7th district................	259,379	−10.1	—	—
8th district................	299,190	+ 3.6	—	—
9th district................	267,663	− 7.3	—	—
10th district...............	295,297	+ 2.3	—	—
11th district...............	292,284	+ 1.3	—	—
12th district...............	304,935	+ 5.6	—	—
13th district...............	289,795	+ 0.4	—	—
14th district...............	294,683	+ 2.1	—	—
New Mexico°..............	423,317	—	528,687	—
New York.................	12,588,066	—	13,379,622	—
Average per district........	292,746	—	311,154	—
1st district................	637,022	+117.6	—	—
2d district................	776,425	+165.2	—	—
3d district................	187,953	−35.8	—	—
4th district................	211,826	−27.6	—	—
5th district................	246,215	−15.9	—	—
6th district................	452,275	+54.5	—	—
7th district................	205,043	−30.0	—	—
8th district................	799,407	+173.1	—	—
9th district................	370,457	+26.5	—	—
10th district...............	217,015	−25.9	—	—
11th district...............	218,545	−25.3	—	—
12th district...............	90,671	−69.0	—	—
13th district...............	111,696	−61.8	—	—
14th district...............	119,794	−59.1	—	—
15th district...............	121,675	−58.4	—	—
16th district...............	142,496	−51.3	—	—
17th district...............	207,648	−29.1	—	—
18th district...............	144,945	−50.5	—	—
19th district...............	259,334	−11.4	—	—
20th district...............	150,523	−48.6	—	—
21st district...............	381,212	+30.2	—	—
22d district...............	210,138	−28.2	—	—
23d district...............	688,454	+135.2	—	—
24th district...............	672,121	+129.6	—	—
25th district...............	352,210	+20.3	—	—
26th district...............	249,589	−14.7	274,367	−11.8
27th district...............	220,519	−30.8	214,457	−3·11

POPULATION OF DISTRICTS—*Continued*

State and District	Census of 1930		Census of 1940	
	Population	*Departure from State Average (Per cent)*	Population	*Departure from State Average (Per cent)*
New York—*Continued*				
28th district..............	252,280	−13.8	—	—
29th district..............	223,424	−23.7	—	—
30th district..............	235,586	−19.5	232,824	−25.2
31st district..............	217,300	−25.8	221,040	−29.0
32d district..............	216,456	−26.1	216,450	−30.4
33d district..............	262,769	−10.2	263,178	−15.4
34th district..............	269,560	− 7.9	288,095	− 7.4
35th district..............	323,315	+10.4	327,594	+ 5.3
36th district..............	210,853	−28.0	215,166	−30.8
37th district..............	237,230	−19.0	240,319	−22.8
38th district..............	327,072	+11.7	—	—
39th district..............	236,396	−19.2	—	—
40th district..............	405,109	+38.4	—	—
41st district..............	258,163	−11.8	—	—
42d district..............	248,465	−15.1	—	—
43d district..............	236,880	−19.1	234,929	−24.5
At large.................	—	—	—	—
At large.................	—	—	—	—
North Carolina.............	3,170,276	—	3,563,174	—
Average per district........	288,207	—	323,925	—
1st district..............	224,768	−22.0	238,988	−26.2
2d district..............	276,795	− 4.0	292,418	− 9.7
3d district..............	226,465	−21.4	251,615	−22.3
4th district..............	322,346	+11.8	358,491	+10.7
5th district..............	293,779	+ 1.9	323,183	− 0.2
6th district..............	263,517	− 8.6	312,226	− 3.6
7th district..............	268,579	− 6.8	314,942	− 2.8
8th district..............	316,614	+ 9.9	340,948	+ 5.3
9th district..............	262,213	− 9.0	310,069	− 4.3
10th district..............	414,808	+43.9	478,723	+47.8
11th district..............	300,392	+ 4.2	341,571	+ 5.4
North Dakota[d].............	680,845	—	639,690	—
Ohio.....................	6,646,697	—	6,889,623	—
Average per district........	302,123	—	313,165	—
1st district..............	296,533	− 1.9	—	—
2d district..............	292,823	− 3.1	—	—
3d district..............	410,020	+35.7	439,795	+40.4
4th district..............	236,783	−21.6	243,908	−22.1
5th district..............	159,679	−47.1	163,416	−47.8
6th district..............	190,828	−36.8	207,214	−33.8
7th district..............	286,374	− 5.2	302,199	− 3.5
8th district..............	182,329	−39.7	183,038	−41.6
9th district..............	371,818	+23.1	366,489	+17.0
10th district..............	171,054	−43.4	181,635	−42.0
11th district..............	168,281	−44.3	180,865	−42.2
12th district..............	361,055	+19.5	387,397	+23.7
13th district..............	213,825	−29.2	218,552	−30.2
14th district..............	525,696	+74.0	527,588	+68.5
15th district..............	198,291	−34.4	199,120	−36.4
16th district..............	353,727	+17.1	370,997	+18.5
17th district..............	237,061	−21.5	253,971	−18.9
18th district..............	304,411	+ 0.8	319,217	+ 1.9
19th district..............	427,566	+41.5	439,754	+40.4

[d] Two representatives at large.

POPULATION OF DISTRICTS—*Continued*

State and District	Census of 1930		Census of 1940	
	Population	Departure from State Average (Per cent)	Population	Departure from State Average (Per cent)
Ohio—*Continued*				
20th district..............	301,964	− 0.1	—	—
21st district..............	322,901	+ 6.9	—	—
22d district..............	633,678	+109.7	—	—
At large................	—	—	—	—
At large................	—	—	—	—
Oklahoma.................	2,396,040	—	2,329,808	—
Average per district........	299,505	—	291,226	—
1st district..............	404,981	+35.2	415,615	+42.7
2d district..............	238,281	−20.4	238,799	−18.0
3d district..............	287,397	− 4.0	316,277	+ 8.6
4th district..............	360,468	+20.4	323,670	+11.1
5th district..............	376,738	+25.8	397,811	+36.6
6th district..............	263,164	−12.1	241,962	−16.9
7th district..............	240,944	−19.6	189,414	−35.0
8th district..............	224,067	−25.2	206,260	−29.2
At large................	—	—	—	—
Oregon...................	953,786	—	1,087,717	—
Average per district........	317,929	—	362,572	—
1st district..............	432,572	+36.1	521,285	+43.8
2d district..............	182,973	−42.4	210,996	−41.8
3d district..............	338,241	+ 6.4	355,436	− 2.0
Pennsylvania..............	9,631,350	—	9,891,709	—
Average per district........	283,275	—	290,933	—
1st district..............	286,462	+ 1.1	—	—
2d district..............	247,068	−12.8	—	—
3d district..............	298,461	+ 5.4	—	—
4th district..............	274,376	− 3.1	—	—
5th district..............	269,564	− 4.8	—	—
6th district..............	291,720	+ 3.0	—	—
7th district.....	283,310	0.0	—	—
8th district..............	280,264	− 1.1	310,172	+ 6.6
9th district..............	269,620	− 4.8	285,053	− 2.0
10th district	323,511	+14.2	347,870	+19.6
11th district..............	310,397	+ 9.6	301,083	+ 3.5
12th district..............	445,109	+57.1	440,246	+51.3
13th district..............	364,009	+28.5	354,608	+21.9
14th district..............	231,717	−18.2	241,860	−16.9
15th district..............	205,084	−27.6	211,803	−27.2
16th district..............	235,574	−16.8	244,452	−16.0
17th district..............	265,804	− 6.2	288,856	− 0.7
18th district..............	198,269	−30.0	215,064	−26.1
19th district..............	300,570	+ 6.1	324,807	+11.6
20th district..............	277,067	− 2.2	286,018	− 1.7
21st district..............	260,970	− 7.9	260,557	−10.4
22d district..............	269,273	− 4.9	286,571	− 1.5
23d district..............	272,861	− 3.7	284,721	− 2.1
24th district..............	279,306	− 1.4	287,768	− 1.1
25th district..............	246,569	−13.0	255,163	−12.3
26th district..............	326,800	+15.4	341,360	+17.3
27th district..............	409,953	+44.7	429,222	+47.5
28th district..............	294,995	+ 4.1	302,850	+ 4.1
29th district..............	238,257	−15.9	248,949	−14.4
30th district..............	265,235	− 6.4	—	—
31st district..............	312,312	+10.3	—	—

POPULATION OF DISTRICTS—*Continued*

State and District	Census of 1930		Census of 1940	
	Population	Departure from State Average (Per cent)	Population	Departure from State Average (Per cent)
Pennsylvania—*Continued*				
32d district...............	213,060	−24.8	—	—
33d district...............	282,119	− 0.4	—	—
34th district..............	301,584	+ 6.5	—	—
Rhode Island..............	687,497	—	711,669	—
Average per district........	343,749	—	355,835	—
1st district...............	341,016	− 0.8	—	—
2d district................	346,481	+ 0.8	—	—
South Carolina.............	1,738,765	—	1,905,815	—
Average per district........	289,794	—	317,636	—
1st district...............	260,439	−10.1	289,004	− 9.0
2d district................	338,668	+16.9	369,015	+16.2
3d district................	291,053	+ 0.4	304,225	− 4.2
4th district...............	306,346	+ 5.7	340,650	+ 7.2
5th district...............	235,093	−18.9	250,795	−21.0
6th district...............	307,166	+ 6.0	352,126	+10.9
South Dakota..............	692,849	—	641,134	—
Average per district........	346,425	—	320,567	—
1st district...............	524,769	+51.5	484,584	+51.2
2d district................	168,080	−51.5	156,550	−51.2
Tennessee..................	2,616,556	—	2,910,992	—
Average per district........	290,728	—	323,444	—
1st district...............	333,746	+14.8	383,401	+18.5
2d district................	368,172	+26.6	420,256	+29.9
3d district................	295,760	+ 1.7	329,250	+ 1.8
4th district...............	292,638	+ 0.7	320,188	− 1.0
5th district...............	343,328	+18.1	387,044	+19.7
6th district...............	194,915	−33.0	213,796	−33.9
7th district...............	240,422	−17.3	250,797	−22.5
8th district...............	241,093	−17.1	248,640	−23.1
9th district...............	306,482	+ 5.4	357,620	+10.6
Texas.....................	5,824,715	—	6,418,321	—
Average per district........	277,367	—	305,634	—
1st district...............	294,426	+ 6.2	306,730	+ 0.4
2d district................	304,279	+ 9.7	329,942	+ 8.0
3d district................	214,306	−22.7	292,465	− 4.3
4th district...............	257,879	− 7.0	259,110	−15.2
5th district...............	325,691	+17.4	398,049	+30.2
6th district...............	288,538	+ 4.0	275,498	− 9.9
7th district...............	277,601	+ 0.1	294,009	− 3.8
8th district...............	359,328	+29.5	529,479	+73.2
9th district...............	323,009	+16.5	354,290	+15.9
10th district..............	264,952	− 4.5	285,507	− 6.6
11th district..............	261,147	− 5.8	251,942	−17.6
12th district..............	259,424	− 6.5	286,138	− 6.4
13th district..............	292,579	+ 5.5	279,824	− 8.4
14th district..............	309,516	+11.6	368,638	+20.6
15th district..............	283,291	+ 2.1	333,357	+ 9.1
16th district..............	210,621	−24.1	230,011	−24.7
17th district..............	238,671	−14.0	230,176	−24.7
18th district..............	254,825	− 8.1	239,408	−21.7
19th district..............	254,367	− 8.3	277,756	− 9.1
20th district..............	292,533	+ 5.5	337,557	+10.4
21st district..............	257,732	− 7.1	258,435	−15.4

POPULATION OF DISTRICTS—*Continued*

State and District	Census of 1930		Census of 1940	
	Population	*Departure from State Average (Per cent)*	Population	*Departure from State Average (Per cent)*
Utah.....................	507,847	—	548,393	—
Average per district........	253,924	—	274,197	—
1st district...............	241,290	*– 5.0*	255,814	*– 6.7*
2d district...............	266,557	*+ 5.0*	292,579	*+ 6.7*
Vermont°.................	359,611	—	357,598	—
Virginia..................	2,421,851	—	2,664,847	—
Average per district........	269,095	—	296,094	—
1st district...............	239,757	*–10.9*	244,314	*–17.5*
2d district...............	302,715	*+12.5*	331,688	*+12.0*
3d district...............	281,064	*+ 4.4*	307,012	*+ 3.7*
4th district...............	242,204	*–10.0*	242,778	*–18.0*
5th district...............	271,794	*+ 1.0*	300,896	*+ 1.6*
6th district...............	280,708	*+ 4.3*	301,610	*+ 1.9*
7th district...............	242,778	*– 9.8*	258,714	*–12.6*
8th district...............	256,511	*– 4.7*	317,792	*+ 7.3*
9th district...............	304,320	*+13.1*	360,043	*+21.6*
Washington...............	1,563,396	—	1,721,376	—
Average per district........	260,566	—	286,896	—
1st district...............	396,359	*+52.1*	—	—
2d district...............	236,238	*– 9.3*	—	—
3d district...............	235,372	*– 9.7*	253,945	*–11.5*
4th district...............	209,433	*–19.6*	244,094	*–14.9*
5th district...............	250,064	*– 4.0*	274,435	*– 4.3*
6th district...............	235,930	*– 9.5*	—	—
West Virginia...............	1,729,205	—	1,900,217	—
Average per district........	288,201	—	316,703	—
1st district...............	273,185	*– 5.2*	281,262	*–11.2*
2d district...............	277,001	*– 3.9*	296,585	*– 6.4*
3d district...............	294,334	*+ 2.1*	315,890	*– 0.3*
4th district...............	296,484	*+ 2.9*	322,445	*+ 1.8*
5th district...............	279,342	*– 3.1*	305,619	*– 3.5*
6th district...............	308,859	*+ 7.2*	378,416	*+19.5*
Wisconsin..................	2,939,006	—	3,125,881	—
Average per district........	293,901	—	312,588	—
1st district...............	280,628	*– 4.5*	293,580	*– 6.1*
2d district...............	284,475	*– 3.2*	317,608	*+ 1.6*
3d district...............	274,488	*– 6.6*	290,496	*– 7.1*
4th district...............	353,521	*+20.3*	—	—
5th district...............	371,742	*+26.5*	—	—
6th district...............	268,533	*– 8.6*	283,948	*– 9.2*
7th district...............	276,625	*– 5.9*	294,128	*– 5.9*
8th district...............	300,734	*+ 2.3*	329,075	*+ 5.3*
9th district...............	283,588	*– 3.5*	294,072	*– 5.9*
10th district...............	244,672	*–16.8*	257,494	*–17.6*
Wyoming°.................	225,565	—	246,763	—

APPENDIXES

APPENDIX A

PRIORITY LISTS BASED ON 1930 CENSUS

The tables on the following pages give priority lists based on the census of 1930 for the five modern methods of apportionment. They are reproduced through the courtesy of the Bureau of the Census, which prepared them. These lists were computed in the manner described on page 8; the multipliers used in the computation are given in the several sections of Chapter III describing the five methods.

Figures are given for any size of House up to 454 members; the lists may be extended by multiplying the population of each state by the appropriate multipliers given in Chapter III.

In order to determine the apportionment for any size of House a line is drawn below the number in the first column (total number of representatives from each state), which shows the size of House determined upon. Then for each state the last entry above the line in the fourth column (cumulative total of representatives for each state) shows the number of representatives to which the state is entitled.

As the membership of the House was fixed at 435 in 1929, a line is drawn in the lists at this point. The last entry for each state above the line is shown in black-face type, and the figure in the last column is the apportionment.

PRIORITY LIST, METHOD OF MAJOR FRACTIONS, CENSUS OF 1930

Total Number of Representatives from All States	Priority Numbers	State	Cumulative Total of Representatives from Each State	Total Number of Representatives from All States	Priority Numbers	State	Cumulative Total of Representatives from Each State
49	8,391,978	N.Y.	2	105	1,259,609	Calif.	5
50	6,420,866	Pa.	2	106	1,252,999	Kans.	2
51	5,086,925	Ill.	2	107	1,236,296	Ark.	2
52	5,035,187	N.Y.	3	108	1,214,171	Mass.	4
53	4,431,089	Ohio	2	109	1,208,479	Ohio	6
54	3,883,067	Tex.	2	110	1,198,854	N.Y.	11
55	3,852,520	Pa.	3	111	1,173,906	Ill.	7
56	3,778,827	Calif.	2	112	1,172,688	Wis.	3
57	3,596,562	N.Y.	4	113	1,163,378	Ga.	3
58	3,228,035	Mich.	2	114	1,159,173	S.C.	2
59	3,052,155	Ill.	3	115	1,154,663	N.J.	4
60	2,833,065	Mass.	2	116	1,152,799	W.Va.	2
61	2,797,326	N.Y.	5	117	1,133,094	Pa.	9
62	2,751,800	Pa.	4	118	1,094,606	N.Y.	12
63	2,694,213	N.J.	2	119	1,087,681	Md.	2
64	2,658,653	Ohio	3	120	1,076,012	Mich.	5
65	2,419,407	Mo.	2	121	1,071,265	Conn.	2
66	2,329,840	Tex.	3	122	1,059,018	Tex.	6
67	2,288,721	N.Y.	6	123	1,058,497	Ala.	3
68	2,267,296	Calif.	3	124	1,046,599	Tenn.	3
69	2,180,111	Ill.	4	125	1,045,830	Ky.	3
70	2,158,987	Ind.	2	126	1,036,889	Mo.	4
71	2,140,289	Pa.	5	127	1,034,949	Wash.	2
72	2,111,516	N.C.	2	128	1,030,589	Calif.	6
73	1,954,481	Wis.	2	129	1,022,559	Ohio	7
74	1,938,964	Ga.	2	130	1,020,633	Minn.	3
75	1,936,821	Mich.	3	131	1,017,385	Ill.	8
76	1,936,610	N.Y.	7	132	1,013,821	Pa.	10
77	1,899,038	Ohio	4	133	1,007,037	N.Y.	13
78	1,764,161	Ala.	2	134	988,168	Iowa	3
79	1,751,145	Pa.	6	135	978,794	Fla.	2
80	1,744,331	Tenn.	2	136	968,732	Va.	3
81	1,743,050	Ky.	2	137	952,889	Okla.	3
82	1,701,055	Minn.	2	138	944,355	Mass.	5
83	1,699,839	Mass.	3	139	932,442	N.Y.	14
84	1,695,642	Ill.	5	140	925,280	Ind.	4
85	1,678,396	N.Y.	8	141	917,267	Pa.	11
86	1,664,172	Tex.	4	142	916,749	Nebr.	2
87	1,646,947	Iowa	2	143	904,935	N.C.	4
88	1,619,497	Calif.	4	144	898,071	N.J.	5
89	1,616,528	N.J.	3	145	897,693	Ill.	9
90	1,614,553	Va.	2	146	896,092	Tex.	7
91	1,588,148	Okla.	2	147	886,218	Ohio	8
92	1,481,738	Pa.	7	148	880,373	Mich.	6
93	1,480,937	N.Y.	9	149	872,037	Calif.	7
94	1,477,030	Ohio	5	150	868,136	N.Y.	15
95	1,451,644	Mo.	3	151	840,637	La.	3
96	1,401,062	La.	2	152	837,635	Wis.	4
97	1,387,343	Ill.	6	153	837,504	Pa.	12
98	1,383,443	Mich.	4	154	830,985	Ga.	4
99	1,338,769	Miss.	2	155	812,127	N.Y.	16
100	1,325,049	N.Y.	10	156	806,469	Mo.	5
101	1,295,392	Ind.	3	157	803,262	Miss.	3
102	1,294,356	Tex.	5	158	803,199	Ill.	10
103	1,284,173	Pa.	8	159	781,957	Ohio	9
104	1,266,910	N.C.	3	160	776,613	Tex.	8

PRIORITY LIST, METHOD OF MAJOR FRACTIONS, CENSUS OF 1930—*Continued*

Total Number of Representatives from All States	Priority Numbers	State	Cumulative Total of Representatives from Each State	Total Number of Representatives from All States	Priority Numbers	State	Cumulative Total of Representatives from Each State
161	772,654	Mass.	6	217	573,758	Miss.	4
162	770,504	Pa.	13	218	569,653	Mich.	9
163	762,907	N.Y.	17	219	567,018	Minn.	5
164	756,069	Ala.	4	220	566,613	Mass.	8
165	755,765	Calif.	8	221	565,214	Ill.	14
166	751,799	Kans.	3	222	559,465	N.Y.	23
167	747,571	Tenn.	4	223	558,325	Mo.	7
168	747,021	Ky.	4	224	554,724	Tex.	11
169	744,931	Mich.	7	225	550,360	Pa.	18
170	741,778	Ark.	3	226	550,049	Nebr.	3
171	734,785	N.J.	6	227	548,982	Iowa	5
172	729,024	Minn.	4	228	539,832	Calif.	11
173	726,704	Ill.	11	229	538,843	N.J.	8
174	719,662	Ind.	5	230	538,184	Va.	5
175	719,312	N.Y.	18	231	536,999	Kans.	4
176	713,430	Pa.	14	232	535,658	N.Y.	24
177	705,834	Iowa	4	233	533,040	Wis.	6
178	703,839	N.C.	5	234	531,731	Ohio	13
179	699,646	Ohio	10	235	531,612	Maine	2
180	695,504	S.C.	3	236	529,841	Ark.	4
181	691,951	Va.	4	237	529,383	Okla.	5
182	691,680	W.Va.	3	238	528,808	Ga.	6
183	689,899	Colo.	2	239	526,234	Ill.	15
184	685,247	Tex.	9	240	520,611	Pa.	19
185	680,635	Okla.	4	241	513,795	N.Y.	25
186	680,431	N.Y.	19	242	509,690	Mich.	10
187	666,852	Calif.	9	243	506,487	Tex.	12
188	664,228	Pa.	15	244	499,953	Mass.	9
189	663,512	Ill.	12	245	498,228	Ind.	7
190	659,838	Mo.	6	246	496,789	S.C.	4
191	653,784	Mass.	7	247	494,057	W.Va.	4
192	652,609	Md.	3	248	493,913	Pa.	20
193	651,494	Wis.	5	249	493,646	N.Y.	26
194	646,321	Ga.	5	250	492,891	Calif.	12
195	645,607	Mich.	8	251	492,343	Ohio	14
196	645,537	N.Y.	20	252	492,283	Ill.	16
197	642,759	Conn.	3	253	487,273	N.C.	7
198	633,586	Oreg.	2	254	483,881	Mo.	8
199	633,013	Ohio	11	255	481,135	Ala.	6
200	621,741	N.J.	7	256	475,727	Tenn.	6
201	621,374	Pa.	16	257	475,449	N.J.	9
202	620,969	Wash.	3	258	475,377	Ky.	6
203	614,047	N.Y.	21	259	475,018	N.Y.	27
204	613,116	Tex.	10	260	469,819	Pa.	21
205	610,431	Ill.	13	261	467,021	La.	5
206	600,455	La.	4	262	466,149	Md.	4
207	596,657	Calif.	10	263	465,968	Tex.	13
208	588,815	Ind.	6	264	463,924	Minn.	6
209	588,054	Ala.	5	265	462,448	Ill.	17
210	587,276	Fla.	3	266	461,148	Mich.	11
211	585,487	N.Y.	22	267	459,113	Conn.	4
212	583,715	Pa.	17	268	458,388	Ohio	15
213	581,444	Tenn.	5	**269**	**458,331**	**R.I.**	**2**
214	581,017	Ky.	5	270	457,744	N.Y.	28
215	577,968	Ohio	12	271	453,459	Calif.	13
216	575,868	N.C.	6	272	451,034	Wis.	7

PRIORITY LIST, METHOD OF MAJOR FRACTIONS, CENSUS OF 1930—*Continued*

Total Number of Representatives from All States	Priority Numbers	State	Cumulative Total of Representatives from Each State	Total Number of Representatives from All States	Priority Numbers	State	Cumulative Total of Representatives from Each State
273	449,167	Iowa	6	329	375,760	N.Y.	34
274	**448,893**	**N.Dak.**	**2**	330	372,620	N.C.	9
275	**448,670**	**S.Dak.**	**2**	331	372,589	Va.	7
276	447,967	Pa.	22	332	372,214	Ill.	21
277	447,453	Ga.	7	333	369,530	Mass.	12
278	447,326	Mass.	10	334	366,496	Okla.	7
279	446,256	Miss.	5	335	365,693	Calif.	16
280	443,549	Wash.	4	336	365,119	Miss.	6
281	441,683	N.Y.	29	337	364,869	N.Y.	35
282	440,333	Va.	6	338	363,445	Pa.	27
283	436,022	Ill.	18	339	362,560	Md.	5
284	433,131	Okla.	6	340	359,277	Ohio	19
285	431,797	Ind.	8	341	358,671	Mich.	14
286	431,452	Tex.	14	342	357,088	Conn.	5
287	428,815	Ohio	16	343	354,902	Ill.	22
288	428,058	Pa.	23	344	354,591	N.Y.	36
289	426,954	Mo.	9	345	353,006	Tex.	17
290	426,711	N.Y.	30	346	352,832	Ala.	8
291	425,402	N.J.	10	347	351,419	N.J.	12
292	422,303	N.C.	8	348	350,229	Pa.	28
293	421,048	Mich.	12	**349**	**349,819**	**Mont.**	**2**
294	419,870	Calif.	14	350	348,866	Tenn.	8
295	419,483	Fla.	4	351	348,610	Ky.	8
296	417,666	Kans.	5	352	345,630	Mo.	11
297	413,940	Colo.	3	353	344,983	Wash.	5
298	412,720	N.Y.	31	354	344,908	Wis.	9
299	412,453	Ill.	19	355	344,876	N.Y.	37
300	412,099	Ark.	5	356	343,530	Calif.	17
301	409,843	Pa.	24	357	342,170	Ga.	9
302	407,114	Ala.	7	358	341,727	Kans.	6
303	404,724	Mass.	11	359	340,893	Ind.	10
304	402,826	Ohio	17	360	340,853	Ohio	20
305	402,538	Tenn.	7	361	340,211	Minn.	8
306	402,242	Ky.	7	362	339,968	Mass.	13
307	401,697	Tex.	15	363	339,128	Ill.	23
308	399,618	N.Y.	32	364	337,940	Pa.	29
309	393,114	Pa.	25	365	337,172	Ark.	6
310	392,892	Nebr.	4	**366**	**337,161**	**Utah**	**2**
311	392,551	Minn.	7	367	335,679	N.Y.	38
312	391,302	Ill.	20	368	333,935	Mich.	15
313	390,913	Calif.	15	369	333,397	N.C.	10
314	390,896	Wis.	8	370	332,834	Tex.	18
315	387,793	Ga.	8	371	329,389	Iowa	8
316	387,364	Mich.	13	372	326,960	N.Y.	39
317	387,322	N.Y.	33	373	326,485	Pa.	30
318	386,391	S.C.	5	**374**	**326,265**	**Fla.**	**5**
319	384,888	N.J.	11	375	324,697	Ill.	24
320	384,266	W.Va.	5	376	324,226	Ohio	21
321	382,108	La.	6	377	323,899	Calif.	18
322	382,012	Mo.	10	378	323,322	La.	7
323	380,998	Ind.	9	379	323,306	N.J.	13
324	**380,152**	**Oreg.**	**3**	380	322,911	Va.	8
325	380,065	Iowa	7	**381**	**318,967**	**Maine**	**3**
326	379,808	Ohio	18	382	318,683	N.Y.	40
327	377,698	Pa.	26	383	317,630	Okla.	8
328	375,781	Tex.	16	**384**	**316,138**	**S.C.**	**6**

PRIORITY LIST, METHOD OF MAJOR FRACTIONS, CENSUS OF 1930—*Continued*

Total Number of Representatives from All States	Priority Numbers	State	Cumulative Total of Representatives from Each State	Total Number of Representatives from All States	Priority Numbers	State	Cumulative Total of Representatives from Each State
385	315,780	Pa.	31	421	290,638	Iowa	9
386	315,575	Mo.	12	422	290,329	Mo.	13
387	314,843	Tex.	19	423	289,379	N.Y.	44
388	314,785	Mass.	14	424	289,154	Kans.	7
389	314,400	W.Va.	6	425	287,939	Ill.	27
390	312,390	Mich.	16	426	287,501	Pa.	34
391	311,444	Ill.	25	427	285,299	Ark.	7
392	311,323	Ala.	9	428	284,921	Va.	9
393	310,814	N.Y.	41	429	284,127	Tex.	21
394	310,195	N.H.	2	430	282,876	N.Y.	45
395	309,146	Ohio	22	431	282,835	Ohio	24
396	308,947	Miss.	7	432	282,259	Wash.	6
397	308,602	Wis.	10	433	281,607	Ind.	12
398	308,427	Ind.	11	434	280,261	Okla.	9
399	307,823	Tenn.	9	435	280,212	La.	8
400	307,597	Ky.	9	436	279,212	Wis.	11
401	306,391	Calif.	19				
402	306,152	Ga.	10	437	279,168	Pa.	35
403	305,756	Pa.	32	438	278,712	N.J.	15
404	305,583	Nebr.	5	439	278,552	Ala.	10
405	303,325	N.Y.	42	440	277,469	Ill.	28
406	301,645	N.C.	11	441	276,995	Ga.	11
407	300,186	Minn.	9	442	276,689	Mich.	18
408	299,357	N.J.	14	443	276,659	N.Y.	46
409	299,231	Ill.	26	444	276,500	Calif.	21
410	298,697	Tex.	20	445	275,421	Tenn.	10
411	296,640	Md.	6	446	275,415	N.C.	12
412	296,348	Pa.	33	447	275,218	Ky.	10
413	296,187	N.Y.	43	448	274,999	R.I.	3
414	295,671	Colo.	4	449	274,168	Mass.	16
415	295,406	Ohio	23	450	271,537	Oreg.	4
416	294,357	Idaho	2	451	271,304	Pa.	36
417	293,458	Mich.	17	452	271,291	Ohio	25
418	293,076	Mass.	15	453	270,912	Tex.	22
419	292,163	Conn.	6	454	270,709	N.Y.	47
420	290,679	Calif.	20				

With a House of 435 members the following states do not appear in the priority list for the method of major fractions and receive one member each:

Arizona	New Mexico
Delaware	Vermont
Nevada	Wyoming

PRIORITY LIST, METHOD OF EQUAL PROPORTIONS, CENSUS OF 1930

Total Number of Representatives from All States	Priority Numbers	State	Cumulative Total of Representatives from Each State	Total Number of Representatives from All States	Priority Numbers	State	Cumulative Total of Representatives from Each State
49	8,901,037	N.Y.	2	105	1,293,034	N.C.	3
50	6,810,357	Pa.	2	106	1,287,036	Pa.	8
51	5,395,499	Ill.	2	107	1,267,457	Calif.	5
52	5,139,016	N.Y.	3	108	1,229,489	S.C.	2
53	4,699,879	Ohio	2	109	1,226,753	Mass.	4
54	4,118,615	Tex.	2	110	1,222,728	W.Va.	2
55	4,008,052	Calif.	2	111	1,213,504	Ohio	6
56	3,931,961	Pa.	3	112	1,200,216	N.Y.	11
57	3,633,833	N.Y.	4	113	1,196,870	Wis.	3
58	3,423,848	Mich.	2	114	1,187,368	Ga.	3
59	3,115,093	Ill.	3	115	1,177,394	Ill.	7
60	3,004,920	Mass.	2	116	1,166,628	N.J.	4
61	2,857,644	N.J.	2	117	1,153,660	Md.	2
62	2,814,755	N.Y.	5	118	1,136,248	Conn.	2
63	2,780,316	Pa.	4	119	1,135,059	Pa.	9
64	2,713,477	Ohio	3	120	1,097,729	Wash.	2
65	2,566,168	Mo.	2	121	1,095,642	N.Y.	12
66	2,377,883	Tex.	3	122	1,082,716	Mich.	5
67	2,314,050	Calif.	3	123	1,080,324	Ala.	3
68	2,298,238	N.Y.	6	124	1,068,180	Tenn.	3
69	2,289,951	Ind.	2	125	1,067,396	Ky.	3
70	2,239,601	N.C.	2	126	1,063,422	Tex.	6
71	2,202,703	Ill.	4	127	1,047,634	Mo.	4
72	2,153,624	Pa.	5	128	1,041,679	Minn.	3
73	2,073,040	Wis.	2	129	1,038,168	Fla.	2
74	2,056,581	Ga.	2	130	1,034,875	Calif.	6
75	1,976,759	Mich.	3	131	1,025,597	Ohio	7
76	1,942,365	N.Y.	7	132	1,019,653	Ill.	8
77	1,918,717	Ohio	4	133	1,015,228	Pa.	10
78	1,871,176	Ala.	2	134	1,008,545	Iowa	3
79	1,850,143	Tenn.	2	135	1,007,844	N.Y.	13
80	1,848,784	Ky.	2	136	988,708	Va.	3
81	1,804,242	Minn.	2	137	972,538	Okla.	3
82	1,758,427	Pa.	6	138	972,359	Nebr.	2
83	1,746,851	Iowa	2	139	950,239	Mass.	5
84	1,734,891	Mass.	3	140	934,869	Ind.	4
85	1,712,492	Va.	2	141	933,082	N.Y.	14
86	1,706,207	Ill.	5	142	918,309	Pa.	11
87	1,684,485	Okla.	2	143	914,313	N.C.	4
88	1,682,138	N.Y.	8	144	903,666	N.J.	5
89	1,681,417	Tex.	4	145	899,250	Ill.	9
90	1,649,862	N.J.	3	146	898,755	Tex.	7
91	1,636,280	Calif.	4	147	888,194	Ohio	8
92	1,486,232	Ohio	5	148	884,034	Mich.	6
93	1,486,141	Pa.	7	149	874,628	Calif.	7
94	1,486,051	La.	2	150	868,653	N.Y.	15
95	1,483,506	N.Y.	9	151	857,972	La.	3
96	1,481,578	Mo.	3	152	846,315	Wis.	4
97	1,419,973	Miss.	2	153	839,596	Ga.	4
98	1,397,780	Mich.	4	154	838,297	Pa.	12
99	1,393,112	Ill.	6	155	819,825	Miss.	3
100	1,329,006	Kans.	2	156	812,549	N.Y.	16
101	1,326,889	N.Y.	10	157	811,494	Mo.	5
102	1,322,104	Ind.	3	158	804,314	Ill.	10
103	1,311,290	Ark.	2	159	783,313	Ohio	9
104	1,302,420	Tex.	5	160	778,345	Tex.	8

PRIORITY LIST, METHOD OF EQUAL PROPORTIONS, CENSUS OF 1930—*Continued*

Total Number of Representatives from All States	Priority Numbers	State	Cumulative Total of Representatives from Each State	Total Number of Representatives from All States	Priority Numbers	State	Cumulative Total of Representatives from Each State
161	775,867	Mass.	6	217	578,263	N.C.	6
162	771,121	Pa.	13	218	570,641	Mich.	9
163	767,302	Kans.	3	219	570,551	Minn.	5
164	763,904	Ala.	4	220	567,876	Mass.	8
165	763,258	N.Y.	17	221	565,602	Ill.	14
166	757,450	Calif.	8	222	563,860	Maine	2
167	757,074	Ark.	3	223	561,392	Nebr.	3
168	755,318	Tenn.	4	224	559,984	Mo.	7
169	754,763	Ky.	4	225	559,603	N.Y.	23
170	747,145	Mich.	7	226	555,354	Tex.	11
171	737,840	N.J.	6	227	552,403	Iowa	5
172	736,578	Minn.	4	228	550,585	Pa.	18
173	731,749	Colo.	2	229	542,564	Kans.	4
174	727,529	Ill.	11	230	541,537	Va.	5
175	724,146	Ind.	5	231	540,446	Calif.	11
176	719,606	N.Y.	18	232	540,044	N.J.	8
177	713,919	Pa.	14	233	535,779	N.Y.	24
178	713,148	Iowa	4	234	535,332	Ark.	4
179	709,846	S.C.	3	235	535,257	Wis.	6
180	708,224	N.C.	5	236	532,681	Okla.	5
181	705,943	W.Va.	3	237	532,157	Ohio	13
182	700,617	Ohio	10	238	531,007	Ga.	6
183	699,122	Va.	4	239	526,547	Ill.	15
184	672,019	Oreg.	2	240	520,801	Pa.	19
185	687,688	Okla.	4	241	513,901	N.Y.	25
186	686,436	Tex.	9	242	510,397	Mich.	10
187	680,679	N.Y.	19	243	506,966	Tex.	12
188	668,008	Calif.	9	244	501,937	S.C.	4
189	666,066	Md.	3	245	500,820	Mass.	9
190	664,623	Pa.	15	246	499,708	Ind.	7
191	664,140	Ill.	12	247	499,177	W.Va.	4
192	662,582	Mo.	6	248	494,075	Pa.	20
193	656,013	Conn.	3	249	493,740	N.Y.	26
194	655,727	Mass.	7	250	493,357	Calif.	12
195	655,553	Wis.	5	251	492,681	Ohio	14
196	650,348	Ga.	5	252	492,539	Ill.	16
197	647,046	Mich.	8	253	488,721	N.C.	7
198	645,749	N.Y.	20	254	486,134	R.I.	2
199	633,774	Wash.	3	255	484,960	Mo.	8
200	633,732	Ohio	11	256	483,136	Ala.	6
201	623,589	N.J.	7	257	477,867	Ga.	7
202	621,697	Pa.	16	258	477,705	Tenn.	6
203	614,230	N.Y.	21	259	477,354	Ky.	6
204	613,967	Tex.	10	260	476,274	N.J.	9
205	610,920	Ill.	13	261	476,123	N.Dak.	2
206	606,678	La.	4	262	475,886	S.Dak.	2
207	599,386	Fla.	3	263	475,103	N.Y.	27
208	597,485	Calif.	10	264	470,980	Md.	4
209	591,718	Ala.	5	265	469,959	Pa.	21
210	591,263	Ind.	6	266	469,930	La.	5
211	585,645	N.Y.	22	267	466,341	Tex.	13
212	585,067	Tenn.	5	268	465,322	Minn.	6
213	584,623	Ky.	5	269	463,871	Conn.	4
214	583,983	Pa.	17	270	462,660	Ill.	17
215	579,704	Miss.	4	271	461,672	Mich.	11
216	578,515	Ohio	12	272	458,662	Ohio	15

PRIORITY LIST, METHOD OF EQUAL PROPORTIONS, CENSUS OF 1930—*Continued*

Total Number of Representatives from All States	Priority Numbers	State	Cumulative Total of Representatives from Each State	Total Number of Representatives from All States	Priority Numbers	State	Cumulative Total of Representatives from Each State
273	457,819	N.Y.	28	329	375,802	N.Y.	34
274	453,823	Calif.	13	330	373,696	Va.	7
275	452,374	Wis.	7	331	373,267	N.C.	9
276	451,035	Iowa	6	332	372,325	Ill.	21
277	449,037	Miss.	5	**333**	**371,039**	**Mont.**	**2**
278	448,146	Wash.	4	334	369,880	Mass.	12
279	448,088	Pa.	22	335	367,585	Okla.	7
280	447,947	Mass.	10	336	366,637	Miss.	6
281	442,163	Va.	6	337	365,883	Calif.	16
282	441,751	N.Y.	29	338	364,908	N.Y.	35
283	436,200	Ill.	18	339	364,819	Md.	5
284	434,932	Okla.	6	340	363,510	Pa.	27
285	432,760	Ind.	8	341	359,409	Ohio	19
286	431,748	Tex.	14	342	359,313	Conn.	5
287	429,038	Ohio	16	343	358,917	Mich.	14
288	428,163	Pa.	23	**344**	**357,613**	**Utah**	**2**
289	427,695	Mo.	9	345	354,998	Ill.	22
290	426,772	N.Y.	30	346	354,625	N.Y.	36
291	425,993	N.J.	10	347	353,619	Ala.	8
292	423,830	Fla.	4	348	353,168	Tex.	17
293	423,245	N.C.	8	349	351,752	N.J.	12
294	422,475	Colo.	3	350	350,286	Pa.	28
295	421,446	Mich.	12	351	349,644	Tenn.	8
296	420,269	Kans.	5	352	349,387	Ky.	8
297	420,156	Calif.	14	353	347,132	Wash.	5
298	414,666	Ark.	5	354	346,022	Mo.	11
299	412,776	N.Y.	31	355	345,507	Wis.	9
300	412,604	Ill.	19	356	344,908	N.Y.	37
301	409,935	Pa.	24	357	343,688	Calif.	17
302	408,324	Ala.	7	358	343,148	Kans.	6
303	405,183	Mass.	11	359	342,764	Ga.	9
304	403,734	Tenn.	7	360	341,366	Ind.	10
305	403,438	Ky.	7	361	340,970	Minn.	8
306	403,011	Ohio	17	362	340,965	Ohio	20
307	401,936	Tex.	15	363	340,240	Mass.	13
308	399,668	N.Y.	32	364	339,212	Ill.	23
309	396,964	Nebr.	4	365	338,574	Ark.	6
310	393,718	Minn.	7	366	337,992	Pa.	29
311	393,196	Pa.	25	367	335,708	N.Y.	38
312	391,768	Wis.	8	368	334,134	Mich.	15
313	391,431	Ill.	20	369	333,860	N.C.	10
314	391,146	Calif.	15	370	332,970	Tex.	18
315	388,799	S.C.	5	371	330,124	Iowa	8
316	388,657	Ga.	8	**372**	**328,304**	**N.H.**	**2**
317	**387,991**	**Oreg.**	**3**	373	328,297	Fla.	5
318	387,675	Mich.	13	374	326,988	N.Y.	39
319	387,368	N.Y.	33	375	326,532	Pa.	30
320	386,660	W.Va.	5	**376**	**325,545**	**Maine**	**3**
321	385,325	N.J.	11	377	324,771	Ill.	24
322	383,697	La.	6	378	324,322	Ohio	21
323	382,542	Mo.	10	379	324,283	La.	7
324	381,658	Ind.	9	380	324,032	Calif.	18
325	381,194	Iowa	7	381	323,630	Va.	8
326	379,963	Ohio	18	382	323,565	N.J.	13
327	377,770	Pa.	26	383	318,708	N.Y.	40
328	375,976	Tex.	16	384	318,338	Okla.	8

PRIORITY LIST, METHOD OF EQUAL PROPORTIONS, CENSUS OF 1930—*Continued*

Total Number of Representatives from All States	Priority Numbers	State	Cumulative Total of Representatives from Each State	Total Number of Representatives from All States	Priority Numbers	State	Cumulative Total of Representatives from Each State
385	317,453	S.C.	6	421	290,774	Calif.	20
386	315,873	Mo.	12	422	290,561	Mo.	13
387	315,823	Pa.	31	423	290,013	Kans.	7
388	315,707	W.Va.	6	424	289,397	N.Y.	44
389	315,001	Mass.	14	425	287,991	Ill.	27
390	314,958	Texas	19	426	287,534	Pa.	34
391	312,553	Mich.	16	427	286,147	Ark.	7
392	312,213	Idaho	2	428	285,415	Va.	9
393	311,863	Ala.	9	429	284,211	Tex.	21
394	311,509	Ill.	25	430	283,432	Wash.	6
395	310,837	N.Y.	41	431	282,899	Ohio	24
396	309,865	Miss.	7	432	282,893	N.Y.	45
397	309,229	Ohio	22	433	281,873	Ind.	12
398	309,031	Wis.	10	434	280,837	La.	8
399	308,777	Ind.	11	435	280,747	Okla.	9
400	308,357	Tenn.	9	436	280,669	R.I.	3
401	308,131	Ky.	9				
402	307,487	Nebr.	5	437	280,001	N.Mex.	2
403	306,577	Ga.	10	438	279,529	Wis.	11
404	306,503	Calif.	19	439	279,198	Pa.	35
				440	278,939	Ala.	10
405	305,794	Pa.	32				
406	303,346	N.Y.	42	441	278,878	N.J.	15
407	301,988	N.C.	11	442	277,514	Ill.	28
408	300,707	Minn.	9	443	277,310	Ga.	11
				444	276,802	Mich.	18
409	299,562	N.J.	14				
410	299,288	Ill.	26	445	276,675	N.Y.	46
411	298,796	Tex.	20	446	276,582	Calif.	21
412	298,735	Colo.	4	447	275,803	Tenn.	10
				448	275,676	N.C.	12
413	297,874	Md.	6				
414	296,383	Pa.	33	449	275,601	Ky.	10
415	296,207	N.Y.	43	450	275,330	Ariz.	2
416	295,479	Ohio	23	451	274,890	N.Dak.	3
				452	274,753	S.Dak.	3
417	293,592	Mich.	17				
418	293,378	Conn.	6	453	274,351	Oreg.	4
419	293,250	Mass.	15	454	274,310	Mass.	16
420	291,142	Iowa	9				

With a House of 435 members the following states do not appear in the priority list for the method of equal proportions and are assigned one member each:

Arizona	New Mexico
Delaware	Vermont
Nevada	Wyoming

PRIORITY LIST, METHOD OF HARMONIC MEAN, CENSUS OF 1930

Total Number of Representatives from All States	Priority Numbers	State	Cumulative Total of Representatives from Each State	Total Number of Representatives from All States	Priority Numbers	State	Cumulative Total of Representatives from Each State
49	9,440,975	N.Y.	2	105	1,310,535	Tex.	5
50	7,223,474	Pa.	2	106	1,304,070	S.C.	2
51	5,722,791	Ill.	2	107	1,296,899	W.Va.	2
52	5,244,985	N.Y.	3	108	1,289,905	Pa.	8
53	4,984,975	Ohio	2	109	1,275,354	Calif.	5
54	4,368,451	Tex.	2	110	1,239,466	Mass.	4
55	4,251,181	Calif.	2	111	1,223,642	Md.	2
56	4,013,041	Pa.	3	112	1,221,550	Wis.	3
57	3,671,490	N.Y.	4	113	1,218,549	Ohio	6
58	3,631,539	Mich.	2	114	1,211,852	Ga.	3
59	3,187,198	Mass.	2	115	1,205,173	Conn.	2
60	3,179,328	Ill.	3	116	1,201,578	N.Y.	11
61	3,030,989	N.J.	2	117	1,180,893	Ill.	7
62	2,832,293	N.Y.	5	118	1,178,718	N.J.	4
63	2,809,128	Pa.	4	119	1,164,317	Wash.	2
64	2,769,430	Ohio	3	120	1,137,028	Pa.	9
65	2,721,832	Mo.	2	121	1,102,601	Ala.	3
66	2,428,860	Ind.	2	122	1,101,143	Fla.	2
67	2,426,917	Tex.	3	123	1,096,679	N.Y.	12
68	2,375,456	N.C.	2	124	1,090,207	Tenn.	3
69	2,361,767	Calif.	3	125	1,089,462	Mich.	5
70	2,307,794	N.Y.	6	126	1,089,406	Ky.	3
71	2,225,529	Ill.	4	127	1,067,843	Tex.	6
72	2,198,791	Wis.	2	128	1,063,159	Minn.	3
73	2,181,334	Ga.	2	129	1,058,490	Mo.	4
74	2,167,042	Pa.	5	130	1,039,177	Calif.	6
75	2,017,521	Mich.	3	131	1,031,342	Nebr.	2
76	1,984,682	Ala.	2	132	1,029,342	Iowa	3
77	1,962,373	Tenn.	2	133	1,028,646	Ohio	7
78	1,960,931	Ky.	2	134	1,021,926	Ill.	8
79	1,948,138	N.Y.	7	135	1,016,637	Pa.	10
80	1,938,601	Ohio	4	136	1,009,095	Va.	3
81	1,913,687	Minn.	2	137	1,008,651	N.Y.	13
82	1,852,815	Iowa	2	138	992,592	Okla.	3
83	1,816,372	Va.	2	139	956,160	Mass.	5
84	1,786,666	Okla.	2	140	944,556	Ind.	4
85	1,770,666	Mass.	3	141	933,723	N.Y.	14
86	1,765,738	Pa.	6	142	923,788	N.C.	4
87	1,716,837	Ill.	5	143	919,351	Pa.	11
88	1,698,842	Tex.	4	144	909,297	N.J.	5
89	1,685,888	N.Y.	8	145	901,426	Tex.	7
90	1,683,883	N.J.	3	146	900,809	Ill.	9
91	1,653,237	Calif.	4	147	890,174	Ohio	8
92	1,576,195	La.	2	148	887,709	Mich.	6
93	1,512,129	Mo.	3	149	877,228	Calif.	7
94	1,506,116	Miss.	2	150	875,664	La.	3
95	1,495,492	Ohio	5	151	869,169	N.Y.	15
96	1,490,558	Pa.	7	152	855,085	Wis.	4
97	1,486,078	N.Y.	9	153	848,297	Ga.	4
98	1,412,265	Mich.	4	154	839,090	Pa.	12
99	1,409,624	Kans.	2	155	836,731	Miss.	3
100	1,398,904	Ill.	6	156	816,550	Mo.	5
101	1,390,833	Ark.	2	157	812,972	N.Y.	16
102	1,349,366	Ind.	3	158	805,429	Ill.	10
103	1,328,729	N.Y.	10	159	784,672	Ohio	9
104	1,319,697	N.C.	3	160	783,124	Kans.	3

PRIORITY LIST, METHOD OF HARMONIC MEAN, CENSUS OF 1930—*Continued*

Total Number of Representatives from All States	Priority Numbers	State	Cumulative Total of Representatives from Each State	Total Number of Representatives from All States	Priority Numbers	State	Cumulative Total of Representatives from Each State
161	780,080	Tex.	8	217	580,667	N.C.	6
162	779,093	Mass.	6	218	579,063	Ohio	12
163	776,137	Colo.	2	219	574,106	Minn.	5
164	772,685	Ark.	3	220	572,968	Nebr.	3
165	771,821	Ala.	4	221	571,631	Mich.	9
166	771,739	Pa.	13	222	569,142	Mass.	8
167	763,607	N.Y.	17	223	565,990	Ill.	14
168	763,145	Tenn.	4	224	561,648	Mo.	7
169	762,584	Ky.	4	225	559,742	N.Y.	23
170	759,139	Calif.	8	226	555,984	Tex.	11
171	749,365	Mich.	7	227	555,844	Iowa	5
172	744,212	Minn.	4	228	550,809	Pa.	18
173	740,908	N.J.	6	229	548,187	Kans.	4
174	728,658	Ind.	5	230	544,912	Va.	5
175	728,355	Ill.	11	231	541,248	N.J.	8
176	724,483	S.C.	3	232	541,059	Calif.	11
177	720,539	Iowa	4	233	540,879	Ark.	4
178	720,499	W.Va.	3	234	537,482	Wis.	6
179	719,900	N.Y.	18	235	536,000	Okla.	5
180	714,409	Pa.	14	236	535,901	N.Y.	24
181	712,784	Oreg.	2	237	533,215	Ga.	6
182	712,637	N.C.	5	238	532,583	Ohio	13
183	706,367	Va.	4	239	526,860	Ill.	15
184	701,589	Ohio	10	240	520,992	Pa.	19
185	694,815	Okla.	4	241	515,623	R.I.	2
186	687,626	Tex.	9	242	514,008	N.Y.	25
187	680,928	N.Y.	19	243	511,105	Mich.	10
188	679,801	Md.	3	244	507,446	Tex.	12
189	669,540	Conn.	3	245	507,138	S.C.	4
190	669,167	Calif.	9	246	505,005	N.Dak.	2
191	665,337	Mo.	6	247	504,754	S.Dak.	2
192	665,018	Pa.	15	248	504,350	W.Va.	4
193	664,769	Ill.	12	249	501,688	Mass.	9
194	659,637	Wis.	5	250	501,193	Ind.	7
195	657,676	Mass.	7	251	494,237	Pa.	20
196	654,400	Ga.	5	252	493,835	N.Y.	26
197	648,489	Mich.	8	253	493,824	Calif.	12
198	646,843	Wash.	3	254	493,019	Ohio	14
199	645,960	N.Y.	20	255	492,796	Ill.	16
200	634,451	Ohio	11	256	490,173	N.C.	7
201	625,442	N.J.	7	257	486,041	Mo.	8
202	622,021	Pa.	16	258	485,144	Ala.	6
203	614,819	Tex.	10	259	479,691	Tenn.	6
204	614,412	N.Y.	21	260	479,339	Ky.	6
205	612,964	La.	4	261	477,100	N.J.	9
206	611,746	Fla.	3	262	475,860	Md.	4
207	611,409	Ill.	13	263	475,186	N.Y.	27
208	598,314	Calif.	10	264	472,858	La.	5
209	598,064	Maine	2	265	470,099	Pa.	21
210	595,404	Ala.	5	266	468,678	Conn.	4
211	593,721	Ind.	6	267	467,790	Minn.	6
212	588,712	Tenn.	5	268	466,715	Tex.	13
213	588,279	Ky.	5	269	462,872	Ill.	17
214	585,802	N.Y.	22	270	462,196	Mich.	11
215	585,711	Miss.	4	271	458,934	Ohio	15
216	584,251	Pa.	17	272	457,895	N.Y.	28

PRIORITY LIST, METHOD OF HARMONIC MEAN, CENSUS OF 1930—*Continued*

Total Number of Representatives from All States	Priority Numbers	State	Cumulative Total of Representatives from Each State	Total Number of Representatives from All States	Priority Numbers	State	Cumulative Total of Representatives from Each State
273	454,186	Calif.	13	329	377,843	Pa.	26
274	453,719	Wis.	7	330	376,172	Tex.	16
275	452,910	Iowa	6	331	375,843	N.Y.	34
276	452,790	Wash.	4	332	374,807	Va.	7
277	451,835	Miss.	5	333	373,914	N.C.	9
278	450,117	Ga.	7	334	372,435	Ill.	21
279	448,568	Mass.	10	335	370,230	Mass.	12
280	448,209	Pa.	22	336	368,677	Okla.	7
281	444,002	Va.	6	337	368,161	Miss.	6
282	441,819	N.Y.	29	338	367,092	Md.	5
283	436,741	Okla.	6	339	336,074	Calif.	16
284	436,378	Ill.	18	340	364,944	N.Y.	35
285	433,725	Ind.	8	341	363,574	Pa.	27
286	432,044	Tex.	14	342	361,552	Conn.	5
287	431,187	Colo.	3	343	359,540	Ohio	19
288	429,261	Ohio	16	344	359,163	Mich.	14
289	428,436	Mo.	9	345	355,093	Ill.	22
290	428,269	Pa.	23	346	354,661	N.Y.	36
291	428,222	Fla.	4	347	354,407	Ala.	8
292	426,833	N.Y.	30	348	353,330	Tex.	17
293	426,583	N.J.	10	349	352,085	N.J.	12
294	424,188	N.C.	8	350	350,425	Tenn.	8
295	422,887	Kans.	5	351	350,344	Pa.	28
296	421,845	Mich.	12	352	350,166	Ky.	8
297	420,446	Calif.	14	353	349,295	Wash.	5
298	417,250	Ark.	5	354	348,969	N.H.	2
299	412,830	N.Y.	31	355	346,415	Mo.	11
300	412,755	Ill.	19	356	346,106	Wis.	9
301	410,028	Pa.	24	357	344,941	N.Y.	37
302	409,537	Ala.	7	358	344,575	Kans.	6
303	405,643	Mass.	11	359	343,845	Calif.	17
304	404,934	Tenn.	7	360	343,358	Ga.	9
305	404,637	Ky.	7	361	341,839	Ind.	10
306	403,196	Ohio	17	362	341,730	Minn.	8
307	402,175	Tex.	15	363	341,077	Ohio	20
308	401,077	Nebr.	4	364	340,513	Mass.	13
309	399,718	N.Y.	32	365	339,981	Ark.	6
310	**395,991**	**Oreg.**	**3**	366	339,296	Ill.	23
311	394,888	Minn.	7	367	338,044	Pa.	29
312	**393,547**	**Mont.**	**2**	368	335,739	N.Y.	38
313	393,278	Pa.	25	369	334,332	Mich.	15
314	392,641	Wis.	8	370	334,323	N.C.	10
315	391,559	Ill.	20	371	333,106	Tex.	18
316	391,378	Calif.	15	**372**	**332,257**	**Maine**	**3**
317	391,221	S.C.	5	**373**	**331,152**	**Idaho**	**2**
318	389,524	Ga.	8	374	330,860	Iowa	8
319	389,070	W.Va.	5	**375**	**330,343**	**Fla.**	**5**
320	387,985	Mich.	13	376	327,015	N.Y.	39
321	387,414	N.Y.	33	377	326,578	Pa.	30
322	385,762	N.J.	11	**378**	**325,247**	**La.**	**7**
323	385,292	La.	6	379	324,845	Ill.	24
324	383,073	Mo.	10	380	324,419	Ohio	21
325	382,327	Iowa	7	381	324,352	Va.	8
326	382,320	Ind.	9	382	324,164	Calif.	18
327	380,118	Ohio	18	383	323,824	N.J.	13
328	**379,306**	**Utah**	**2**	**384**	**319,047**	**Okla.**	**8**

PRIORITY LIST, METHOD OF HARMONIC MEAN, CENSUS OF 1930—*Continued*

Total Number of Representatives from All States	Priority Numbers	State	Cumulative Total of Representatives from Each State	Total Number of Representatives from All States	Priority Numbers	State	Cumulative Total of Representatives from Each State
385	318,773	S.C.	6	421	292,031	Ariz.	2
386	318,734	N.Y.	40	422	291,647	Iowa	9
387	317,020	W.Va.	6	423	290,875	Kans.	7
388	316,172	Mo.	12	424	290,870	Calif.	20
389	315,864	Pa.	31	425	290,794	Mo.	13
390	315,217	Mass.	14	426	289,416	N.Y.	44
391	315,074	Tex.	19	427	288,041	Ill.	27
392	312,716	Mich.	16	428	287,565	Pa.	34
393	312,403	Ala.	9	429	286,997	Ark.	7
394	311,574	Ill.	25	430	286,457	R.I.	3
395	310,861	N.Y.	41	431	285,910	Va.	9
396	310,786	Miss.	7	432	284,611	Wash.	6
397	309,459	Wis.	10	433	284,296	Tex.	21
398	309,403	Nebr.	5	434	282,964	Ohio	24
399	309,312	Ohio	22	435	282,911	N.Y.	45
400	309,127	Ind.	11				
				436	282,140	Ind.	12
401	308,892	Tenn.	9				
402	308,665	Ky.	9	437	281,463	La.	8
403	307,002	Ga.	10	438	281,234	Okla.	9
404	306,616	Calif.	19	439	280,558	N.Dak.	3
				440	280,419	S.Dak.	3
405	305,832	Pa.	32				
406	303,367	N.Y.	42	441	279,846	Wis.	11
407	302,331	N.C.	11	442	279,325	Ala.	10
408	301,831	Colo.	4	443	279,226	Pa.	35
				444	279,043	N.J.	15
409	301,228	Minn.	9				
410	299,768	N.J.	14	445	277,624	Ga.	11
411	299,345	Ill.	26	446	277,560	Ill.	28
412	299,112	Md.	6	447	277,194	Oreg.	4
				448	276,915	Mich.	18
413	298,893	Tex.	20				
414	296,986	N.Mex.	2	449	276,691	N.Y.	46
415	296,418	Pa.	33	450	276,664	Calif.	21
416	296,228	N.Y.	43	451	276,186	Tenn.	10
				452	275,983	Ky.	10
417	295,552	Ohio	23				
418	294,598	Conn.	6	453	275,937	N.C.	12
419	293,727	Mich.	17	454	274,453	Mass.	16
420	293,425	Mass.	15				

With a House of 435 members the following states do not appear in the priority list for the method of harmonic mean and received one member each.

Delaware   Vermont

Nevada   Wyoming

Priority List, Method of Smallest Divisors, Census of 1930

Total Number of Representatives from All States	Priority Numbers	State	Cumulative Total of Representatives from Each State	Total Number of Representatives from All States	Priority Numbers	State	Cumulative Total of Representatives from Each State
49	12,587,967	N.Y.	2	105	1,583,637	N.C.	3
50	9,631,299	Pa.	2	106	1,573,496	N.Y.	9
51	7,630,388	Ill.	2	107	1,552,423	Wash.	2
52	6,646,633	Ohio	2	108	1,526,078	Ill.	6
53	6,293,984	N.Y.	3	109	1,468,191	Fla.	2
54	5,824,601	Tex.	2	110	1,465,861	Wis.	3
55	5,668,241	Calif.	2	111	1,456,151	Tex.	5
56	4,842,052	Mich.	2	112	1,454,223	Ga.	3
57	4,815,650	Pa.	3	113	1,417,060	Calif.	5
58	4,249,598	Mass.	2	114	1,416,533	Mass.	4
59	4,195,989	N.Y.	4	115	1,398,663	N.Y.	10
60	4,041,319	N.J.	2	116	1,375,899	Pa.	8
61	3,815,194	Ill.	3	117	1,375,123	Nebr.	2
62	3,629,110	Mo.	2	118	1,347,106	N.J.	4
63	3,323,317	Ohio	3	119	1,329,327	Ohio	6
64	3,238,480	Ind.	2	120	1,323,121	Ala.	3
65	3,210,433	Pa.	4	121	1,308,249	Tenn.	3
66	3,167,274	N.C.	2	122	1,307,288	Ky.	3
67	3,146,992	N.Y.	5	123	1,275,792	Minn.	3
68	2,931,721	Wis.	2	124	1,271,732	Ill.	7
69	2,912,301	Tex.	3	125	1,258,197	N.Y.	11
70	2,908,446	Ga.	2	126	1,235,210	Iowa	3
71	2,834,121	Calif.	3	127	1,210,915	Va.	3
72	2,646,242	Ala.	2	128	1,210,513	Mich.	5
73	2,616,497	Tenn.	2	129	1,209,703	Mo.	4
74	2,614,575	Ky.	2	130	1,203,912	Pa.	9
75	2,551,583	Minn.	2	131	1,191,111	Okla.	3
76	2,543,462	Ill.	4	132	1,164,920	Tex.	6
77	2,517,593	N.Y.	6	133	1,144,361	N.Y.	12
78	2,470,420	Iowa	2	134	1,133,648	Calif.	6
79	2,421,829	Va.	2	135	1,107,772	Ohio	7
80	2,421,026	Mich.	3	136	1,090,055	Ill.	8
81	2,407,825	Pa.	5	137	1,079,493	Ind.	4
82	2,382,222	Okla.	2	138	1,070,144	Pa.	10
83	2,215,544	Ohio	4	139	1,062,400	Mass.	5
84	2,124,799	Mass.	3	140	1,055,758	N.C.	4
85	2,101,593	La.	2	141	1,050,797	La.	3
86	2,097,995	N.Y.	7	142	1,048,997	N.Y.	13
87	2,020,660	N.J.	3	143	1,034,849	Colo.	2
88	2,008,154	Miss.	2	144	1,010,330	N.J.	5
89	1,941,533	Tex.	4	145	1,004,077	Miss.	3
90	1,926,260	Pa.	6	146	977,240	Wis.	4
91	1,907,597	Ill.	5	147	970,767	Tex.	7
92	1,889,413	Calif.	4	148	969,482	Ga.	4
93	1,879,498	Kans.	2	149	968,410	Mich.	6
94	1,854,444	Ark.	2	150	968,305	N.Y.	14
95	1,814,555	Mo.	3	151	963,130	Pa.	11
96	1,798,280	N.Y.	8	152	953,799	Ill.	9
97	1,738,760	S.C.	2	153	950,379	Oreg.	2
98	1,729,199	W.Va.	2	154	949,519	Ohio	8
99	1,661,659	Ohio	5	155	944,707	Calif.	7
100	1,631,522	Md.	2	156	939,749	Kans.	3
101	1,619,240	Ind.	3	157	927,222	Ark.	3
102	1,614,017	Mich.	4	158	907,278	Mo.	5
103	1,606,897	Conn.	2	159	899,141	N.Y.	15
104	1,605,217	Pa.	7	160	882,081	Ala.	4

PRIORITY LIST, METHOD OF SMALLEST DIVISORS, CENSUS OF 1930—*Continued*

Total Number of Representatives from All States	Priority Numbers	State	Cumulative Total of Representatives from Each State	Total Number of Representatives from All States	Priority Numbers	State	Cumulative Total of Representatives from Each State
161	875,573	Pa.	12	217	635,865	Ill.	13
162	872,166	Tenn.	4	218	633,455	N.C.	6
163	871,525	Ky.	4	219	629,804	Calif.	10
164	869,380	S.C.	3	220	629,398	N.Y.	21
165	864,600	W.Va.	3	221	626,499	Kans.	4
166	850,528	Minn.	4	222	618,148	Ark.	4
167	849,920	Mass.	6	223	617,605	Iowa	5
168	847,821	Ill.	10	224	607,085	Mass.	8
169	839,198	N.Y.	16	225	605,458	Va.	5
170	832,086	Tex.	8	226	605,257	Mich.	9
171	830,829	Ohio	9	227	604,852	Mo.	7
172	823,473	Iowa	4	228	604,239	Ohio	12
173	815,761	Md.	3	229	601,957	Pa.	17
174	809,748	Calif.	8	230	599,426	N.Y.	22
175	809,620	Ind.	5	231	595,556	Okla.	5
176	808,264	N.J.	6	232	586,953	Ill.	14
177	807,276	Va.	4	233	586,344	Wis.	6
178	807,009	Mich.	7	234	582,460	Tex.	11
179	803,449	Conn.	3	235	581,689	Ga.	6
180	802,608	Pa.	13	236	579,587	S.C.	4
181	797,418	Maine	2	237	577,331	N.J.	8
182	794,074	Okla.	4	238	576,400	W.Va.	4
183	791,819	N.C.	5	239	572,180	N.Y.	23
184	786,748	N.Y.	17	240	566,824	Calif.	11
185	776,212	Wash.	3	241	566,547	Pa.	18
186	763,039	Ill.	11	242	553,886	Ohio	13
187	740,868	Pa.	14	243	547,303	N.Y.	24
188	740,470	N.Y.	18	244	545,028	Ill.	15
189	738,515	Ohio	10	245	543,841	Md.	4
190	734,096	Fla.	3	246	539,747	Ind.	7
191	732,931	Wis.	5	247	538,006	Mich.	10
192	728,075	Tex.	9	248	535,632	Conn.	4
193	727,112	Ga.	5	249	535,073	Pa.	19
194	725,822	Mo.	6	250	531,200	Mass.	9
195	708,530	Calif.	9	251	529,509	Tex.	12
196	708,266	Mass.	7	252	529,248	Ala.	6
197	700,531	La.	4	253	527,879	N.C.	7
198	699,332	N.Y.	19	254	525,398	La.	5
199	693,672	Ill.	12	255	524,729	Mont.	2
200	691,722	Mich.	8	256	524,499	N.Y.	25
201	687,950	Pa.	15	257	523,299	Tenn.	6
202	687,562	Nebr.	3	258	522,915	Ky.	6
203	687,497	R.I.	2	259	518,444	Mo.	8
204	673,553	N.J.	7	260	517,474	Wash.	4
205	673,340	N.Dak.	2	261	517,425	Colo.	3
206	673,005	S.Dak.	2	262	515,295	Calif.	12
207	669,385	Miss.	4	263	511,280	Ohio	14
208	664,663	Ohio	11	264	510,317	Minn.	6
209	662,525	N.Y.	20	265	508,693	Ill.	16
210	661,561	Ala.	5	266	506,911	Pa.	20
211	654,125	Tenn.	5	267	505,741	Utah	2
212	653,644	Ky.	5	268	505,165	N.J.	9
213	647,696	Ind.	6	269	503,519	N.Y.	26
214	647,178	Tex.	10	270	502,039	Miss.	5
215	642,087	Pa.	16	271	494,084	Iowa	6
216	637,896	Minn.	5	272	489,397	Fla.	4

PRIORITY LIST, METHOD OF SMALLEST DIVISORS, CENSUS OF 1930—*Continued*

Total Number of Representatives from All States	Priority Numbers	State	Cumulative Total of Representatives from Each State	Total Number of Representatives from All States	Priority Numbers	State	Cumulative Total of Representatives from Each State
273	488,620	Wis.	7	329	401,724	Conn.	5
274	485,383	Tex.	13	330	401,631	Miss.	6
275	484,741	Ga.	7	331	401,600	Ill.	20
276	484,366	Va.	6	332	401,304	Pa.	25
277	484,205	Mich.	11	333	398,709	Maine	3
278	484,152	N.Y.	27	334	397,037	Okla.	7
279	481,565	Pa.	21	335	395,982	N.Mex.	2
280	476,899	Ill.	17	336	395,909	N.C.	9
281	476,444	Okla.	6	337	393,374	N.Y.	33
282	475,190	Oreg.	3	338	390,978	Ohio	18
283	474,760	Ohio	15	339	389,375	Ariz.	2
284	472,353	Calif.	13	340	388,307	Tex.	16
285	472,178	Mass.	10	341	388,106	Wash.	5
286	469,875	Kans.	5	342	386,327	Mass.	12
287	466,221	N.Y.	28	343	385,252	Pa.	26
288	465,292	N.H.	2	344	381,519	Ill.	21
289	463,611	Ark.	5	345	381,453	N.Y.	34
290	462,640	Ind.	8	346	378,034	Ala.	8
291	458,633	Pa.	22	347	377,883	Calif.	16
292	458,374	Nebr.	4	348	375,900	Kans.	6
293	453,639	Mo.	9	349	373,785	Tenn.	8
294	452,468	N.C.	8	350	373,511	Ky.	8
295	449,570	N.Y.	29	351	372,466	Mich.	14
296	449,035	N.J.	10	352	370,889	Ark.	6
297	448,846	Ill.	18	353	370,434	Pa.	27
298	448,046	Tex.	14	354	370,235	N.Y.	35
299	443,109	Ohio	16	355	369,258	Ohio	19
300	441,536	Idaho	2	356	367,393	N.J.	12
301	441,040	Ala.	7	357	367,048	Fla.	5
302	440,187	Mich.	12	358	366,465	Wis.	9
303	437,786	Pa.	23	359	364,512	Minn.	8
304	436,083	Tenn.	7	360	364,038	Tex.	17
305	436,019	Calif.	14	361	363,556	Ga.	9
306	435,763	Ky.	7	362	363,351	Ill.	22
307	434,690	S.C.	5	363	362,911	Mo.	11
308	434,068	N.Y.	30	364	359,831	Ind.	10
309	432,300	W.Va.	5	365	359,656	N.Y.	36
310	425,264	Minn.	7	366	359,611	Vt.	2
311	424,960	Mass.	11	367	356,714	Pa.	28
312	423,911	Ill.	19	368	354,265	Calif.	17
313	420,319	La.	6	369	354,133	Mass.	13
314	419,598	N.Y.	31	370	352,917	Iowa	8
315	418,817	Wis.	8	371	351,919	N.C.	10
316	418,753	Pa.	24	372	350,266	La.	7
317	416,043	Tex.	15	373	349,823	Ohio	20
318	415,492	Ga.	8	374	349,666	N.Y.	37
319	415,415	Ohio	17	375	347,752	S.C.	6
320	411,737	Iowa	7	376	346,835	Ill.	23
321	407,881	Md.	5	377	345,975	Va.	8
322	406,064	N.Y.	32	378	345,861	Mich.	15
323	404,815	Calif.	15	379	345,840	W.Va.	6
324	404,810	Ind.	9	380	344,950	Colo.	4
325	404,132	N.J.	11	381	343,975	Pa.	29
326	403,638	Va.	7	382	343,781	Nebr.	5
327	403,504	Mich.	13	383	343,749	R.I.	3
328	403,234	Mo.	10	384	342,623	Tex.	18

PRIORITY LIST, METHOD OF SMALLEST DIVISORS, CENSUS OF 1930—*Continued*

Total Number of Representatives from All States	Priority Numbers	State	Cumulative Total of Representatives from Each State	Total Number of Representatives from All States	Priority Numbers	State	Cumulative Total of Representatives from Each State
385	340,317	Okla.	8	421	309,074	Ark.	7
386	340,215	N.Y.	38	422	308,803	Iowa	9
387	336,776	N.J.	13	423	307,023	N.Y.	42
388	336,670	N.Dak.	3	424	306,558	Tex.	20
389	336,503	S.Dak.	3	425	305,216	Ill.	26
390	334,692	Miss.	7	426	303,543	Mass.	15
391	333,426	Calif.	18	427	302,729	Va.	9
392	332,332	Ohio	21	428	302,628	Mich.	17
393	332,114	Pa.	30	429	302,426	Mo.	13
394	331,756	Ill.	24	430	302,119	Ohio	23
395	331,262	N.Y.	39	431	300,978	Pa.	33
396	330,780	Ala.	9	432	300,227	La.	8
397	329,919	Mo.	12	433	299,713	N.Y.	43
398	327,062	Tenn.	9	434	298,329	Calif.	20
399	326,892	Mass.	14	435	297,778	Okla.	9
400	326,822	Ky.	9	436	294,407	Ind.	12
401	326,304	Md.	6				
402	325,747	Wis.	10	437	294,027	Ala.	10
403	323,848	Ind.	11	438	293,638	Fla.	6
404	323,589	Tex.	19	439	293,476	Ill.	27
				440	293,172	Wis.	11
405	323,161	Ga.	10	441	292,743	N.Y.	44
406	322,804	Mich.	16	442	291,857	Pa.	34
407	322,768	N.Y.	40	443	291,230	Tex.	21
408	321,379	Conn.	6	444	290,845	Ga.	11
409	321,043	Pa.	31	445	290,722	Tenn.	10
410	318,948	Minn.	9	446	290,508	Ky.	10
411	317,933	Ill.	25	447	289,793	S.C.	7
412	316,793	Oreg.	4	448	288,984	Ohio	24
413	316,727	N.C.	11	449	288,666	N.J.	15
414	316,506	Ohio	22	450	288,200	W.Va.	7
415	314,903	Calif.	19	451	287,934	N.C.	12
416	314,699	N.Y.	41	452	286,879	Miss.	8
417	313,250	Kans.	7	453	286,091	N.Y.	45
418	310,871	N.J.	14	454	284,826	Mich.	18
419	310,687	Pa.	32				
420	310,485	Wash.	6				

With a House of 435 members the following states do not appear in the priority list for the method of smallest divisors, and receive one member each:

Delaware   Wyoming
Nevada

PRIORITY LIST, METHOD OF GREATEST DIVISORS, CENSUS OF 1930

Total Number of Representatives from All States	Priority Number	State	Cumulative Total of Representatives from Each State	Total Number of Representatives from All States	Priority Numbers	State	Cumulative Total of Representatives from Each State
49	6,293,984	N.Y.	2	105	1,079,493	Ind.	3
50	4,815,656	Pa.	2	106	1,070,144	Pa.	9
51	4,195,989	N.Y.	3	107	1,062,400	Mass.	4
52	3,815,194	Ill.	2	108	1,055,758	N.C.	3
53	3,323,317	Ohio	2	109	1,050,797	La.	2
54	3,210,433	Pa.	3	110	1,048,997	N.Y.	12
55	3,146,992	N.Y.	4	111	1,010,330	N.J.	4
56	2,912,301	Tex.	2	112	1,004,077	Miss.	2
57	2,834,121	Calif.	2	113	977,240	Wis.	3
58	2,543,462	Ill.	3	114	970,767	Tex.	6
59	2,517,593	N.Y.	5	115	969,482	Ga.	3
60	2,421,026	Mich.	2	116	968,410	Mich.	5
61	2,407,825	Pa.	4	117	968,305	N.Y.	13
62	2,215,544	Ohio	3	118	963,130	Pa.	10
63	2,124,799	Mass.	2	119	953,799	Ill.	8
64	2,097,995	N.Y.	6	120	949,519	Ohio	7
65	2,020,660	N.J.	2	121	944,707	Calif.	6
66	1,941,533	Tex.	3	122	939,749	Kans.	2
67	1,926,260	Pa.	5	123	927,222	Ark.	2
68	1,907,597	Ill.	4	124	907,278	Mo.	4
69	1,889,413	Calif.	3	125	899,141	N.Y.	14
70	1,814,555	Mo.	2	126	882,081	Ala.	3
71	1,798,280	N.Y.	7	127	875,573	Pa.	11
72	1,661,659	Ohio	4	128	872,166	Tenn.	3
73	1,619,240	Ind.	2	129	871,525	Ky.	3
74	1,614,017	Mich.	3	130	869,380	S.C.	2
75	1,605,217	Pa.	6	131	864,600	W.Va.	2
76	1,583,637	N.C.	2	132	850,528	Minn.	3
77	1,573,496	N.Y.	8	133	849,920	Mass.	5
78	1,526,078	Ill.	5	134	847,821	Ill.	9
79	1,465,861	Wis.	2	135	839,198	N.Y.	15
80	1,456,151	Tex.	4	136	832,086	Tex.	7
81	1,454,223	Ga.	2	137	830,829	Ohio	8
82	1,417,060	Calif.	4	138	823,473	Iowa	3
83	1,416,533	Mass.	3	139	815,761	Md.	2
84	1,398,663	N.Y.	9	140	809,748	Calif.	7
85	1,375,899	Pa.	7	141	809,620	Ind.	4
86	1,347,106	N.J.	3	142	808,264	N.J.	5
87	1,329,327	Ohio	5	143	807,276	Va.	3
88	1,323,121	Ala.	2	144	807,009	Mich.	6
89	1,308,249	Tenn.	2	145	803,449	Conn.	2
90	1,307,288	Ky.	2	146	802,608	Pa.	12
91	1,275,792	Minn.	2	147	794,074	Okla.	3
92	1,271,732	Ill.	6	148	791,819	N.C.	4
93	1,258,797	N.Y.	10	149	786,748	N.Y.	16
94	1,235,210	Iowa	2	150	776,212	Wash.	2
95	1,210,919	Va.	2	151	763,039	Ill.	10
96	1,210,513	Mich.	4	152	740,868	Pa.	13
97	1,209,703	Mo.	3	153	740,470	N.Y.	17
98	1,203,912	Pa.	8	154	738,515	Ohio	9
99	1,191,111	Okla.	2	155	734,096	Fla.	2
100	1,164,920	Tex.	5	156	732,931	Wis.	4
101	1,144,361	N.Y.	11	157	728,075	Tex.	8
102	1,133,648	Calif.	5	158	727,112	Ga.	4
103	1,107,772	Ohio	6	159	725,822	Mo.	5
104	1,090,055	Ill.	7	160	708,530	Calif.	8

PRIORITY LIST, METHOD OF GREATEST DIVISIONS, CENSUS OF 1930—*Continued*

Total Number of Representatives from All States	Priority Numbers	State	Cumulative Total of Representatives from Each State	Total Number of Representatives from All States	Priority Numbers	State	Cumulative Total of Representatives from Each State
161	708,266	Mass.	6	217	524,499	N.Y.	24
162	700,531	La.	3	218	523,299	Tenn.	5
163	699,332	N.Y.	18	219	522,915	Ky.	5
164	693,672	Ill.	11	220	518,444	Mo.	7
165	691,722	Mich.	7	221	517,474	Wash.	3
166	687,950	Pa.	14	222	517,425	Colo.	2
167	687,562	Nebr.	2	223	515,295	Calif.	11
168	673,553	N.J.	6	224	511,280	Ohio	13
169	669,385	Miss.	3	225	510,317	Minn.	5
170	664,663	Ohio	10	226	508,693	Ill.	15
171	662,525	N.Y.	19	227	506,911	Pa.	19
172	661,561	Ala.	4	228	505,165	N.J.	8
173	654,125	Tenn.	4	229	503,519	N.Y.	25
174	653,644	Ky.	4	230	502,039	Miss.	4
175	647,696	Ind.	5	231	494,084	Iowa	5
176	647,178	Tex.	9	232	489,397	Fla.	3
177	642,087	Pa.	15	233	488,620	Wis.	6
178	637,896	Minn.	4	234	485,383	Tex.	12
179	635,865	Ill.	12	235	484,741	Ga.	6
180	633,455	N.C.	5	236	484,366	Va.	5
181	629,804	Calif.	9	237	484,205	Mich.	10
182	629,398	N.Y.	20	238	484,152	N.Y.	26
183	626,499	Kans.	3	239	481,565	Pa.	20
184	618,148	Ark.	3	240	476,899	Ill.	16
185	617,605	Iowa	4	241	476,444	Okla.	5
186	607,085	Mass.	7	242	475,190	Oreg.	2
187	605,458	Va.	4	243	474,760	Ohio	14
188	605,257	Mich.	8	244	472,353	Calif.	12
189	604,852	Mo.	6	245	472,178	Mass.	9
190	604,239	Ohio	11	246	469,875	Kans.	4
191	601,957	Pa.	16	247	466,221	N.Y.	27
192	599,426	N.Y.	21	248	463,611	Ark.	4
193	595,556	Okla.	4	249	462,640	Ind.	7
194	586,953	Ill.	13	250	458,633	Pa.	21
195	586,344	Wis.	5	251	458,374	Nebr.	3
196	582,460	Tex.	10	252	453,639	Mo.	8
197	581,689	Ga.	5	253	452,468	N.C.	7
198	579,587	S.C.	3	254	449,570	N.Y.	28
199	577,331	N.J.	7	255	449,035	N.J.	9
200	576,400	W.Va.	3	256	448,846	Ill.	17
201	572,180	N.Y.	22	257	448,046	Tex.	13
202	566,824	Calif.	10	258	443,109	Ohio	15
203	566,547	Pa.	17	259	441,040	Ala.	6
204	553,886	Ohio	12	260	440,187	Mich.	11
205	547,303	N.Y.	23	261	437,786	Pa.	22
206	545,028	Ill.	14	262	436,083	Tenn.	6
207	543,841	Md.	3	263	436,019	Calif.	13
208	539,747	Ind.	6	264	435,763	Ky.	6
209	538,006	Mich.	9	265	434,690	S.C.	4
210	535,632	Conn.	3	266	434,068	N.Y.	29
211	535,073	Pa.	18	267	432,300	W.Va.	4
212	531,200	Mass.	8	268	425,264	Minn.	6
213	529,509	Tex.	11	269	424,960	Mass.	10
214	529,248	Ala.	5	270	423,911	Ill.	18
215	527,879	N.C.	6	271	420,319	La.	5
216	525,398	La.	4	272	419,598	N.Y.	30

PRIORITY LIST, METHOD OF GREATEST DIVISIONS, CENSUS OF 1930—*Continued*

Total Number of Representatives from All States	Priority Numbers	State	Cumulative Total of Representatives from Each State	Total Number of Representatives from All States	Priority Numbers	State	Cumulative Total of Representatives from Each State
273	418,817	Wis.	7	329	349,666	N.Y.	36
274	418,753	Pa.	23	330	347,752	S.C.	5
275	416,043	Tex.	14	331	346,835	Ill.	22
276	415,492	Ga.	7	332	345,975	Va.	7
277	415,415	Ohio	16	333	345,861	Mich.	14
278	411,737	Iowa	6	334	345,840	W.Va.	5
279	407,881	Md.	4	335	344,950	Colo.	3
280	406,064	N.Y.	31	336	343,975	Pa.	28
281	404,875	Calif.	14	337	343,781	Nebr.	4
282	404,810	Ind.	8	338	343,749	R.I.	2
283	404,132	N.J.	10	339	342,623	Tex.	17
284	403,638	Va.	6	340	340,317	Okla.	7
285	403,504	Mich.	12	341	340,215	N.Y.	37
286	403,234	Mo.	9	342	336,776	N.J.	12
287	401,724	Conn.	4	343	336,670	N.Dak.	2
288	401,631	Miss.	5	344	336,503	S.Dak.	2
289	401,600	Ill.	19	345	334,692	Miss.	6
290	401,304	Pa.	24	346	333,426	Calif.	17
291	398,709	Maine	2	347	332,332	Ohio	20
292	397,037	Okla.	6	348	332,114	Pa.	29
293	395,909	N.C.	8	349	331,756	Ill.	23
294	393,374	N.Y.	32	350	331,262	N.Y.	38
295	390,978	Ohio	17	351	330,780	Ala.	8
296	388,307	Tex.	15	352	329,919	Mo.	11
297	388,106	Wash.	4	353	327,062	Tenn.	8
298	386,327	Mass.	11	354	326,892	Mass.	13
299	385,252	Pa.	25	355	326,822	Ky.	8
300	381,519	Ill.	20	356	326,304	Md.	5
301	381,453	N.Y.	33	357	325,747	Wis.	9
302	378,034	Ala.	7	358	323,848	Ind.	10
303	377,883	Calif.	15	359	323,589	Tex.	18
304	375,900	Kans.	5	360	323,161	Ga.	9
305	373,785	Tenn.	7	361	322,804	Mich.	15
306	373,511	Ky.	7	362	322,768	N.Y.	39
307	372,466	Mich.	13	363	321,379	Conn.	5
308	370,889	Ark.	5	364	321,043	Pa.	30
309	370,434	Pa.	26	365	318,948	Minn.	8
310	370,235	N.Y.	34	366	317,933	Ill.	24
311	369,258	Ohio	18	367	316,793	Oreg.	3
312	367,393	N.J.	11	368	316,727	N.C.	10
313	367,048	Fla.	4	369	316,506	Ohio	21
314	366,465	Wis.	8	370	314,903	Calif.	18
315	364,512	Minn.	7	371	314,699	N.Y.	40
316	364,038	Tex.	16	372	313,250	Kans.	6
317	363,556	Ga.	8	373	310,871	N.J.	13
318	363,351	Ill.	21	374	310,687	Pa.	31
319	362,911	Mo.	10	375	310,485	Wash.	5
320	359,831	Ind.	9	376	309,074	Ark.	6
321	359,656	N.Y.	35	377	308,803	Iowa	8
322	356,714	Pa.	27	378	307,023	N.Y.	41
323	354,265	Calif.	16	379	306,558	Tex.	19
324	354,133	Mass.	12	380	305,216	Ill.	25
325	352,917	Iowa	7	381	303,543	Mass.	14
326	351,919	N.C.	9	382	302,729	Va.	8
327	350,266	La.	6	383	302,628	Mich.	16
328	349,823	Ohio	19	384	302,426	Mo.	12

PRIORITY LIST, METHOD OF GREATEST DIVISIONS, CENSUS OF 1930—*Continued*

Total Number of Representatives from All States	Priority Numbers	State	Cumulative Total of Representatives from Each State	Total Number of Representatives from All States	Priority Numbers	State	Cumulative Total of Representatives from Each State
385	302,119	Ohio	22	421	274,491	Iowa	9
386	300,978	Pa.	32	422	273,651	N.Y.	46
387	300,227	La.	7	423	272,514	Ill.	28
388	299,713	N.Y.	42	424	271,920	Md.	6
389	298,329	Calif.	19	425	269,916	Calif.	21
390	297,778	Okla.	8	426	269,873	Ind.	12
391	294,407	Ind.	11	427	269,421	N.J.	15
392	294,027	Ala.	9	428	269,092	Va.	9
393	293,638	Fla.	5	429	269,003	Mich.	18
394	293,476	Ill.	26	430	268,500	Kans.	7
395	293,172	Wis.	10	431	267,829	N.Y.	47
396	292,743	N.Y.	43	432	267,816	Conn.	6
397	291,857	Pa.	33	433	267,536	Pa.	36
398	291,230	Tex.	20	434	266,520	Wis.	11
399	290,845	Ga.	10	435	265,865	Ohio	25
400	290,722	Tenn.	9	436	265,806	Maine	3
401	290,508	Ky.	9				
402	289,793	S.C.	6	437	265,600	Mass.	16
403	288,984	Ohio	23	438	264,920	Ark.	7
404	288,666	N.J.	14	439	264,754	Tex.	22
405	288,200	W.Va.	6	440	264,691	Okla.	9
406	287,934	N.C.	11	441	264,624	Ala.	10
407	286,879	Miss.	7	442	264,404	Ga.	11
408	286,091	N.Y.	44	443	263,939	N.C.	12
409	284,826	Mich.	17	444	263,117	Ill.	29
410	283,509	Minn.	9	445	262,699	La.	8
411	283,412	Calif.	20	446	262,365	Mont.	2
412	283,307	Mass.	15	447	262,249	N.Y.	48
413	283,274	Pa.	34	448	261,650	Tenn.	10
414	282,607	Ill.	27	449	261,458	Ky.	10
415	279,732	N.Y.	45	450	260,305	Pa.	37
416	279,162	Mo.	13	451	259,222	Mo.	14
417	277,362	Tex.	21	452	258,737	Wash.	6
418	276,943	Ohio	24	453	258,712	Colo.	4
419	275,180	Pa.	35	454	257,647	Calif.	22
420	275,025	Nebr.	5				

With a House of 435 members the following states do not appear in the priority list for the method of greatest divisors, and received one member each.

Arizona	New Hampshire
Delaware	New Mexico
Idaho	Utah
Montana	Vermont
Nevada	Wyoming

APPENDIX B
PRIORITY LISTS BASED ON 1940 CENSUS

The tables on the following pages give priority lists based on the census of 1940 for the methods of major fractions and equal proportions. They are reproduced through the courtesy of the Bureau of the Census, which prepared them.

Figures are given for any size of House up to 500 members; the list may be extended by multiplying the population of each state by the appropriate multipliers given in Chapter III.

In order to determine the apportionment for any size of House a line is drawn below the number in the first column (total number of representatives from each state), which shows the size of House determined upon. Then for each state the last entry above the line in the fourth column (cumulative total of representatives for each state) shows the number of representatives to which the state is entitled.

As the membership of the House was fixed at 435 in 1929 a line is drawn in the lists at this point. The last entry for each state above the line is shown in black-face type, and the figure in the last column is the apportionment.

Priority List, Method of Major Fractions, Census of 1940

Total Number of Representatives from All States	Priority Numbers	State	Cumulative Total of Representatives from Each State	Total Number of Representatives from All States	Priority Numbers	State	Cumulative Total of Representatives from Each State
49	8,986,095	N.Y.	2	105	1,320,024	Pa.	8
50	6,600,120	Pa.	2	106	1,299,591	Ark.	2
51	5,391,657	N.Y.	3	107	1,283,728	N.Y.	11
52	5,264,827	Ill.	2	108	1,267,983	W.Va.	2
53	4,605,075	Ohio	2	109	1,266,536	S.C.	2
54	4,604,925	Calif.	2	110	1,264,943	Fla.	2
55	4,276,549	Tex.	2	111	1,255,929	Ohio	6
56	3,960,072	Pa.	3	112	1,255,889	Calif.	6
57	3,851,183	N.Y.	4	113	1,255,035	Wis.	3
58	3,504,071	Mich.	2	114	1,249,489	Ga.	3
59	3,158,896	Ill.	3	115	1,233,349	Mass.	4
60	2,995,365	N.Y.	5	116	1,214,960	Ill.	7
61	2,877,814	Mass.	2	117	1,214,163	Md.	2
62	2,828,623	Pa.	4	118	1,200,685	Kans.	2
63	2,773,443	N.J.	2	119	1,188,619	N.J.	4
64	2,763,045	Ohio	3	120	1,172,099	N.Y.	12
65	2,762,955	Calif.	3	121	1,168,024	Mich.	5
66	2,565,930	Tex.	3	122	1,166,336	Tenn.	3
67	2,523,109	Mo.	2	123	1,166,332	Tex.	6
68	2,450,753	N.Y.	6	124	1,164,727	Pa.	9
69	2,381,082	N.C.	2	125	1,157,461	Wash.	2
70	2,285,197	Ind.	2	126	1,139,495	Conn.	2
71	2,256,355	Ill.	4	127	1,138,251	Ky.	3
72	2,200,040	Pa.	5	128	1,133,184	Ala.	3
73	2,102,442	Mich.	3	129	1,116,920	Minn.	3
74	2,091,725	Wis.	2	130	1,081;333	Mo.	4
75	2,082,482	Ga.	2	131	1,078,331	N.Y.	13
76	2,073,714	N.Y.	7	132	1,071,109	Va.	3
77	1,973,603	Ohio	4	133	1,062,710	Ohio	7
78	1,973,539	Calif.	4	134	1,062,675	Calif.	7
79	1,943,894	Tenn.	2	135	1,052,965	Ill.	8
80	1,897,085	Ky.	2	136	1,042,124	Pa.	10
81	1,888,641	Ala.	2	137	1,020,464	N.C.	4
82	1,861,533	Minn.	2	138	1,015,307	Iowa	3
83	1,832,807	Tex.	4	139	998,455	N.Y.	14
84	1,800,033	Pa.	6	140	986,896	Tex.	7
85	1,797,219	N.Y.	8	141	979,370	Ind.	4
86	1,785,182	Va.	2	142	959,271	Mass.	5
87	1,754,942	Ill.	5	143	955,656	Mich.	6
88	1,726,688	Mass.	3	144	945,552	La.	3
89	1,692,179	Iowa	2	145	942,874	Pa.	11
90	1,664,066	N.J.	3	146	934,574	Okla.	3
91	1,585,781	N.Y.	9	147	929,596	N.Y.	15
92	1,575,920	La.	2	148	929,087	Ill.	9
93	1,557,623	Okla.	2	149	924,481	N.J.	5
94	1,535,025	Ohio	5	150	921,015	Ohio	8
95	1,534,975	Calif.	5	151	920,985	Calif.	8
96	1,523,105	Pa.	7	152	896,453	Wis.	4
97	1,513,866	Mo.	3	153	892,492	Ga.	4
98	1,501,745	Mich.	4	154	877,223	Nebr.	2
99	1,455,864	Miss.	2	155	873,518	Miss.	3
100	1,435,862	Ill.	6	156	869,622	N.Y.	16
101	1,428,649	N.C.	3	157	860,885	Pa.	12
102	1,425,516	Tex.	5	158	855,310	Tex.	8
103	1,418,857	N.Y.	10	159	841,036	Mo.	5
104	1,371,118	Ind.	3	160	833,097	Tenn.	4

PRIORITY LIST, METHOD OF MAJOR FRACTIONS, CENSUS OF 1940—*Continued*

Total Number of Representatives from All States	Priority Numbers	State	Cumulative Total of Representatives from Each State	Total Number of Representatives from All States	Priority Numbers	State	Cumulative Total of Representatives from Each State
161	831,289	Ill.	10	217	620,511	Minn.	5
162	816,918	N.Y.	17	218	618,365	Mich.	9
163	813,036	Ky.	4	219	610,936	Tex.	11
164	812,660	Ohio	9	220	600,662	Ohio	12
165	812,634	Calif.	9	221	600,642	Calif.	12
166	809,417	Ala.	4	222	600,011	Pa.	17
167	808,632	Mich.	7	223	599,073	N.Y.	23
168	797,800	Minn.	4	224	595,061	Va.	5
169	793,694	N.C.	5	225	584,981	Ill.	14
170	792,014	Pa.	13	226	582,256	Mo.	7
171	784,858	Mass.	6	227	575,563	Mass.	8
172	779,755	Ark.	3	228	573,580	N.Y.	24
173	770,237	N.Y.	18	229	570,470	Wis.	6
174	765,078	Va.	4	230	567,950	Ga.	6
175	761,732	Ind.	5	231	565,725	Pa.	18
176	760,790	W.Va.	3	232	564,817	Maine	2
177	759,922	S.C.	3	233	564,060	Iowa	5
178	758,966	Fla.	3	234	557,811	Tex.	12
179	756,394	N.J.	6	235	556,968	Ark.	4
180	754,685	Tex.	9	236	554,689	N.J.	8
181	752,118	Ill.	11	237	553,274	Mich.	10
182	748,864	Colo.	2	238	552,609	Ohio	13
183	733,347	Pa.	14	239	552,591	Calif.	13
184	728,602	N.Y.	19	240	550,169	N.Y.	25
185	728,498	Md.	3	241	549,480	N.C.	7
186	727,117	Ohio	10	242	544,637	Ill.	15
187	727,093	Calif.	10	243	543,421	W.Va.	4
188	726,456	Oreg.	2	244	542,801	S.C.	4
189	725,219	Iowa	4	245	542,118	Fla.	4
190	720,411	Kans.	3	246	535,145	Pa.	19
191	700,814	Mich.	8	247	530,153	Tenn.	6
192	697,242	Wis.	5	248	528,594	N.Y.	26
193	694,476	Wash.	3	249	527,353	Ind.	7
194	694,161	Ga.	5	250	526,334	Nebr.	3
195	691,238	N.Y.	20	251	525,307	La.	5
196	688,121	Mo.	6	252	520,355	Md.	4
197	686,717	Ill.	12	253	519,208	Okla.	5
198	683,697	Conn.	3	254	517,387	Ky.	6
199	682,771	Pa.	15	255	515,084	Ala.	6
200	675,394	La.	4	256	514,579	Kans.	4
201	675,245	Tex.	10	257	513,186	Tex.	13
202	667,553	Okla.	4	258	511,675	Ohio	14
203	664,111	Mass.	7	259	511,658	Calif.	14
204	657,868	Ohio	11	260	509,499	Ill.	16
205	657,846	Calif.	11	261	508,647	N.Y.	27
206	657,519	N.Y.	21	262	507,850	Mass.	9
207	649,386	N.C.	6	263	507,702	Pa.	20
208	647,965	Tenn.	5	264	507,691	Minn.	6
209	640,025	N.J.	7	265	504,622	Mo.	8
210	638,721	Pa.	16	266	500,582	Mich.	11
211	632,362	Ky.	5	267	496,055	Wash.	4
212	631,779	Ill.	13	268	490,151	N.Y.	28
213	629,547	Ala.	5	269	489,431	N.J.	9
214	626,937	N.Y.	22	270	488,355	Conn.	4
215	623,942	Miss.	4	271	486,868	Va.	6
216	623,236	Ind.	6	272	485,288	Miss.	5

PRIORITY LIST, METHOD OF MAJOR FRACTIONS, CENSUS OF 1940—*Continued*

Total Number of Representatives from All States	Priority Numbers	State	Cumulative Total of Representatives from Each State	Total Number of Representatives from All States	Priority Numbers	State	Cumulative Total of Representatives from Each State
273	482,936	Pa.	21	329	400,228	Kans.	5
274	482,706	Wis.	7	330	398,386	Mo.	10
275	480,573	Ga.	7	331	397,054	Miss.	6
276	478,621	Ill.	17	332	396,206	N.J.	11
277	476,387	Ohio	15	333	394,721	Ohio	18
278	476,372	Calif.	15	334	394,708	Calif.	18
279	476,216	N.C.	8	335	390,700	N.Y.	35
280	**475,564**	**R.I.**	**2**	336	390,503	Iowa	7
281	475,172	Tex.	14	337	389,341	Mich.	14
282	472,952	N.Y.	29	338	388,779	Tenn.	8
283	461,503	Iowa	6	339	388,777	Tex.	17
284	460,474	Pa.	22	340	388,242	Pa.	26
285	457,053	Mich.	12	341	385,820	Wash.	5
286	457,039	Ind.	8	342	385,231	Ill.	21
287	456,920	N.Y.	30	343	379,832	Conn.	5
288	454,392	Mass.	10	344	379,694	N.Y.	36
289	451,271	Ill.	18	345	379,417	Ky.	8
290	449,318	Colo.	3	346	377,728	Ala.	8
291	448,591	Tenn.	7	347	375,960	N.C.	10
292	445,652	Ohio	16	**348**	**375,953**	**Nebr.**	**4**
293	445,638	Calif.	16	349	375,367	Mass.	12
294	445,255	Mo.	9	350	373,592	Pa.	27
295	442,402	Tex.	15	351	373,384	Ohio	19
296	441,939	N.Y.	31	352	373,372	Calif.	19
297	440,008	Pa.	23	**353**	**372,971**	**Mont.**	**2**
298	437,912	N.J.	10	354	372,307	Minn.	8
299	437,789	Ky.	7	355	369,292	N.Y.	37
300	435,874	Oreg.	3	356	369,128	Wis.	9
301	435,840	Ala.	7	357	367,497	Ga.	9
302	433,197	Ark.	5	358	367,314	Ill.	22
303	429,796	La.	6	**359**	**366,873**	**Utah**	**2**
304	429,585	Minn.	7	360	366,561	Tex.	18
305	**428,641**	**S.Dak.**	**2**	361	363,674	La.	7
306	**427,957**	**N.Dak.**	**2**	362	362,490	Mich.	15
307	427,909	N.Y.	32	363	361,753	N.J.	12
308	426,878	Ill.	19	364	360,821	Ind.	10
309	424,806	Okla.	6	365	360,444	Mo.	11
310	422,661	W.Va.	5	366	360,007	Pa.	28
311	422,179	S.C.	5	367	359,451	Okla.	7
312	421,648	Fla.	5	368	359,444	N.Y.	38
313	421,284	Pa.	24	369	357,036	Va.	8
314	420,488	Mich.	13	**370**	**354,545**	**N.Mex.**	**2**
315	420,191	N.C.	9	**371**	**354,434**	**Ark.**	**6**
316	418,643	Ohio	17	372	354,237	Ohio	20
317	418,630	Calif.	17	373	354,225	Calif.	20
318	418,345	Wis.	8	374	350,988	Ill.	23
319	416,496	Ga.	8	375	350,108	N.Y.	39
320	414,743	N.Y.	33	**376**	**349,915**	**Idaho**	**2**
321	413,860	Tex.	16	377	347,375	Pa.	29
322	411,965	Va.	7	378	346,747	Tex.	19
323	411,116	Mass.	11	**379**	**345,813**	**W.Va.**	**6**
324	404,987	Ill.	20	**380**	**345,419**	**S.C.**	**6**
325	404,721	Md.	5	381	345,338	Mass.	13
326	404,089	Pa.	25	**382**	**344,984**	**Fla.**	**6**
327	403,270	Ind.	9	383	343,040	Tenn.	9
328	402,362	N.Y.	34	384	341,244	N.Y.	40

PRIORITY LIST, METHOD OF MAJOR FRACTIONS, CENSUS OF 1940—*Continued*

Total Number of Representatives from All States	Priority Numbers	State	Cumulative Total of Representatives from Each State	Total Number of Representatives from All States	Priority Numbers	State	Cumulative Total of Representatives from Each State
385	340,155	N.C.	11	437	299,540	Ky.	10
386	339,104	Mich.	16	438	298,818	Wis.	11
387	338,890	Maine	3	439	298,620	Iowa	9
388	338,436	Iowa	8	440	298,364	Tex.	22
389	336,957	Ohio	21	441	298,207	Ala.	10
390	336,946	Calif.	21	442	298,069	Ind.	12
391	336,053	Ill.	24	443	298,009	Ill.	27
392	335,969	Miss.	7	444	297,705	Mass.	15
393	335,599	Pa.	30	445	297,497	Ga.	11
394	334,780	Ky.	9	446	296,245	N.Y.	46
395	333,290	Ala.	9	447	295,527	Pa.	34
396	332,841	Ariz.	2	448	293,941	Ohio	24
397	332,818	N.Y.	41	449	293,931	Calif.	24
398	332,813	N.J.	13	450	293,926	Minn.	10
399	331,135	Md.	6	451	292,611	W.Va.	7
400	330,272	Wis.	10	452	292,408	Nebr.	5
401	329,101	Mo.	12	453	292,278	S.C.	7
402	328,965	Tex.	20	454	291,910	Fla.	7
403	328,813	Ga.	10	455	291,173	Miss.	8
404	328,506	Minn.	9	456	289,874	N.Y.	47
405	327,683	N.H.	2	457	287,172	Ill.	28
406	327,460	Kans.	6	458	286,962	Pa.	35
407	326,457	Ind.	11	459	286,908	N.J.	15
408	324,799	N.Y.	42	460	285,730	N.C.	13
409	324,596	Pa.	31	461	285,338	R.I.	3
410	322,336	Ill.	25	462	285,103	Tex.	23
411	321,284	Ohio	22	463	284,114	Mich.	19
412	321,274	Calif.	22	464	283,771	N.Y.	48
413	320,942	Colo.	4	465	281,943	Ohio	25
414	319,757	Mass.	14	466	281,934	Calif.	25
415	318,552	Mich.	17	467	281,871	Va.	10
416	317,156	N.Y.	43	468	280,346	Mo.	14
417	315,671	Wash.	6	469	280,191	Md.	7
418	315,184	La.	8	470	278,878	Pa.	36
419	315,032	Va.	9	471	278,498	Mass.	16
420	314,291	Pa.	32	472	278,104	La.	9
421	312,918	Tex.	21	473	277,920	N.Y.	49
422	311,525	Okla.	8	474	277,699	Tenn.	11
423	311,338	Oreg.	4	475	277,096	Ill.	29
424	310,771	Conn.	6	476	277,081	Kans.	7
425	310,576	N.C.	12	477	274,875	Okla.	9
426	309,865	N.Y.	44	478	274,224	Ind.	13
427	309,696	Ill.	26	479	272,971	Tex.	24
428	308,160	N.J.	14	480	272,834	Wis.	12
429	307,005	Ohio	23	481	272,306	N.Y.	50
430	306,995	Calif.	23	482	271,628	Ga.	12
431	306,931	Tenn.	10	483	271,238	Pa.	37
432	304,621	Pa.	33	484	271,012	Ky.	11
433	302,902	N.Y.	45	485	270,887	Ohio	26
434	302,773	Mo.	13	486	270,878	Calif.	26
435	300,349	Mich.	18	487	269,806	Ala.	11
436	299,906	Ark.	7	488	269,544	Mich.	20

PRIORITY LIST, METHOD OF MAJOR FRACTIONS, CENSUS OF 1940—*Continued*

Total Number of Representatives from All States	Priority Numbers	State	Cumulative Total of Representatives from Each State	Total Number of Representatives from All States	Priority Numbers	State	Cumulative Total of Representatives from Each State
489	268,398	N.J.	16	495	264,565	N.C.	14
490	267,703	Ill.	30	496	264,005	Pa.	38
491	267,186	Iowa	10				
492	267,106	Wash.	7	497	262,960	Conn.	7
				498	261,830	Tex.	25
493	266,914	N.Y.	51	499	261,731	N.Y.	52
494	265,933	Minn.	11	500	261,619	Mass.	17

With a House of 435 members the following states do not appear in the priority list for the method of major fractions and receive one member each.

Delaware   Vermont

Nevada   Wyoming

PRIORITY LIST, METHOD OF EQUAL PROPORTIONS, CENSUS OF 1940

Total Number of Representatives from All States	Priority Numbers	State	Cumulative Total of Representatives from Each State	Total Number of Representatives from All States	Priority Numbers	State	Cumulative Total of Representatives from Each State
49	9,531,193	N.Y.	2	81	1,993,991	Calif.	4
50	7,000,484	Pa.	2	82	1,974,454	Minn.	2
51	5,584,193	Ill.	2	83	1,893,471	Va.	2
52	5,502,837	N.Y.	3	84	1,851,800	Tex.	4
53	4,884,419	Ohio	2	85	1,807,517	Pa.	6
54	4,884,260	Calif.	2	86	1,801,226	N.Y.	8
55	4,535,966	Tex.	2	87	1,794,827	Iowa	2
56	4,041,732	Pa.	3	88	1,765,877	Ill.	5
57	3,891,093	N.Y.	4	89	1,762,294	Mass.	3
58	3,716,628	Mich.	2	90	1,698,380	N.J.	3
59	3,224,035	Ill.	3	91	1,671,516	La.	2
60	3,052,383	Mass.	2	92	1,652,108	Okla.	2
61	3,014,028	N.Y.	5	93	1,588,532	N.Y.	9
62	2,941,681	N.J.	2	94	1,545,083	Mo.	3
63	2,857,936	Pa.	4	95	1,544,589	Ohio	5
64	2,820,021	Ohio	3	96	1,544,539	Calif.	5
65	2,819,929	Calif.	3	97	1,544,177	Miss.	2
66	2,676,162	Mo.	2	98	1,527,631	Pa.	7
67	2,618,841	Tex.	3	99	1,517,307	Mich.	4
68	2,525,519	N.C.	2	100	1,458,109	N.C.	3
69	2,460,943	N.Y.	6	101	1,441,832	Ill.	6
70	2,423,818	Ind.	2	102	1,434,398	Tex.	5
71	2,279,737	Ill.	4	103	1,420,826	N.Y.	10
72	2,218,609	Wis.	2	104	1,399,392	Ind.	3
73	2,213,748	Pa.	5	105	1,378,425	Ark.	2
74	2,208,806	Ga.	2	106	1,344,899	W.Va.	2
75	2,145,796	Mich.	3	107	1,343,364	S.C.	2
76	2,079,877	N.Y.	7	108	1,341,674	Fla.	2
77	2,061,811	Tenn.	2	109	1,322,967	Pa.	8
78	2,012,162	Ky.	2	110	1,287,814	Md.	2
79	2,003,206	Ala.	2	111	1,285,186	N.Y.	11
80	1,994,056	Ohio	4	112	1,280,915	Wis.	3

PRIORITY LIST, METHOD OF EQUAL PROPORTIONS, CENSUS OF 1940—*Continued*

Total Number of Representatives from All States	Priority Numbers	State	Cumulative Total of Representatives from Each State	Total Number of Representatives from All States	Priority Numbers	State	Cumulative Total of Representatives from Each State
113	1,275,255	Ga.	3	169	798,639	N.C.	5
114	1,273,519	Kans.	2	170	795,834	Ark.	3
115	1,261,152	Ohio	6	171	794,290	Colo.	2
116	1,261,111	Calif.	6	172	792,649	Pa.	13
117	1,246,130	Mass.	4	173	788,122	Mass.	6
118	1,227,672	Wash.	2	174	776,478	W.Va.	3
119	1,218,571	Ill.	7	175	775,592	S.C.	3
120	1,208,617	Conn.	2	176	774,616	Fla.	3
121	1,200,936	N.J.	4	177	773,006	Va.	4
122	1,190,387	Tenn.	3	178	770,551	N.Y.	18
123	1,175,301	Mich.	5	179	770,523	Oreg.	2
124	1,173,209	N.Y.	12	180	766,478	Ind.	5
125	1,171,181	Tex.	6	181	759,539	N.J.	6
126	1,166,747	Pa.	9	182	755,994	Tex.	9
127	1,161,722	Ky.	3	183	752,972	Ill.	11
128	1,156,551	Ala.	3	184	743,520	Md.	3
129	1,139,952	Minn.	3	185	735,267	Kans.	3
130	1,093,196	Va.	3	186	733,850	Pa.	14
131	1,092,538	Mo.	4	187	732,735	Iowa	4
132	1,079,195	N.Y.	13	188	728,869	N.Y.	19
133	1,065,868	Ohio	7	189	728,126	Ohio	10
134	1,065,833	Calif.	7	190	728,103	Calif.	10
135	1,055,313	Ill.	8	191	708,797	Wash.	3
136	1,043,571	Pa.	10	192	702,377	Mich.	8
137	1,036,244	Iowa	3	193	701,586	Wis.	5
138	1,031,039	N.C.	4	194	698,486	Ga.	5
139	999,140	N.Y.	14	195	697,795	Conn.	3
140	989,829	Tex.	7	196	691,465	N.Y.	20
141	989,519	Ind.	4	197	690,982	Mo.	6
142	965,248	Mass.	5	198	687,367	Ill.	12
143	965,050	La.	3	199	683,177	Pa.	15
144	959,629	Mich.	6	200	682,393	La.	4
145	953,845	Okla.	3	201	676,182	Tex.	10
146	943,945	Pa.	11	202	674,470	Okla.	4
147	930,699	Ill.	9	203	666,084	Mass.	7
148	930,435	Nebr.	2	204	658,615	Ohio	11
149	930,241	N.J.	5	205	658,594	Calif.	11
150	930,149	N.Y.	15	206	657,715	N.Y.	21
151	923,068	Ohio	8	207	652,086	N.C.	6
152	923,038	Calif.	8	208	652,002	Tenn.	5
153	905,743	Wis.	4	209	641,927	N.J.	7
154	901,741	Ga.	4	210	639,054	Pa.	16
155	891,531	Miss.	3	211	636,302	Ky.	5
156	870,075	N.Y.	16	212	633,469	Ala.	5
157	861,700	Pa.	12	213	632,285	Ill.	13
158	857,217	Tex.	8	214	630,408	Miss.	4
159	846,277	Mo.	5	215	627,106	N.Y.	22
160	841,731	Tenn.	4	216	625,827	Ind.	6
161	832,442	Ill.	10	217	624,377	Minn.	5
162	821,462	Ky.	4	218	619,438	Mich.	9
163	817,805	Ala.	4	219	611,629	Tex.	11
164	817,293	N.Y.	17	220	601,230	Ohio	12
165	814,070	Ohio	9	221	601,211	Calif.	12
166	814,043	Calif.	9	222	600,287	Pa.	17
167	811,035	Mich.	7	223	599,221	N.Y.	23
168	806,068	Minn.	4	224	599,079	Maine	2

PRIORITY LIST, METHOD OF EQUAL PROPORTIONS, CENSUS OF 1940—*Continued*

Total Number of Representatives from All States	Priority Numbers	State	Cumulative Total of Representatives from Each State	Total Number of Representatives from All States	Priority Numbers	State	Cumulative Total of Representatives from Each State
225	598,768	Va.	5	281	475,498	Tex.	14
226	585,382	Ill.	14	282	473,025	N.Y.	29
227	583,986	Mo.	7	283	463,422	Iowa	6
228	576,846	Mass.	8	284	460,598	Pa.	22
229	573,710	N.Y.	24	285	458,584	Colo.	3
230	572,842	Wis.	6	286	458,059	Ind.	8
231	570,311	Ga.	6	287	457,485	Mich.	12
232	567,574	Iowa	5	288	456,986	N.Y.	30
233	565,956	Pa.	18	289	455,022	Mass.	10
234	562,740	Ark.	4	290	454,642	S.Dak.	2
235	558,339	Tex.	12	291	453,917	N.Dak.	2
236	555,925	N.J.	8	292	451,455	Ill.	18
237	554,042	Mich.	10	293	449,924	Tenn.	7
238	553,052	Ohio	13	294	446,027	Mo.	9
239	553,034	Calif.	13	295	445,884	Ohio	16
240	551,113	N.C.	7	296	445,870	Calif.	16
241	550,284	N.Y.	25	297	444,862	Oreg.	3
242	549,053	W.Va.	4	298	442,665	Tex.	15
243	548,426	S.C.	4	299	441,998	N.Y.	31
244	547,736	Fla.	4	300	440,117	Pa.	23
245	544,961	Ill.	15	301	439,090	Ky.	7
246	537,187	Nebr.	3	302	438,520	N.J.	10
247	535,340	Pa.	19	303	437,135	Ala.	7
248	532,357	Tenn.	6	304	435,896	Ark.	5
249	528,920	Ind.	7	305	431,583	La.	6
250	528,695	N.Y.	26	306	430,861	Minn.	7
251	528,580	La.	5	307	427,963	N.Y.	32
252	525,748	Md.	4	308	427,034	Ill.	19
253	522,443	Okla.	5	309	426,573	Okla.	6
254	519,912	Kans.	4	310	425,294	W.Va.	5
255	519,538	Ky.	6	311	424,809	S.C.	5
256	517,226	Ala.	6	312	424,275	Fla.	5
257	513,597	Tex.	13	313	421,380	Pa.	24
258	512,026	Ohio	14	314	420,920	N.C.	9
259	512,010	Calif.	14	315	420,825	Mich.	13
260	509,802	Minn.	6	316	419,278	Wis.	8
261	509,765	Ill.	16	317	418,836	Ohio	17
262	508,737	N.Y.	27	318	418,822	Calif.	17
263	508,730	Mass.	9	319	417,425	Ga.	8
264	507,869	Pa.	20	320	414,792	N.Y.	33
265	505,747	Mo.	8	321	414,075	Tex.	16
266	504,412	R.I.	2	322	413,189	Va.	7
267	501,195	Wash.	4	323	411,583	Mass.	11
268	501,150	Mich.	11	324	407,243	Md.	5
269	493,416	Conn.	4	325	405,120	Ill.	20
270	490,280	N.J.	9	326	404,173	Pa.	25
271	490,232	N.Y.	28	327	403,970	Ind.	9
272	488,892	Va.	6	328	402,722	Kans.	5
273	488,312	Miss.	5	329	402,407	N.Y.	34
274	484,140	Wis.	7	330	398,939	Mo.	10
275	483,079	Pa.	21	331	398,705	Miss.	6
276	482,001	Ga.	7	332	396,656	N.J.	11
277	478,841	Ill.	17	333	395,595	Mont.	2
278	477,278	N.C.	8	334	394,882	Ohio	18
279	476,671	Ohio	15	335	394,869	Calif.	18
280	476,655	Calif.	15	336	391,663	Iowa	7

PRIORITY LIST, METHOD OF EQUAL PROPORTIONS, CENSUS OF 1940—*Continued*

Total Number of Representatives from All States	Priority Numbers	State	Cumulative Total of Representatives from Each State	Total Number of Representatives from All States	Priority Numbers	State	Cumulative Total of Representatives from Each State
337	390,741	N.Y.	35	393	336,967	Miss.	7
338	389,646	Tenn.	8	394	336,129	Ill.	24
339	389,608	Mich.	14	395	335,648	Pa.	30
340	389,128	Utah	2	396	335,360	Ky.	9
341	388,956	Tex.	17	397	333,868	Ala.	9
342	388,317	Pa.	26	398	333,080	N.J.	13
343	388,224	Wash.	5	399	332,844	N.Y.	41
344	385,346	Ill.	21	400	332,512	Md.	6
345	382,198	Conn.	5	401	330,731	Wis.	10
346	380,263	Ky.	8	402	329,413	Mo.	12
347	379,849	Nebr.	4	403	329,269	Ga.	10
348	379,732	N.Y.	36	404	329,076	Minn.	9
349	378,570	Ala.	8	405	329,074	Tex.	20
350	376,482	N.C.	10	406	328,821	Kans.	6
351	376,052	N.Mex.	2	407	326,828	Ind.	11
352	375,722	Mass.	12	408	324,822	N.Y.	42
353	373,658	Pa.	27	409	324,640	Pa.	31
354	373,521	Ohio	19	410	324,268	Colo.	4
355	373,509	Calif.	19	411	322,404	Ill.	25
356	373,137	Minn.	8	412	321,371	Ohio	22
357	371,141	Idaho	2	413	321,361	Calif.	22
358	369,768	Wis.	9	414	319,977	Mass.	14
359	369,326	N.Y.	37	415	318,698	Mich.	17
360	368,134	Ga.	9	416	317,178	N.Y.	43
361	367,413	Ill.	22	417	316,984	Wash.	6
362	366,711	Tex.	18	418	315,887	La.	8
363	364,755	La.	7	419	315,578	Va.	9
364	362,706	Mich.	15	420	314,565	Oreg.	4
365	362,096	N.J.	12	421	314,331	Pa.	32
366	361,321	Ind.	10	422	313,011	Tex.	21
367	360,854	Mo.	11	423	312,219	Okla.	8
368	360,520	Okla.	7	424	312,063	Conn.	6
369	360,066	Pa.	28	425	310,870	N.C.	12
370	359,476	N.Y.	38	426	309,886	N.Y.	44
371	357,832	Va.	8	427	309,755	Ill.	26
372	355,908	Ark.	6	428	308,372	N.J.	14
373	354,353	Ohio	20	429	307,357	Tenn.	10
374	354,341	Calif.	20	430	307,081	Ohio	23
375	353,031	Ariz.	2	431	307,071	Calif.	23
376	351,075	Ill.	23	432	304,657	Pa.	33
377	350,137	N.Y.	39	433	303,016	Mo.	13
378	347,560	N.H.	2	434	302,921	N.Y.	45
379	347,428	Pa.	29	435	300,797	Ark.	7
380	347,251	W.Va.	6	436	300,472	Mich.	18
381	346,874	Tex.	19	437	299,956	Ky.	10
382	346,855	S.C.	6	438	299,157	Wis.	11
383	346,419	Fla.	6	439	299,138	Iowa	9
384	345,879	Maine	3	440	298,620	Ala.	10
385	345,614	Mass.	13	441	298,445	Tex.	22
386	343,635	Tenn.	9	442	298,351	Ind.	12
387	341,271	N.Y.	40	443	298,062	Ill.	27
388	340,541	N.C.	11	444	297,882	Mass.	15
389	339,280	Mich.	16	445	297,835	Ga.	11
390	339,190	Iowa	8	446	296,262	N.Y.	46
391	337,057	Ohio	21	447	295,561	Pa.	34
392	337,046	Calif.	21	448	294,334	Minn.	10

PRIORITY LIST, METHOD OF EQUAL PROPORTIONS, CENSUS OF 1940—*Continued*

Total Number of Representatives from All States	Priority Numbers	State	Cumulative Total of Representatives from Each State	Total Number of Representatives from All States	Priority Numbers	State	Cumulative Total of Representatives from Each State
449	294,229	Neb.	5	475	277,905	Kans.	7
450	294,007	Ohio	24	476	277,139	Ill.	29
451	293,998	Calif.	24				
452	293,481	W.Va.	7	477	275,351	Okla.	9
				478	274,443	Ind.	13
453	293,146	S.C.	7	479	273,092	Wis.	12
454	292,777	Fla.	7	480	273,033	Tex.	24
455	291,822	Miss.	8				
456	291,222	R.I.	3	481	272,320	N.Y.	50
				482	271,885	Ga.	12
457	289,891	N.Y.	47	483	271,320	Ky.	11
458	287,219	Ill.	28	484	271,263	Pa.	37
459	287,079	N.J.	15				
460	286,992	Pa.	35	485	270,939	Ohio	26
				486	270,930	Calif.	26
461	285,959	N.C.	13	487	270,112	Ala.	11
462	285,174	Tex.	23	488	269,633	Mich.	20
463	284,218	Mich.	19				
464	283,787	N.Y.	48	489	268,537	N.J.	16
				490	267,900	Wash.	7
465	282,262	Va.	10	491	267,742	Ill.	30
466	282,002	Ohio	25	492	267,557	Iowa	10
467	281,993	Calif.	25				
468	281,024	Md.	7	493	266,927	N.Y.	51
				494	266,235	Minn.	11
469	280,538	Mo.	14	495	264,746	N.C.	14
470	278,906	Pa.	36	496	264,028	Pa.	38
471	278,643	Mass.	16				
472	278,586	La.	9	497	263,742	Conn.	7
				498	262,488	S.Dak.	3
473	278,015	Tenn.	11	499	262,069	N.Dak.	3
474	277,935	N.Y.	49	500	261,884	Tex.	25

With a House of 435 members the following states do not appear in the priority list for the method of equal proportions, and receive one member each.

Delaware   Vermont
Nevada   Wyoming

TOTAL AND APPORTIONMENT POPU-
LATION AND APPORTIONMENT
FOR EACH CENSUS

The following tables show the constitutional apportionment, or that prescribed by the Constitution in 1789, and the total population, the apportionment population, and the assignment of representatives after each census.[1] The apportionment prior to the census of 1790, here called the constitutional apportionment, was prescribed by the Constitution. It was based on an estimate.[2]

Up to and including 1860, the apportionment population included only three-fifths of the slaves, and excluded Indians not taxed. Beginning with 1870, the apportionment population includes all inhabitants except the Indians not taxed. In 1880 and 1890, however, apparently no Indians were included in the figures for total population, and the figures for the total and the apportionment populations are the same for those years.

For 1840, 1870, and 1880 the total population figures for some states do not agree with those given in the recent census reports. This is because the original figures have been revised. The original figures are used here, as they were contemporary with the apportionment. The difference is not material.

There was no apportionment after the census of 1920, and the apportionment prescribed after the census of 1910 continued in effect. The figures for 1920 show also the distribution of members of the House if the apportionment had been made by the method of major fractions, which had been used after the census of 1910. In 1940 the apportionment population was the same as the total population, as all Indians were regarded as subject to taxation.

---

[1] In the older reports the apportionment population is variously called the constitutional population, the federal population, and the representative population.

[2] Estimates used in the Constitutional Convention are given in Max Farrand, *The Records of Federal Convention of 1787*, Vol. 1, pp. 190, 572; Vol. 3, p. 253. Other estimates of the colonial population are given in Carroll D. Wright, *History and Growth of the United States Census*, 1900, pp. 8–11.

TOTAL POPULATION, APPORTIONMENT POPULATION, AND REPRESENTATIVES
AFTER EACH CENSUS

State	Consti-tutional Appor-tionment	1790			1800		
		Total Population	Apportion-ment Population	Number of Repre-senta-tives	Total Population	Apportion-ment Population	Number of Repre-senta-tives
Connecticut.....	5	237,946	236,841	7	251,002	250,622	7
Delaware.......	1	59,096	55,540	1	64,273	61,812	1
Georgia.........	3	82,548	70,835	2	162,686	138,807	4
Kentucky.......	—	73,677	68,705	2	220,955	204,822	6
Maryland.......	6	319,728	278,514	8	341,548	306,610	9
Massachusetts...	8	475,327	475,327	14	574,564	574,564	17
New Hampshire..	3	141,885	141,822	4	183,858	183,855	5
New Jersey......	4	184,139	179,570	5	211,149	206,181	6
New York.......	6	340,120	331,589	10	589,051	577,805	17
North Carolina...	5	393,751	353,523	10	478,103	424,785	12
Pennsylvania....	8	434,373	432,879	13	602,365	601,863	18
Rhode Island....	1	68,825	68,446	2	69,122	68,970	2
South Carolina...	5	249,073	206,236	6	345,591	287,131	8
Tennessee.......	—	—	—	—	105,602	100,169	3
Vermont.......	—	85,539	85,533	2	154,465	154,465	4
Virginia.........	10	747,610	630,560	19	880,200	747,362	22
Total.........	65	3,893,637	3,615,920	105	5,234,534	4,889,823	141

TOTAL POPULATION, APPORTIONMENT POPULATION, AND REPRESENTATIVES
AFTER EACH CENSUS—*Continued*

State	1810			1820		
	Total Population	Apportion-ment Population	Number of Repre-sentatives	Total Population	Apportion-ment Population	Number of Repre-sentatives
Alabama..........	—	—	—	127,901	111,147	3
Connecticut........	261,942	261,818	7	275,248	275,208	6
Delaware.........	72,674	71,004	2	72,749	70,943	1
Georgia...........	252,433	210,346	6	340,989	281,126	7
Illinois............	—	—	—	55,211	54,843	1
Indiana...........	—	—	—	147,178	147,102	3
Kentucky.........	406,511	374,287	10	564,317	513,623	12
Louisiana.........	—	—	—	153,407	125,779	3
Maine............	—	—	—	298,335	298,335	7
Maryland..........	380,546	335,946	9	407,350	364,389	9
Massachusetts......	700,745	700,745	20	523,287	523,287	13
Mississippi........	—	—	—	75,448	62,320	1
Missouri..........	—	—	—	66,586	62,496	1
New Hampshire.....	214,460	214,460	6	244,161	244,161	6
New Jersey.........	245,562	241,222	6	277,575	274,551	6
New York.........	959,049	953,043	27	1,372,812	1,368,775	34
North Carolina.....	555,500	497,971	13	638,829	556,821	13
Ohio.............	230,760	230,760	6	581,434	581,434	14
Pennsylvania.......	810,091	809,773	23	1,049,458	1,049,449	26
Rhode Island.......	76,931	76,888	2	83,059	83,038	2
South Carolina......	415,115	336,569	9	502,741	399,351	9
Tennessee.........	261,727	243,913	6	422,823	390,569	9
Vermont..........	217,895	217,895	6	235,981	235,764	5
Virginia............	974,600	817,615	23	1,065,366	895,303	22
Total............	7,036,541	6,594,255	181	9,582,245	8,969,814	213

TOTAL POPULATION, APPORTIONMENT POPULATION, AND REPRESENTATIVES
AFTER EACH CENSUS—*Continued*

State	1830			1840		
	Total Population	Apportion- ment Population	Number of Repre- sentatives	Total Population	Apportion- ment Population	Number of Repre- sentatives
Alabama............	309,527	262,508	5	590,756	489,343	7
Arkansas............	—	—	—	97,574	89,600	1
Connecticut........	297,675	297,665	6	310,015	310,008	4
Delaware..........	76,748	75,432	1	78,085	77,043	1
Georgia............	516,823	429,811	9	691,392	579,014	8
Illinois.............	157,445	157,147	3	476,183	476,051	7
Indiana............	343,031	343,031	7	685,866	685,865	10
Kentucky..........	687,917	621,832	13	779,828	706,925	10
Louisiana..........	215,739	171,694	3	352,411	285,030	4
Maine.............	399,455	399,437	8	501,793	501,793	7
Maryland..........	447,040	405,843	8	470,019	434,124	6
Massachusetts......	610,408	610,408	12	737,699	737,699	10
Michigan..........	—	—	—	212,267	212,267	3
Mississippi.........	136,621	110,358	2	375,651	297,567	4
Missouri...........	140,455	130,419	2	383,702	360,406	5
New Hampshire.....	269,328	269,326	5	284,574	284,574	4
New Jersey.........	320,823	319,922	6	373,306	373,036	5
New York.........	1,918,608	1,918,553	40	2,428,921	2,428,919	34
North Carolina.....	737,987	639,747	13	753,419	655,092	9
Ohio..............	937,903	935,884	19	1,519,467	1,519,466	21
Pennsylvania.......	1,348,233	1,348,072	28	1,724,033	1,724,007	24
Rhode Island.......	97,199	97,194	2	108,830	108,828	2
South Carolina......	581,185	455,025	9	594,074	463,583	7
Tennessee..........	681,904	625,263	13	829,210	755,986	11
Vermont...........	280,652	280,657	5	291,948	291,948	4
Virginia...........	1,211,405	1,023,503	21	1,239,797	1,060,202	15
Total..........	12,724,111	11,928,731	240	16,890,820	15,908,376	223

TOTAL POPULATION, APPORTIONMENT POPULATION, AND REPRESENTATIVES
AFTER EACH CENSUS—*Continued*

State	1850			1860		
	Total Population	Apportion-ment Population	Number of Repre-sentatives	Total Population	Apportion-ment Population	Number of Repre-sentatives[a]
Alabama..........	771,671	634,514	7	964,201	790,169	6
Arkansas..........	209,639	190,846	2	435,450	391,004	3
California.........	165,000[b]	165,000[b]	2	379,994	362,196	3
Connecticut.......	370,791	370,791	4	460,147	460,147	4
Delaware.........	91,535	90,619	1	112,216	111,496	1
Florida..........	87,401	71,667	1	140,424	115,726	1
Georgia..........	905,999	753,326	8	1,057,286	872,406	7
Illinois............	851,470	851,470	9	1,711,951	1,711,951	13
Indiana...........	988,416	988,416	11	1,350,428	1,350,428	11
Iowa.............	192,214	192,214	2	674,913	674,913	5
Kansas...........	—	—	—	107,206	107,206	1
Kentucky.........	982,405	898,012	10	1,155,684	1,065,490	8
Louisiana.........	517,739	419,824	4	708,002	575,311	5
Maine............	583,188	583,188	6	628,279	628,279	5
Maryland.........	583,035	546,887	6	687,049	652,173	5
Massachusetts......	994,499	994,499	11	1,231,066	1,231,066	10
Michigan.........	397,654	397,654	4	749,113	749,113	6
Minnesota........	—	—	—	172,023	172,023	1
Mississippi........	606,555	482,595	5	791,305	616,652	5
Missouri..........	682,043	647,074	7	1,182,012	1,136,039	9
New Hampshire.:...	317,964	317,964	3	326,073	326,073	3
New Jersey........	489,555	489,466	5	672,035	672,027	5
New York.........	3,097,394	3,097,394	33	3,880,735	3,880,735	31
North Carolina.....	868,903	753,538	8	992,622	860,197	7
Ohio..............	1,980,408	1,980,408	21	2,339,511	2,339,511	18
Oregon............	—	—	—	52,465	52,465	1
Pennsylvania.......	2,311,786	2,311,786	25	2,906,215	2,906,115	23
Rhode Island.......	147,544	147,544	2	174,620	174,620	1
South Carolina.....	668,507	514,513	6	703,708	542,745	4
Tennessee.........	1,002,625	906,840	10	1,109,801	999,513	8
Texas	212,592	189,327	2	604,215	531,188	4
Vermont..........	314,120	314,120	3	315,098	315,098	2
Virginia...........	1,421,661	1,232,649	13	1,596,318	1,399,972	11
Wisconsin.........	305,191	305,191	3	775,881	775,881	6
Total...........	23,119,504	21,839,336	234	31,148,046	29,549,928	233

[a] This was the original apportionment made by the Secretary of the Interior July 5, 1861. The act of Mar. 4, 1862 (12 Stat. L. 533), assigned an additional representative each to Illinois, Iowa, Kentucky, Minnesota, Ohio, Pennsylvania, Rhode Island and Vermont, making the total membership 241.
[b] Estimated in the official report.

TOTAL POPULATION, APPORTIONMENT POPULATION, AND REPRESENTATIVES
AFTER EACH CENSUS—*Continued*

State	1870			1880		
	Total Population	Apportionment Population	Number of Representatives[a]	Total Population	Apportionment Population	Number of Representatives
Alabama............	996,992	996,992	7	1,262,794	1,262,794	8
Arkansas..........	484,471	484,471	4	802,564	802,564	5
California.........	582,031	560,247	4	864,686	864,686	6
Colorado..........	—	—	—	194,649	194,649	1
Connecticut	537,454	537,454	4	622,683	622,683	4
Delaware	125,015	125,015	1	146,654	146,654	1
Florida............	188,248	187,748	1	267,351	267,351	2
Georgia...........	1,184,109	1,184,109	9	1,539,048	1,539,048	10
Illinois...........	2,539,891	2,539,891	19	3,078,769	3,078,769	20
Indiana...........	1,680,637	1,680,637	12	1,978,362	1,978,362	13
Iowa..............	1,194,320	1,194,020	9	1,624,620	1,624,620	11
Kansas............	373,299	364,399	3	995,966	995,966	7
Kentucky..........	1,321,011	1,321,011	10	1,648,708	1,648,708	11
Louisiana..........	726,915	726,915	5	940,103	940,103	6
Maine.............	626,915	626,915	5	648,945	648,945	4
Maryland..........	780,894	780,894	6	934,632	934,632	6
Massachusetts......	1,457,351	1,457,351	11	1,783,012	1,783,012	12
Michigan..........	1,187,234	1,184,059	9	1,636,331	1,636,331	11
Minnesota.........	446,056	439,706	3	780,806	780,806	5
Mississippi........	827,922	827,922	6	1,131,592	1,131,592	7
Missouri..........	1,721,295	1,721,295	13	2,168,804	2,168,804	14
Nebraska..........	129,322	122,993	1	452,433	452,433	3
Nevada............	58,711	42,491	1	62,265	62,265	1
New Hampshire.....	318,300	318,300	2	346,984	346,984	2
New Jersey.........	906,096	906,096	7	1,130,983	1,130,983	7
New York..........	4,387,464	4,382,759	32	5,083,810	5,083,810	34
North Carolina.....	1,071,361	1,071,361	8	1,400,047	1,400,047	9
Ohio..............	2,665,260	2,665,260	20	3,198,239	3,198,239	21
Oregon............	101,883	90,923	1	174,767	174,767	1
Pennsylvania.......	3,522,050	3,521,951	26	4,282,786	4,282,786	28
Rhode Island.......	217,353	217,353	2	276,528	276,528	2
South Carolina.....	705,606	705,606	5	995,622	995,622	7
Tennessee..........	1,258,520	1,258,520	9	1,542,463	1,542,463	10
Texas.............	818,899	818,579	6	1,592,574	1,592,574	11
Vermont...........	330,551	330,551	2	332,286	332,286	2
Virginia...........	1,225,163	1,225,163	9	1,512,806	1,512,806	10
West Virginia.......	442,014	442,014	3	618,443	618,443	4
Wisconsin..........	1,064,985	1,054,670	8	1,315,480	1,315,480	9
Total............	38,205,598	38,115,641	283	49,369,595	49,369,595	325

[a] This was the original apportionment made by the act of Feb. 2, 1872 (17 Stat. L. 28). A supplemental
act of May 30, 1872 (17 Stat. L. 192), assigned one additional representative each to Alabama, Florida,
Indiana, Louisiana, New Hampshire, New York, Pennsylvania, Tennessee, and Vermont.

TOTAL POPULATION, APPORTIONMENT POPULATION, AND REPRESENTATIVES
AFTER EACH CENSUS—*Continued*

State	1890			1900		
	Total Population	Apportion-ment Population	Number of Repre-sentatives	Total Population	Apportion-ment Population	Number of Repre-sentatives
Alabama............	1,513,017	1,513,017	9	1,828,697	1,828,697	9
Arkansas..........	1,128,179	1,128,179	6	1,311,564	1,311,564	7
California..........	1,208,130	1,208,130	7	1,485,053	1,483,504	8
Colorado..........	412,198	412,198	2	539,700	539,103	3
Connecticut.......	746,258	746,258	4	908,420	908,420	5
Delaware..........	168,493	168,493	1	184,735	184,735	1
Florida............	391,422	391,422	2	528,542	528,542	3
Georgia...........	1,837,353	1,837,353	11	2,216,331	2,216,331	11
Idaho.............	84,385	84,385	1	161,772	159,475	1
Illinois............	3,826,351	3,826,351	22	4,821,550	4,821,550	25
Indiana...........	2,192,404	2,192,404	13	2,516,462	2,516,462	13
Iowa..............	1,911,896	1,911,896	11	2,231,853	2,231,853	11
Kansas..	1,427,096	1,427,096	8	1,470,495	1,470,495	8
Kentucky..........	1,858,635	1,858,635	11	2,147,174	2,147,174	11
Louisiana.........	1,118,587	1,118,587	6	1,381,625	1,381,625	7
Maine.............	661,086	661,086	4	694,466	694,466	4
Maryland..........	1,042,390	1,042,390	6	1,188,044	1,188,044	6
Massachusetts......	2,238,943	2,238,943	13	2,805,346	2,805,346	14
Michigan..........	2,093,889	2,093,889	12	2,420,982	2,420,982	12
Minnesota.	1,301,826	1,301,826	7	1,751,394	1,749,626	9
Mississippi.........	1,289,600	1,289,600	7	1,551,270	1,551,270	8
Missouri...........	2,679,184	2,679,184	15	3,106,665	3,106,665	16
Montana...........	132,159	132,159	1	243,329	232,583	1
Nebraska..........	1,058,910	1,058,910	6	1,066,300	1,066,300	6
Nevada............	45,761	45,761	1	42,335	40,670	1
New Hampshire.....	376,530	376,530	2	411,588	411,588	2
New Jersey.........	1,444,933	1,444,933	8	1,883,669	1,883,669	10
New York..........	5,997,853	5,997,853	34	7,268,894	7,264,183	37
North Carolina.....	1,617,947	1,617,947	9	1,893,810	1,893,810	10
North Dakota......	182,719	182,719	1	319,146	314,454	2
Ohio..............	3,672,316	3,672,316	21	4,157,545	4,157,545	21
Oregon............	313,767	313,767	2	413,536	413,536	2
Pennsylvania.......	5,258,014	5,258,014	30	6,302,115	6,302,115	32
Rhode Island.......	345,506	345,506	2	428,556	428,556	2
South Carolina.....	1,151,149	1,151,149	7	1,340,316	1,340,316	7
South Dakota......	328,808	328,808	2	401,570	390,638	2
Tennessee.........	1,767,518	1,767,518	10	2,020,616	2,020,616	10
Texas.............	2,235,523	2,235,523	13	3,048,710	3,048,710	16
Utah..............	—	—	—	276,749	275,277	1
Vermont...........	332,422	332,422	2	343,641	343,641	2
Virginia...........	1,655,980	1,655,980	10	1,854,184	1,854,184	10
Washington........	349,390	349,390	2	518,103	515,572	3
West Virginia.......	762,794	762,794	4	958,800	958,800	5
Wisconsin..........	1,686,880	1,686,880	10	2,069,042	2,067,385	11
Wyoming..........	60,705	60,705	1	92,531	92,531	1
Total...........	61,908,906	61,908,906	356	74,607,225	74,562,608	386

TOTAL POPULATION, APPORTIONMENT POPULATION, AND REPRESENTATIVES
AFTER EACH CENSUS—*Continued*

State	1910			1920			
	Total Population	Apportionment Population	Number of Representatives	Total Population	Apportionment Population	Number of Representatives	
						Actual[a]	Computed by Method Used in 1910[b]
Alabama	2,138,093	2,138,093	10	2,348,174	2,348,174	10	10
Arizona	—	—	—	334,162	309,495	1	1
Arkansas	1,574,449	1,574,449	7	1,752,204	1,752,204	7	7
California	2,377,549	2,376,561	11	3,426,861	3,426,031	11	14
Colorado	799,024	798,572	4	939,629	939,161	4	4
Connecticut	1,114,756	1,114,756	5	1,380,631	1,380,631	5	6
Delaware	202,322	202,322	1	223,003	223,003	1	1
Florida	752,619	752,619	4	968,470	968,470	4	4
Georgia	2,609,121	2,609,121	12	2,895,832	2,895,832	12	12
Idaho	325,594	323,440	2	431,866	430,442	2	2
Illinois	5,638,591	5,638,591	27	6,485,280	6,485,280	27	27
Indiana	2,700,876	2,700,876	13	2,930,390	2,930,390	13	12
Iowa	2,224,771	2,224,771	11	2,404,021	2,404,021	11	10
Kansas	1,690,949	1,690,949	8	1,769,257	1,769,257	8	7
Kentucky	2,289,905	2,289,905	11	2,416,630	2,416,630	11	10
Louisiana	1,656,388	1,656,388	8	1,798,509	1,798,509	8	7
Maine	742,371	742,371	4	768,014	768,014	4	3
Maryland	1,295,346	1,295,346	6	1,449,661	1,449,661	6	6
Massachusetts	3,366,416	3,366,416	16	3,852,356	3,852,356	16	16
Michigan	2,810,173	2,810,173	13	3,668,412	3,668,412	13	15
Minnesota	2,075,708	2,074,376	10	2,387,125	2,385,656	10	10
Mississippi	1,797,114	1,797,114	8	1,790,618	1,790,618	8	7
Missouri	3,293,335	3,293,335	16	3,404,055	3,404,055	16	14
Montana	376,053	366,338	2	548,889	541,511	2	2
Nebraska	1,192,214	1,192,214	6	1,296,372	1,296,372	6	5
Nevada	81,875	80,293	1	77,407	75,820	1	1
New Hampshire	430,572	430,572	2	443,083	443,083	2	2
New Jersey	2,537,167	2,537,167	12	3,155,900	3,155,900	12	13
New Mexico	—	—	—	360,350	353,428	1	1
New York	9,113,614	9,108,934	43	10,385,227	10,380,589	43	43
North Carolina	2,206,287	2,206,287	10	2,559,123	2,559,123	10	11
North Dakota	577,056	574,403	3	646,872	643,953	3	3
Ohio	4,767,121	4,767,121	22	5,759,394	5,759,394	22	24
Oklahoma	1,657,155	1,657,155	8	2,028,283	2,028,283	8	8
Oregon	672,765	672,765	3	783,389	783,389	3	3
Pennsylvania	7,665,111	7,665,111	36	8,720,017	8,720,017	36	36
Rhode Island	542,610	542,610	3	604,397	604,397	3	2
South Carolina	1,515,400	1,515,400	7	1,683,724	1,683,724	7	7
South Dakota	583,888	575,676	3	636,547	631,239	3	3
Tennessee	2,184,789	2,184,789	10	2,337,885	2,337,885	10	10
Texas	3,896,542	3,896,542	18	4,663,228	4,663,228	18	19
Utah	373,351	371,864	2	449,396	448,388	2	2
Vermont	355,956	355,956	2	352,428	352,428	2	1
Virginia	2,061,612	2,061,612	10	2,309,187	2,309,187	10	10
Washington	1,141,990	1,140,134	5	1,356,621	1,354,596	5	6
West Virginia	1,221,119	1,221,119	6	1,463,701	1,463,701	6	6
Wisconsin	2,333,860	2,332,853	11	2,632,067	2,631,305	11	11
Wyoming	145,965	144,658	1	194,402	193,487	1	1
Total	91,109,542	91,072,117	433	105,273,049	105,210,729	435	435

[a] There was no apportionment in 1920 and the apportionment of 1910 continued in effect.
[b] Computed according to method of major fractions; numbers according to the four other modern methods are given on p. 64.

Total Population, Apportionment Population, and Representatives
after Each Census—*Continued*

State	1930			1940		
	Total Population	Apportionment Population	Number of Representatives	Apportionment Population[a]	Method of Major Fractions[b]	Method of Equal Proportions
Alabama	2,646,248	2,646,242	9	2,832,961	9	9
Arizona	435,573	389,375	1	499,261	2	2
Arkansas	1,854,482	1,854,444	7	1,949,387	6	7
California	5,677,251	5,668,241	20	6,907,387	23	23
Colorado	1,035,791	1,034,849	4	1,123,296	4	4
Connecticut	1,606,903	1,606,897	6	1,709,242	6	6
Delaware	238,380	238,380	1	266,505	1	1
Florida	1,468,211	1,468,191	5	1,897,414	6	6
Georgia	2,908,506	2,908,446	10	3,123,723	10	10
Idaho	445,032	441,536	2	524,873	2	2
Illinois	7,630,654	7,630,388	27	7,897,241	26	26
Indiana	3,238,503	3,238,480	12	3,427,796	11	11
Iowa	2,470,939	2,470,420	9	2,538,268	8	8
Kansas	1,880,999	1,879,498	7	1,801,028	6	6
Kentucky	2,614,589	2,614,575	9	2,845,627	9	9
Louisiana	2,101,593	2,101,593	8	2,363,880	8	8
Maine	797,423	797,418	3	847,226	3	3
Maryland	1,631,526	1,631,522	6	1,821,244	6	6
Massachusetts	4,249,614	4,249,598	15	4,316,721	14	14
Michigan	4,842,325	4,842,052	17	5,256,106	18	17
Minnesota	2,563,953	2,551,583	9	2,792,300	9	9
Mississippi	2,009,821	2,008,154	7	2,183,796	7	7
Missouri	3,629,367	3,629,110	13	3,784,664	13	13
Montana	537,606	524,729	2	559,456	2	2
Nebraska	1,377,963	1,375,123	5	1,315,834	4	4
Nevada	91,058	86,390	1	110,247	1	1
New Hampshire	465,293	465,292	2	491,524	2	2
New Jersey	4,041,334	4,041,319	14	4,160,165	14	14
New Mexico	423,317	395,982	1	531,818	2	2
New York	12,588,066	12,587,967	45	13,479,142	45	45
North Carolina	3,170,276	3,167,274	11	3,571,623	12	12
North Dakota	680,845	673,340	2	641,935	2	2
Ohio	6,646,697	6,646,633	24	6,907,612	23	23
Oklahoma	2,396,040	2,382,222	9	2,336,434	8	8
Oregon	953,786	950,379	3	1,089,684	4	4
Pennsylvania	9,631,350	9,631,299	34	9,900,180	33	33
Rhode Island	687,497	687,497	2	713,346	2	2
South Carolina	1,738,765	1,738,760	6	1,899,804	6	6
South Dakota	692,849	673,005	2	642,961	2	2
Tennessee	2,616,556	2,616,497	9	2,915,841	10	10
Texas	5,824,715	5,824,601	21	6,414,824	21	21
Utah	507,847	505,741	2	550,310	2	2
Vermont	359,611	359,611	1	359,231	1	1
Virginia	2,421,851	2,421,829	9	2,677,773	9	9
Washington	1,563,396	1,552,423	6	1,736,191	6	6
West Virginia	1,729,205	1,729,199	6	1,901,974	6	6
Wisconsin	2,939,006	2,931,721	10	3,137,587	10	10
Wyoming	225,565	223,630	1	250,742	1	1
Total	122,288,177	122,093,455	435	131,006,184	435	435

[a] The apportionment population is the same as the total population.
[b] This method will be used if Congress takes no action.